JUTLAND 1916

OSPREY
PUBLISHING

Innes McCartney

JUTLAND 1916

THE ARCHAEOLOGY OF A NAVAL BATTLEFIELD

OSPREY PUBLISHING
Bloomsbury Publishing Plc

PO Box 883, Oxford, OX1 9PL, UK
1385 Broadway, 5th Floor, New York, NY 10018, USA
Email: info@ospreypublishing.com
www.ospreypublishing.com

OSPREY is a trademark of Osprey Publishing, a division of Bloomsbury Publishing Plc

This edition first published in Great Britain in 2018 by Osprey Publishing
First Bloomsbury Publishing edition 2016

A CIP record for this book is available from the British Library.

Print ISBN: 978-1-4728-3541-3
ePub ISBN: 978-1-4728-3540-6
ePDF ISBN: 978-1-4728-3539-0

Design by CE Marketing
Typeset in Palatino, Myriad Pro and Helvetica Ultra Compressed
Printed and bound in India through Replika Press Pvt Ltd.

18 19 20 21 22   10 9 8 7 6 5 4 3 2 1

Image acknowledgements
All diagrams and images, unless otherwise indicated, © Innes McCartney, 2016.

Every effort has been made to contact the copyright holders of the illustrations reproduced in this book. If any errors or omissions have inadvertently been made, they will be rectified in future editions provided that written notification is sent to the publishers.

Title spread image: Robert Hunt Library/Windmill Books/UIG via Getty Images.

The Woodland Trust
Osprey Publishing supports the Woodland Trust, the UK's leading woodland conservation charity. Between 2014 and 2018 our donations are being spent on their Centenary Woods project in the UK.

www.ospreypublishing.com
To find out more about our authors and books visit our website. Here you will find extracts, author interviews, details of forthcoming events and the option to sign-up for our newsletter.

In memory of the servicemen and civilians
of all nations and services who perished
at sea during the First World War

CONTENTS

PREFACE

When I was a child my father bought me a book entitled *Great Sea Battles*. Within it was Jutland, a battle full of uncertainties and controversies, which sparked a lifelong interest. Back in 2000, when I was first able to dive the wrecks that were then known, this interest took on another dimension and led me to study modern shipwreck archaeology as an academic discipline and ultimately to this book.

It has always felt like an immense privilege to be able to examine the shipwrecks and unravel the mysteries they contain. Over the past 17 years so much has been achieved that now all but two of the ships sunk in the Jutland battlefield have been found and are described here.

Very little of this would have been possible without Gert Normann Andersen. He has had a lifelong fascination with the shipwrecks off the coast of his native Denmark. Gert's company, JD-Contractor A/S, is the largest underwater contractor in Denmark and has been well situated to gather shipwreck data in the waters off the Danish coast.

In marine archaeology, local knowledge is everything and since 2001 Gert and I have shared information. This culminated in 2015 when he graciously invited me to work as his number two on a groundbreaking survey of the Jutland battlefield, the results of which have finally made this book possible.

The chronology of how the wrecks were found and identified begins with the Royal Navy locating the wreck of HMS *Invincible* in 1919. HMS *Black Prince*, *Queen Mary* and the larger wrecks were located by Danish divers, not least Gert in the 1980s. SMS *Wiesbaden* was probably first located by the German Navy in 1983.

With information from Gert, I was lucky to be among the first dive party to visit HMS *Indefatigable* and *Defence* in 2001. HMS *Nomad* was also located that year. Between 2000 and 2001 I took part in four diving expeditions aboard Deep Blue Diving's *Loyal Watcher* and slowly began to learn what was there.

By 2003 enough was known to make a two-hour television documentary with Ideal World Productions and Channel Four. With assistance from Gert,

I organised and led the underwater filming expedition that was central to the film. The expedition aboard MV *Gorm* was equipped with a remotely operated underwater vehicle (ROV) and side scanning sonar. This was one of the first times geophysics was employed on the Jutland wrecks. Although primitive, the results of the side scans clearly showed that geophysics was the only way to develop an accurate site map of the larger wrecks if used in the calmest of conditions. They are simply too big to be accurately described by only diving or ROV.

Changing times at Jutland: Left, getting ready to jump off MV Gorm *for a dive on HMS* Invincible *during the filming of* Clash of the Dreadnoughts *in 2003. Above, with Gert Normann Andersen aboard MV* Vina *in April 2015 during the groundbreaking multibeam survey of the Jutland battlefield. Note the very flat sea.*

I made one last attempt to dive at Jutland with Deep Blue Diving in 2007, only to be thwarted by the weather, an ever-present menace in the North Sea. But by then it was obvious that the newer technology of multibeam sonar was what was really needed to drive future discoveries at Jutland because it offered the means to accurately map each wreck site, from which deeper interpretations could be made.

In the years that followed there were several abortive attempts to encourage interest in a multibeam-driven survey of the Jutland wrecks, not least two wasted years of talks with the BBC. Ultimately, it was Gert Normann who came up with a survey plan of his own and invited me to partake. JD-Contractor had acquired a state-of-the-art multibeam system made by EIVA Marine Survey Solutions and it proved to be revelatory. But first we had to wait on standby for nearly three months for a weather window that would give us the flattest of sea conditions in which to work.

The April 2015 survey took place aboard JD-Contractor's MV *Vina*. It remains the only expedition ever to go to Jutland for the sole purpose of gathering archaeological data. In all my previous visits to the battlefield, as a diver, diver guide or television producer, the gathering of pure archaeology had come second to the actual purposes behind the trips. This time archaeology drove the agenda. Over eight days we steamed more than 800 nautical miles and examined 106 seabed anomalies, which turned out to be 76 shipwrecks, with many brand-new finds; among them were at least 22 warships sunk during the Battle of Jutland.

Although I knew the multibeam would be very useful in mapping the larger shipwrecks, I had not expected that we would also locate all but two of the destroyers sunk during the battle. Once all of these sites had been identified, we could accurately map the entire battlefield for the first time. The results of this survey and Gert Normann's huge collection of shipwreck artefacts and ephemera are on display in the newly opened Sea War Museum Jutland in Thyborøn, Denmark.

It was also my great pleasure to meet Nick Jellicoe on the 2015 expedition. He provided me with a pristine set of incredibly rare charts of the battle, prepared under the supervision of Captain JET Harper in 1919, which were never published but had been retained by the Jellicoe family. These charts in conjunction with the accurately mapped positions of the wrecks have given us a better picture of what happened on 31 May and 1 June 1916. Ultimately this is the true purpose of archaeology.

I wish to personally acknowledge the following: Patricia McCartney, Jutland explorer and ever patient proofreader, Gert Normann Andersen, all at JD-

Contractor (especially Rasmus Normann Andersen, Sven Heinrichs and Jeppe Ildsvad Jeppesen) and the Sea War Museum Jutland for making this book possible, my agent Ian Drury at Sheil Land Associates, EIVA Marine Survey Solutions, Nick Jellicoe, Dr Jann Witt at the Archiv Deutscher Marinebund, Gary Staff for his generosity in sharing information on SMS *Lützow*, Jeremy Michell and Andrew Choong at the National Maritime Museum, all the incredibly helpful staff at the National Archives, Churchill Archives, Glasgow University Library, Leeds University Library and Imperial War Museum, James Delgado, Nelson Mceachan at the UK Hydrographic Office, Crispin Sadler of Mallinson-Sadler Productions, Hamish Barbour of Ideal World Productions, Andrew Gordon, James Yates, Lawrence Burr, Dr John Brooks, the late David K Brown, Dr Richard Osborne of the World Ship Society, Professor Eric Grove, Matt Skelhorn, Richard Stevenson and Steve Wright of Deep Blue Diving, Doug Friday, Bradley Sheard, Mike Boring, Kevin Pickering, Kevin Gurr and all those I have inadvertently omitted to mention.

INTRODUCTION

On 31 May to 1 June 1916 the two largest battle fleets in the world clashed in the North Sea, off the coast of Denmark (Fig. i). The positions of the wrecks are derived from the record of the battle compiled by the Royal Navy's director of navigation, Captain JET Harper in 1919, commonly referred to as the Harper Record.[1]

The Battle of Jutland was more of a skirmish than a set-piece naval battle. In effect, the German High Seas Fleet 'blundered into the stronger British Grand Fleet while chasing what it assumed to be an isolated part of that fleet'.[2] Facing impossible odds, the High Seas Fleet skilfully turned around and slipped away into the mists of the North Sea, leaving the Royal Navy in command of the battlefield. Germany never risked a fleet encounter again and increasingly turned to the U-boat as a means of pursuing the naval war.

Although a seemingly strategic victory for the Royal Navy, Jutland was no Trafalgar. The German fleet avoided defeat and the price paid by the isolated part of the British fleet, Admiral Beatty's Battlecruiser Fleet, was tragically

Fig. i *Map showing the location of the Battle of Jutland and the routes taken by the British and German fleets. The black crosses mark the historical positions of the shipwrecks as recorded in the* Harper Record. *The battlefield covers more than 3,000 nautical square miles.*

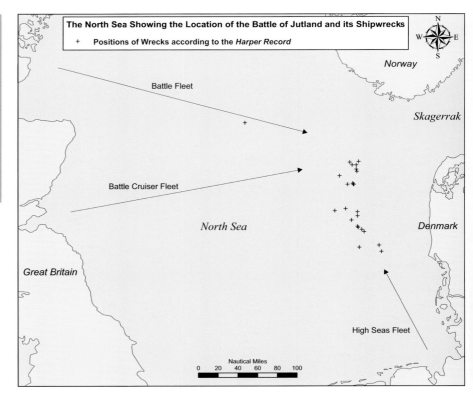

The North Sea Showing the Location of the Battle of Jutland and its Shipwrecks

+ Positions of Wrecks according to the *Harper Record*

Norway

Battle Fleet

Skagerrak

Battle Cruiser Fleet

North Sea

Denmark

Great Britain

High Seas Fleet

Nautical Miles
0 20 40 60 80 100

high. Of the 249 ships that fought in the Battle of Jutland, 25 were sunk, claiming 8,500 lives in the process. The Royal Navy's share of these losses was 14 of the ships and 6,000 of the dead.

More than 5,000 of the British casualties occurred in the five largest warships lost, the battlecruisers HMS *Indefatigable*, *Queen Mary* and *Invincible* and the armoured cruisers HMS *Defence* and *Black Prince*.[3] These ships suffered fatal internal explosions from which very few survived. The disappointment felt in Britain became the source of much acrimony in the years following the battle. More has been published about the Battle of Jutland than any other naval encounter.[4] But aside from my academic papers,[5][6] this book is the first detailed study of the shipwrecks.

The battlefield

The total number of wrecks in the main battlefield area, and under investigation here, is 24. This omits HMS *Warrior*, which sank on her return voyage owing to damage sustained in the battle (see Fig. i, where it is the one wreck plotted between Norway and Scotland, out of the main battlefield).

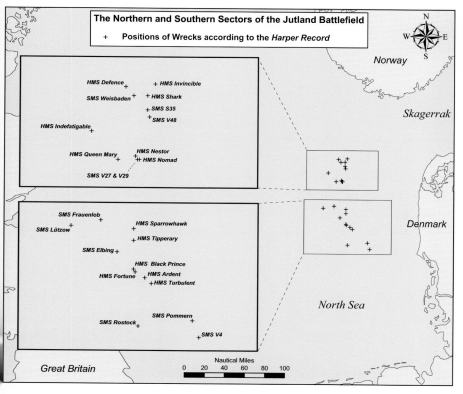

Fig. ii *Map showing the two distinct groupings of wrecks that characterise the Jutland battlefield. The northern sector contains the wrecks of the daylight actions.*

The Battle of Jutland covers an area of around 3,772 nautical square miles. It was fought over 16 hours and in reality was a collection of three different and quite distinct actions; the Battlecruiser Action, the Fleet Action and the Night Action, which fall into two distinct groups of wrecks (Fig. ii).

Battlecruiser Action

Initially the Battlecruiser Action broke out when the Battlecruiser Fleet engaged the German First Scouting Group made up of Admiral Hipper's battlecruisers on what became known as the 'Run to the South' during which time both HMS *Indefatigable* and *Queen Mary* were sunk.

With the arrival from the south-east of the main German battle fleet, the Battlecruiser Fleet turned around and headed towards Jellicoe who was approaching from the north-west. By this time the Battlecruiser Fleet was being protected by the fast battleships of the Fifth Battle Squadron which had been attached to it but had been left behind at the start of the action. This phase of the Battlecruiser Action has become known as the 'Run to the North'. At the apex, where the turn north was made, the opposing light forces clashed; two destroyers (British light vessels) and two torpedo boats (German light vessels) were sunk.

Fleet Action

The Fleet Action is characterised as the period when the British battle fleet deployed into its fighting line, catching the German battle fleet off guard and forcing it to turn away completely on two occasions before it was able to disentangle itself from the British and escape into the enclosing dusk. The British lost the battlecruiser *Invincible*, the armoured cruiser *Defence* and one destroyer, while the Germans lost the light cruiser *Wiesbaden* and two torpedo boats. The distinct nature of the wreck distribution in the Battlecruiser and Fleet actions is shown in Fig. iii.

Night Action

The rest of the battle is characterised by the scuttling of German ships and by a number of clashes between opposing ships at night, usually at extremely short range. During these actions the German fleet managed to pass behind the British fleet as it attempted to screen the coast of Denmark and keep the

German fleet at sea for battle the following day. The German fleet made good its escape and in the morning the British returned to base.

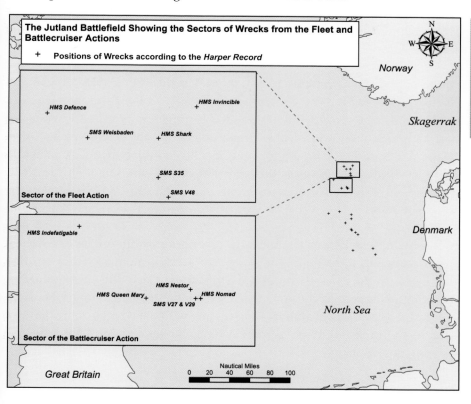

The Jutland Battlefield Showing the Sectors of Wrecks from the Fleet and Battlecruiser Actions

+   Positions of Wrecks according to the *Harper Record*

Sector of the Fleet Action

HMS Defence
SMS Weisbaden
HMS Shark
HMS Invincible
SMS S35
SMS V48

Sector of the Battlecruiser Action

HMS Indefatigable
HMS Nestor
HMS Queen Mary
HMS Nomad
SMS V27 & V29

Great Britain

Nautical Miles
0   20   40   60   80   100

Norway
Skagerrak
Denmark
North Sea

N
W   E
S

Fig. iii Map showing the northern group of wrecks segmented into the lower Battlecruiser Action and the upper Fleet Action.

During the Night Action, Germany lost the battleship SMS *Pommern*, the battlecruiser *Lützow*, the light cruisers *Elbing*, *Rostock* and *Frauenlob* and one torpedo boat, *V4*. The British lost the armoured cruiser *Black Prince* and five destroyers, *Tipperary*, *Sparrowhawk*, *Ardent*, *Fortune* and *Turbulent*.

The ships lost remained unseen to all but a few until 1991 when at the time of the 75th anniversary of the battle, the first of the wrecks (HMS *Queen Mary*, *Invincible* and SMS *Lützow*) were filmed for television. Since then, more of the wrecks have been discovered and modern shipwreck archaeology has emerged as a distinctive field of study.

Modern shipwreck archaeology

The nautical archaeology of modern shipwrecks as a discipline can trace its formative roots back as least as far as the Cold War. Early cases tended to focus on the need to explain why certain military assets had sunk and were largely secret, but their investigative approaches share much with the modern discipline. Everything changed in 1985 with the discovery of RMS *Titanic* which popularised iconic modern shipwrecks. Many other finds followed, not least the first of the Jutland shipwrecks.

In the popular imagination at least, wrecks of this type could confirm and demonstrate exactly what contemporary reports of their sinking stated. In other words, the wrecks initially tended to function as friendly witnesses and, although interesting, were largely incidental to the central historical tale of wreck and loss. (In many ways, this fits in with a broader perception that historical archaeology is little more than the handmaiden of history.) This, however, seriously underestimates the archaeological potential of the wrecks themselves.

Modern shipwrecks can significantly contribute to our understanding of historical events if the bodies of the wrecks are subject to a kind of scrutiny that seeks to go beyond the original historical depiction of the sinking, adopting an approach closer to that used by the investigators of lost Cold War naval assets. I have attempted to do this with the wrecks of the Battle of Jutland and in the study of more than 100 U-boat wrecks and am not alone in using this approach.

While all shipwrecks can offer some element of new information as to how they sank, the scale of the new data obviously varies from case to case. Some wrecks, such as HMS *Queen Mary,* have proven to be revelatory in what they can offer. Others, such as SMS *Lützow,* have told us little aside from the fact that portions of the ship have been salvaged. Yet every wreck has at least revealed something new that has added to our understanding of Jutland.

Importantly, it has become increasingly clear that there is plenty left to learn about the technologies used on the sunken ships. For example, in her time HMS *Queen Mary* was among the most complex structures ever built. No single person would have understood even a small portion of the myriad technologies she contained. Today few people know much about how she really functioned and this is one of the major challenges faced by archaeologists when examining complex modern shipwrecks; something my colleagues who prefer the certainties of ancient dug-out canoes have never had to think about.

Nautical battlefield scale

Battlefield archaeology is not normally associated with nautical contexts. Owing to the unique circumstances of naval conflict, the challenges faced by the nautical archaeologist are different from land contexts. I have previously published a detailed study of the U-boat wrecks in the English Channel from both world wars and have placed the findings in the contexts of the battlefields in which they were lost.[7]

In that case, my approach was to view the wrecks both individually and collectively and compare the results of the 63 wreck surveys with the original Allied documents that, up until then, had been the dominant force in informing the historical record. The results revealed a wide variance in the accuracy of the Allied naval intelligence records and demonstrated the value of examining shipwrecks on the battlefield level.

At Jutland, I've adopted a not entirely dissimilar approach. The distribution of the wrecks has been benchmarked against the best geographically referenced charts of the battle to find differences and similarities. Where the two datasets coincide and conflict with each other they can potentially tell us much about how the records were compiled and how the battle was viewed by its participants.

The *Harper Record*

Original copies of the *Harper Record* are difficult to find. Until recently I only ever worked from two now quite ragged photocopies. But from the first time I saw it I knew that the *Harper Record* was a very useful source document to anyone who sought to explore the battlefield. This is because it seemingly is agenda-free and simply a chronology of the battle, giving the positions of where Harper thought the ships sank – most useful to an archaeologist. The Harper charts are even rarer than the *Record;* I hope readers will appreciate just how useful they are.

It is difficult not to admire the work carried out by Captain JET Harper, his team of four officers and their assistants in compiling what is commonly referred to as the *Harper Record*.[1] It was the first and, as it turned out, the only attempt made by the Admiralty to produce an honest, unvarnished version of events. Other Admiralty portrayals of the battle are sadly contaminated with varying degrees of agenda-laden falsehoods. The reason it failed to see

publication in its original impartial version, with charts, had nothing to do with the quality of Harper's work.

The compilation of the *Harper Record* must have been a colossal undertaking. According to Harper: 'My orders were to prepare a Record, with plans, showing in chronological order what actually occurred in the battle. No comment or criticism was to be included and no oral evidence was to be accepted. All statements made in the Record were to be in accordance with evidence obtainable from Admiralty records.'[8] From February to September 1919 Harper and his team worked through the mass of charts, tracings, gunnery records and other reports. Permission was sought in April to locate the wreck of HMS *Invincible* and it was duly found in July, allowing Beatty's and Jellicoe's tracks to be reconciled.

The *Harper Record* was submitted in October 1919 but not seen in public in anything like its original form until 1927, and even then without its charts. The charts were never officially published. Instead, in 1920 the Admiralty published *Jutland Dispatches*, a compilation of original reports, charts and signals from the battle.[9] Although remarkably detailed, it was unintelligible to the average reader. Some alterations to original documents had also been made, not least to HMS *Lion*'s movements.

By the time the *Harper Record* was published in 1927 (seemingly to conflict with the launch of Harper's *The Truth About Jutland*, published at the same time), Harper had dissociated himself from a number of corrections that he felt had been forced on him, not least on some of the charts which, he felt, erroneously portrayed the movements of Battlecruiser Fleet after 17.00 on 31 May 1916.[10] Harper never hid his bitterness about how the *Record* had been subverted.

The unsightly 'Jutland Scandal' into which the *Harper Record* was drawn is outside the scope of this book, but it was seemingly too soon after the battle to attempt an impartial record of events. The author Leslie Gardiner put it succinctly: 'Too many Jutland veterans were still alive, still engaged in a longer running fight, the promotion battle, still anxious to clear their individual yardarms after the action.'[11] As a consequence, Harper's task was something of a poisoned chalice. It mattered little just how impartial or accurate the *Harper Record* actually was because in any case it would inevitably find its detractors. They came in the form of Admiral Beatty who, having just been made First Sea Lord, found the *Harper Record* awaiting his approval when he arrived at the Admiralty. It was Beatty who blocked its progress through official and unofficial means.

By comparison with Harper, geographical data is missing from many other histories, even though they were published replete with maps. Notably Corbett,[12] Groos[13] and Marder[14] did not geographically reference their diagrams and only some of the charts in *Jutland Dispatches*[9] are geographically referenced. Therefore in the study of the Battle of Jutland at the battlefield level the *Harper Record* is a very important source document. Its geographical referencing means that the charts can be digitised and accurately incorporated into the electronic charting of the battle. This is how the maps in this book were compiled.

Other historical sources

There are a number of other sources that have continually proved of use while researching the wrecks. The National Archives hold a great deal of material on the battle; the reports of commanders and maps and records of the German Navy compiled by the Intelligence Division have all proved invaluable. All sources used have been referenced throughout the text. Of particular use has been the Admiralty translation of the official German history of the Battle of Jutland.[15] The original ship's plans of many of the wrecks sunk at Jutland are housed at the National Maritime Museum and have proven invaluable in deciphering much of the archaeology recorded.

Aside from the archival sources, innumerable published sources have been consulted throughout the years. The most useful include Campbell's *Analysis of the Fighting*,[16] Friedman's compilation of British intelligence sources on the German Navy,[17] March's superb history of British destroyers,[18] Parkes's companion volume on British battleships[19] and Gordon's *Rules of the Game*.[20]

Eyewitness accounts

The most useful eyewitness accounts in researching the shipwrecks tend to be those from survivors of ships that sank or those who witnessed the destruction of others, preferably recorded as soon after events as possible. Eyewitness accounts can be revelatory but also very inconsistent and unreliable. For example, one survivor from HMS *Queen Mary* recalled in 1972 that the ship was torpedoed and took 20 minutes to sink when in reality she took little more than a few seconds to sink after shellfire caused a magazine detonation.[21]

You can also imagine a situation where the ships' crews all talked to each other about the battle in the hours afterwards, affecting each participant's memory of events. By the time the Grand Fleet arrived back in Britain each ship could have, to a greater or lesser degree, developed her own personal account of events. It is important to recognise this and take a somewhat less than sanguine view of what eyewitnesses have to offer.

Inevitably some accounts tend to ring truer than others. Perhaps this is just personal preference, but as much as possible the selection of eyewitness accounts used in this book has been drawn from those that tend to support what the archaeology of the wrecks is telling us; however, this is not always the case. In instances where practically nothing is known of what happened to a ship, whatever eyewitness accounts are available have been used as evidence for consideration.

By far the most valuable published volumes of eyewitness accounts are those by Fawcett & Hooper[22] and Steel & Hart.[23] Accounts from both sides can be found in the National Archives, Leeds University Library and the Imperial War Museum. The researchers Peter Liddle and Robert Church, in particular, are owed a great debt of gratitude for recording the words of so many of Jutland's participants during the 1970s and 80s.

Fieldwork objectives

The purpose of this book is to place a full written record of the fieldwork in which I have been involved on the Jutland shipwrecks in the public domain in time for the 100th anniversary of the battle. Although we now know the exact locations and identities of 22 of the wrecks, this study is not definitive, but it has reached a point where the results have become extensive enough to form a springboard for further research.

The motivation behind my earliest dives on the Jutland wrecks was the sort of curiosity that all explorers seem to share. But as time passed and my understanding of what was there began to grow, it became apparent that the wrecks had a unique story to tell. By examining their remains it was possible to contribute significantly to the history of the battle. The next step was to try to define in archaeological terms what this actually meant. Studying archaeology to PhD level certainly helped me in this as did my surveys of countless submarine wrecks.

Diving or surveying wrecks and seeing how what is there is confirmed by the history books may make nice television, but it is not archaeology. To do that is to fulfil 'the fallacy of affirming the consequent'[24] and once you know what it is, you see it all the time. The acid test is to ask yourself: 'If we know this anyway, why are we here?' It's better to ask how the shipwrecks can shed light on what we do not know, but could find out if we looked.

In the case of the Battle of Jutland, in particular, a major constraint on the archaeologist is the sheer weight of archival and written information about the battle. The archaeologist needs to have a working knowledge of this literature, of a highly complex battle involving highly complex ships, battle fleets' fighting instructions and so on.

Moreover, in common with many modern shipping losses, there is a plethora of eyewitness accounts and descriptions of events which depict, sometimes in great detail, the building, life, roles, purposes and losses of the ships under investigation. This has led some to doubt whether such shipwrecks have any archaeological worth. This debate reached a crescendo over the wreck of the RMS *Titanic* when it was claimed that the site had no archaeological merit.[25]

The case of the USS *Arizona* shares similarities with the Jutland wrecks. There, symbolically laden terms such as 'war-grave' and 'desecration' meant that the archaeologists have undertaken not to enter the wreck and be conscious of how their findings may be displayed.[26] Similarly, the TV producers gave undertakings to the Ministry of Defence (MOD) not to disturb or enter the Jutland wrecks, nor to depict images of a perceived emotive nature when we were making the television documentary *Clash of the Dreadnoughts* in 2003.

Main areas of study

Within the constraints described above, there are two major categories that shaped the fieldwork carried out on the wrecks:

Firstly, the wreck sites offer an opportunity to assess the reports of how the ships were destroyed and the myriad eyewitness accounts and weed out any incorrect interpretations of events. At the same time, they can also contribute new and unique data to what was previously known about how the ships sank. As you'll find out, the extant remains of many of the Jutland wrecks have significantly enhanced the history of the battle, especially in those cases where either the chaos of events or the lack of survivors had led to a great deal of speculation in the past.

Secondly, the accurate wreck positions offer the opportunity to produce a better map of where the losses actually occurred, which could potentially lead to a greater understanding of the battle and help assess the accuracy of various conflicting accounts of what happened. In geographical terms at least, they offer the possibility to measure the accuracy of official track charts and reports. Ultimately the most detailed studies, such as the *Harper Record*, can be re-examined to see how and why elements were either correctly or incorrectly portrayed.

Beyond these two objectives, the surveys were also essential to identify the smaller wrecks and, in so doing, highlighting what remains of them and how they are rapidly deteriorating. Furthermore, they also uncovered an unsavoury record of illegal salvage for profit on several sites.

Before the battlefield could be accurately mapped, the wrecks needed to be identified. There were no real issues with the larger ones because of their comparative uniqueness. However, the destroyers and torpedo boats did need to be specifically identified and this required fieldwork and detailed archaeological analysis.

Along with the examination of the wrecks for archaeological purposes, we assessed just how much remains of them and attempted to gauge how much longer they will remain in a condition in which they remain worthy of study (see Chapter 15). During this type of assessment we realised that increasing numbers of the wrecks had been subject to salvage for profit in recent years, causing damage to the sites and seriously disrupting their archaeological potential.

Surveying the large wrecks

Early on we recognised that the North Sea presents some tricky challenges to those who wish to survey the Jutland wrecks. The cold and the depth of the wrecks are major limiting factors to what divers can hope to achieve in the short duration they have on each dive. On the deeper wrecks, helium-enriched gases are essential, bottom time is short and decompression is long. The limited time and the sheer size of the Jutland wrecks mean that traditional methods of wreck recording by divers are hopelessly impractical. The best way to record what is seen is to use a video camera on every dive, and over time bring together an overall picture of what is present.

Better still is to employ an ROV, which does not labour under the time constraints imposed on divers. The ROV work in 2003 really opened up the potential for detailed study and was the basis behind my papers on HMS *Defence*[5] and HMS *Invincible*.[6] The ROV worked better than diving because of the time that could be spent examining the wrecks, but it was not perfect. The ROV employed on these surveys had the potential to see much, but disorientation was always a possibility as there was no telemetry recorded. What was really required to build up accurate site maps was geophysics.

In 2003 some side scan passes were made, showing the potential of this technology on a dedicated expedition. Multibeam imaging was still not producing the type of resolution required to make it useful on the deeper wrecks. However, by 2008 this had changed. I was involved in the making of a documentary about the loss of the Dreadnought HMS *Audacious* to a mine in 1914. During the filming, multibeam imaging was employed (see Fig.v) and the results were very helpful in mapping the wreck site, understanding how she had sunk and revealing how she had subsequently collapsed as a shipwreck.

Clearly this technology would be essential to figure out what is present on the Jutland battlefield. So it was with great enthusiasm that I accepted the

chance to work as Gert Normann Andersen's number two on a dedicated multibeam survey of the Jutland battlefield in 2015. The EIVA multibeam system in use on MV *Vina* is state of the art and has really helped push the study of the Jutland battlefield to another dimension. This expedition also happily coincided with the discovery of so many of the smaller shipwrecks, which, with one exception, had eluded us during the diving expeditions. The challenge that remained was to identify these smaller wrecks.

Identifying the small wrecks

The multibeam results of the April 2015 survey revealed a number of wrecks that were likely to be torpedo boats and destroyers. Some had been confirmed as such by the ROV. In many cases the wrecks were very corroded; in some cases right down to the boilers being the only remaining recognisable features. So a methodology was needed to try to differentiate the sites.

I decided to develop a typology that could, if the wrecks yielded enough clues, be used to distinguish each wreck down to the class of ship to which she was built. This involved inspecting the original builder's plans of all the classes of destroyers and torpedo boats sunk at Jutland. The 13 smaller ships sunk fell into six classes. The lower deck and hold plans of these classes showed clearly how the heavy machinery within each class was distributed within their hull forms.[17][27] Each class of warship turned out to be sufficiently different to allow a very useful tool to be developed (Fig. vi).

The typology was based on the supposition that what appeared on the multibeam images was likely to be the types of heavy machinery that have survived 100 years underwater, notably the boilers, condensers and turbines. The distribution of these features is significantly different from class to class. For example, HMS *Tipperary* has a unique number of boilers, whereas the German vessels tended to have more compact double engine rooms, thanks to the use of the Föttinger transformer system. British designs tended to have a single engine room and employed both cruising and high-pressure turbines. As it turned out, this typology proved to be useful in differentiating the smaller wrecks down to the class level.

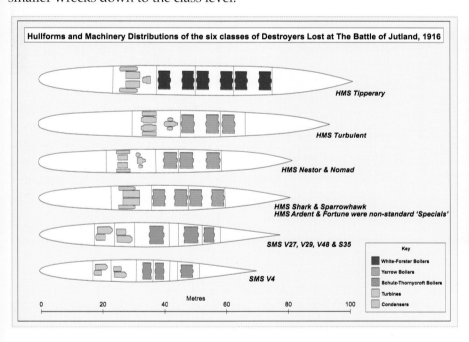

Hullforms and Machinery Distributions of the six classes of Destroyers Lost at The Battle of Jutland, 1916

HMS Tipperary

HMS Turbulent

HMS Nestor & Nomad

HMS Shark & Sparrowhawk
HMS Ardent & Fortune were non-standard 'Specials'

SMS V27, V29, V48 & S35

SMS V4

Key
White-Forster Boilers
Yarrow Boilers
Schulz-Thornycroft Boilers
Turbines
Condensers

Metres
0   20   40   60   80   100

Fig. vi *Typology of the six classes of destroyers and torpedo boats lost at Jutland. The typology is based on the overall dimensions of their hull forms and the distribution of the boilers, turbines and condensers. These tend to be the most common surviving features easily detectable on multibeam, for which this typology was developed alongside.*

One common piece of machinery across nearly all of the warships sunk at Jutland was the three-drum boiler. This was a boiler system that used three drums in a triangular configuration, with the heat source in the middle heating the upper drum, known as the steam drum. There were three different designs in use among the smaller vessels (Fig. vii). We hoped that from the ROV data it would be possible to distinguish the types of boiler on each ship based on these design differences.

Fig. vii shows the subtle differences: The boilers are displayed in a split diagram that shows the internals on one side and what they looked like completed on the other. The boiler in common use in the Royal Navy was the Yarrow type (A), characterised by its absolutely straight water tubes and the oval nature of the bottom two tubes, known as water troughs. The White-Forster type seen exclusively on the wreck of HMS *Tipperary* (B) looked very similar to the Yarrow type, but the tubes are gently curved. The German Navy seems to have almost exclusively used the Schulz-Thornycroft boiler, often called simply the 'marine type'.[28] The version in Fig. vii (C) has four tubes, but this system came in two- to four-tube variants. The Schulz-Thornycroft type is characterised by very obviously curved water tubes and circular water troughs. All three types of boiler are visible on the Jutland wrecks.

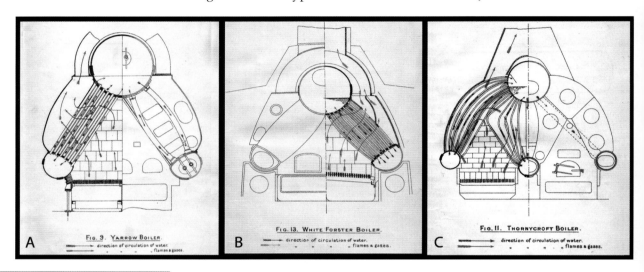

Fig. vii *The three types of three-drum boiler in use in the smaller warships sunk during the Battle of Jutland. Yarrow (A) is the common British type, White-Forster was used in HMS Tipperary (B), and the Schulz-Thornycroft type (C) was in extensive use in the Imperial German Navy. (Picture: Stoker's Manual, 1911)*

Times and measurements

As much as possible, the timings used have been derived from the *Harper Record*. These are British (GMT) time, which is an hour behind the times used by the German High Seas Fleet (CET) and generally seen in German accounts of the battle.

Imperial measurements have been used to describe the ships and events in a historic context, while metric measurements have been used to discuss the archaeology of the wrecks and modern interpretations of the results. This was the simplest convention to use as events happened when Britain used the imperial system and the archaeology developed as a discipline after the metric system came into use.

Notes

1   Harper JET. *Reproduction of the Record of the Battle of Jutland*. London: HMSO; 1927.

2   Gordon, A., 1996. *The Rules of the Game. Jutland and British Naval Command*. London: John Murray: 2.

3   Harper JET. *Reproduction of the Record of the Battle of Jutland*. London: HMSO; 1927. p.117.

4   Campbell NJM. *Jutland: an Analysis of the Fighting*. London: Conway; 1986. p.1.

5   McCartney I. The armoured cruiser HMS *Defence*: a case study in assessing the Royal Navy shipwrecks of the Battle of Jutland 1916 as an archaeological resource. *International Journal of Nautical Archaeology* 2012; 41(1):56–66.

6   McCartney I. Jutland 1916: The archaeology of a modern naval battle: the wreck of HMS *Invincible*, the world's first battlecruiser. *Skyllis* 2012; 2:168-76.

7   McCartney I. *The maritime archaeology of a modern conflict: comparing the archaeology of German submarine wrecks to the historical text*. New York: Routledge; 2014.

8   Temple Patterson A, editor. *The Jellicoe Papers*: Volume II *1916–1935*. London: Navy Records Society; 1968. p.464.

9   Admiralty. *Battle of Jutland: 30th May to 1st June 1916: Official Dispatches with Appendices*. London: HMSO; 1920.

10   Temple Patterson A, editor. *The Jellicoe Papers*: Volume II *1916–1935*. London: Navy Records Society; 1968. pp.462–90.

11   Gardiner L. *The Royal Oak Courts Martial*. Edinburgh: Blackwood; 1965. p.82.

12   Corbett JS. *History of the Great War based on Official Documents: Naval Operations, Vol. III*. London: Longmans, Green and Co.; 1923.

13   Groos O. *Der Krieg zur See 1914–1918. Nordsee Band 5: Kartenband*. Berlin: Mittler & Sohn; 1925.

14   Marder AJ. *From the Dreadnought to Scapa Flow: Volume III*. Oxford: OUP; 1966.

15   National Archives (various dates). Groos O. *The Battle of Jutland: Official German Account*. Translated Bagot WT. ADM 186/626. London: Admiralty; 1926.

16   Campbell NJM. *Jutland: an Analysis of the Fighting*. London: Conway; 1986.

17   Royal Navy. *German Warships of World War I*. London: Greenhill; 1992.

18   March EJ. *British Destroyers: a History of Development 1892–1953*. London: Seeley Service & Co.; 1966.

19   Parkes O. *British Battleships*. London: Seeley Service & Co.; 1970.

20   Gordon A. *The Rules of the Game*. London: John Murray; 1996.

21   Church Papers Misc 1010. WJ Wilkins correspondence, Imperial War Museum (various dates), London.

22   Fawcett HW, Hooper GWW. *The Fighting at Jutland*. Glasgow: Maclure, Macdonald & Co.; 1921.

23   Steel N, Hart P. *Jutland 1916*. London: Cassell; 2003.

24   Gould RA. Beyond exploration: underwater archaeology after the year 2000. *Historical Archaeology* 2000; 34(4):24–28.

25   Bass GF, Searle WF. Epilog. In: Bass GF, editor. *Ships and Shipwrecks of the Americas*. London: Thames and Hudson; 1988.

26   Delgado JP. Recovering the past of USS *Arizona*: symbolism, myth and reality. *Historical Archaeology* 1992; 26(4):69–80.

27   National Maritime Museum (various dates), Controller's Department, Admiralty (undated). Constructor's plans of *HMS Marne*, New torpedo boat destroyers 1911–12, *HMS Tipperary, HMS Trident* and *SMS V25–30*. Ship's plans collection, London.

28   *Jane's Fighting Ships of World War I*. London: Studio Editions; 1990. p.116.

Vice Admirals Beatty, left, and von Hipper, right, the commanders of the opposing battlecruiser forces, clashed in the opening phase of the Battle of Jutland, as they had done at Dogger Bank the year before. On this occasion Hipper emerged ascendant, sinking two British battlecruisers, HMS Indefatigable *and HMS* Queen Mary. *(Pictures: Crown Copyright, left; Archiv Deutscher Marinebund, right)*

PART ONE

THE BATTLECRUISER ACTION

1
BATTLECRUISER
HMS *INDEFATIGABLE*

Sunk by gunfire at 1602 on 31 May

Fig. 1.1 *HMS* Indefatigable. *Displacement: 18,500 tons, length: 555 ft, eight 12-inch guns, sixteen 4-inch guns. (Picture: Topical Press Agency/ Getty Images)*

The remains of HMS Indefatigable, *the first of three British battlecruisers sunk during the battle, are the most challenging to decipher. It was not until the 2015 multibeam survey that the extent of the dispersed nature of the wreck site and the way in which the ship was reported sinking came to be understood.*

The battlecruiser HMS *Indefatigable*, the lead ship of the Indefatigable class, was essentially an elongated *Invincible* (see Chapter 5), making her capable of firing both her wing ('Q' and 'P') turrets in broadside without restriction.[1] She was ordered in the 1908 building programme and constructed at Devonport, launched in October 1909 and completed in February 1911. Her early career was with the Home Fleet as part of the First Cruiser Squadron, later renamed the First Battlecruiser Squadron, but in December 1913 she was transferred to the Mediterranean to serve with the Second Battlecruiser Squadron and was there as war spread through Europe.[2]

So it was on 4 August 1914 that the *Indefatigable,* under the command of Admiral Milne, found herself chasing the German battlecruiser *Goeben* together with HMS *Indomitable,* attempting to stay in contact in time for the British deadline to expire at midnight. Fresh from overhaul, SMS *Goeben* was able to pull ahead slowly and escape, heading for Messina, which she reached unmolested. *Goeben* and *Breslau*'s subsequent escape to the Dardanelles does not need retelling here, suffice to say that the *Indefatigable* did not make contact with them again.[3] Under Admiral Troubridge, HMS *Indefatigable* and HMS *Defence* (see Chapter 4) began to maintain the blockade of the Dardanelles from 20 August 1914 onwards, to prevent the German ships from breaking out.[4]

Now the Dardanelles became a focus of attention in the Mediterranean. In September Troubridge was replaced by Carden and the forces in the area had significantly increased, and included HMS *Indomitable,* two French battleships, light cruisers, destroyers and submarines. Ordered to bombard the outer Dardanelles forts, Carden launched the attack on 3 November. The British battlecruisers attacked the European side and in a ten-minute barrage set off the magazine at the Sedd-el-Bahr battery.[5] In reality this did little more than inform the Turks of the need to reinforce the area and expand the coastal minefield.

On 24 January 1915 the *Indefatigable* left the Dardanelles for refit at Malta. From there she sailed for home waters and on 14 February joined the Second Battlecruiser Squadron of the Grand Fleet's Battlecruiser Fleet. Her service from then until the Battle of Jutland was unremarkable. However, it was during this period that the ship was fitted with director firing, enabling salvoes to be sighted and controlled from a central control position. Other modifications included better protection for the 4-inch guns in the form of casemates, the addition of two AA guns, expansion of the after superstructure, and the topmasts cut down.[6]

HMS *Indefatigable* was at Rosyth with the Battlecruiser Fleet under the command of Acting Vice Admiral Sir David Beatty when she sortied for the Battle of Jutland. The Battlecruiser Fleet's key role was to act as a fast wing of the fleet and to scout ahead of the main battle fleet under the command of Admiral Sir John Jellicoe and, if possible, bring any German elements to battle.

The role of the German battlecruisers denoted as the First Scouting Group under the command of Vice Admiral Franz von Hipper was essentially the same. It was Hipper, attempting to do just this, who turned about to southward on sighting the Battlecruiser Fleet approaching from the west. Beatty pursued and this opening fight of the Battlecruiser Action has become known as the 'Run to the South'. Hipper brought the unsuspecting Beatty to the guns of the approaching German High Seas Fleet. Firing began at around 15.45, with both battle lines commencing simultaneously.[7]

Loss

The Battlecruiser Fleet line consisted of HMS *Lion*, the lead ship and Beatty's flagship, followed by the *Princess Royal*, *Queen Mary*, *Tiger*, *New Zealand* and lastly, the *Indefatigable*. Opposing them the German battlecruiser line consisted of Hipper's flagship, SMS *Lützow*, followed by the *Derfflinger*, *Seydlitz*, *Moltke* and *Von der Tann*. The gunnery duel between the two lines of battlecruisers initially favoured the British not only in the numbers of ships (six against five) but also in weight of shot, with the four leading British ships being equipped with the newer, heavier and longer-ranged 13.5-inch gun.

Fig. 1.2 HMS Indefatigable *allegedly 30 minutes before action at Jutland began. (Picture: Imperial War Museum SP799)*

But it was the Germans who found their range more effectively, aided in part by better visibility. Although hits were achieved by both sides, the German gunners were ascendant, scoring 42 hits on the British battlecruisers in the first hour of action and receiving only 11 in return in the same time.[8] The British line was seen to be surrounded by a 'forest of fountains' as salvoes continually crashed into the sea around it.[9]

At around 15.55 SMS *Seydlitz* was struck on a midship turret. The resulting fire killed all in this turret and in the lower handling room. Magazine flooding averted 'a greater catastrophe'.[9] Similarly, five minutes later, Beatty's flagship, HMS *Lion*, was hit on 'Q' turret. Eighty died in the cordite fire that followed. In this case, a potentially fatal detonation of the underlying magazine was also averted by flooding, which was allegedly ordered by the mortally wounded marine Major Francis Harvey who was consequently awarded the first of the posthumous Victoria Crosses of the Battle of Jutland.

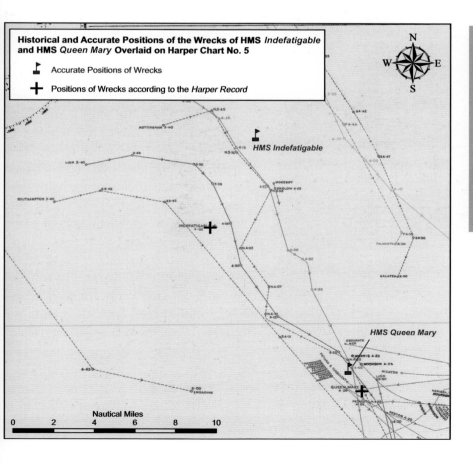

Fig. 1.3 The start of the 'Run to the South' as depicted by Harper, showing his appreciation of where HMS Indefatigable sank and her actual known position as a shipwreck. The track of the Battlecruiser Fleet (HMS Lion) can be seen on her southward run. The First Scouting Group was to the east.

Only minutes were to pass before the devastating consequences of a warship magazine explosion were witnessed at Jutland for the first time. HMS *Indefatigable* had, since opening fire, been in an uninterrupted one-to-one gunnery duel with SMS *Von der Tann*. According to Harper, disaster struck at around 16.02 when she sank killing all but two of her complement of 1,019.[10] Fig. 1.3 depicts the battle situation at this time.

Eyewitness accounts

In the case of HMS *Indefatigable* it was her position as the last ship in the line that meant that the key moment when she was hit had relatively few witnesses. The closest battlecruiser, 500 yards ahead (2.5 cables bridge to bridge), was the *New Zealand*, hotly engaged with the *Moltke*, as her navigating officer recalled:

> *The loss of our next astern happened so suddenly that, almost before we realised she had gone, our attention was entirely absorbed by the battle that was now progressing. The noise of our own salvoes, and the shrieking of the enemy's shells falling over or short, and the throwing up of great sheets of spray, left one with little time to think of anything except the work in hand.*[11]

Fig. 1.4 *King-Hall's sketch of what was last seen of HMS* Indefatigable. *(Picture: King-Hall, Liddle Collection, Burroughs Papers)*

The most common accounts simply depict the smoke that arose from the already sinking ship. Chief Petty Officer William Cave, range taker at the foremast of the light cruiser HMS *Dublin*, of the Second Light Cruiser Squadron on starboard of the battle line, noted the time as 16.05 when he saw one detonation as 'an inferno of flame & smoke, her picket boat was seen in the air, intact before dropping back into the smoke'.[12] In his account of Jutland, witnessed with an unobstructed view from the after control station on the light cruiser HMS *Southampton* (the lead ship of the Second Light Cruiser Squadron), Sub-lieutenant Stephen King-Hall (later the politician Baron King-Hall of Headley) recorded:

> *I was watching the line at 4.15 (approx.) and had just noted with satisfaction that the* Lion *was emerging from a collection of huge fountains of water, when I was horrified to see a colossal column of grey white smoke stand on the water where the* Indefatigable

had been. This column of smoke I estimate was 700 feet high, expanded on top into a great mushroom. The base… then became a fiery red.[13]

Note the difference in timings of around ten minutes, possibly suggesting that the destruction of the ship took longer than is recorded in *Harper* and elsewhere. The issue of timing will be returned to later.

Another, similar account came from Harry Oram on the fore gun of the destroyer HMS *Obdurate* (part of the Thirteenth Destroyer Flotilla to *Lion*'s port), who recalled in his autobiography:

> [M]y sleeve was pulled by one of the gun's crew drawing my attention to Indefatigable, *the last ship in the British line which, enveloped in smoke, had hauled out to starboard… To our horror we saw her hit again and shattered by a violent explosion, the great ship rolled over and sank.*[14]

Greater detail from those who saw the *Indefatigable* hit comes from HMS *New Zealand*. The *Harper Record*'s description of her sinking is cursory:

> Indefatigable *was hit by three shots falling together… The shots appeared to hit the outer edge of the upper deck in line with the after turret. An explosion followed and she fell out of line sinking by the stern. Hit again by another salvo near 'A' turret, she turned over and sank.*[15]

This is very similar to Admiral Pakenham's description, as seen from the upper bridge of HMS *New Zealand*, and Harper must have gleaned his description from it.[16] However, it was the torpedo officer of HMS *New Zealand*, Lieutenant-Commander Lovett-Cameron, stationed in the conning tower, who gave a most detailed account. Without opportunity to fire he was free to witness the event in detail through binoculars:

> [S]he had been hit aft, apparently by the mainmast, and a good deal of smoke was coming from her superstructure aft, but there were no flames visible… We were altering course to port at the time and apparently her steering gear was damaged as she did not follow round in our wake, but held on until she was about 500 yards on our starboard quarter, in full view of the conning tower… she was [then] hit by two shells, one on the fo'c'sle and one on the fore turret. Both shells appeared to explode on impact. Then there was an interval of about 30 seconds, during which there was absolutely no fire or flame or smoke, except the little actually formed by the burst of the two shells, which was not considerable. At the end of the interval of about 30 seconds the ship completely blew up, apparently from forward. The main explosion started with sheets of flame, followed immediately afterwards by dense dark smoke which obscured the ship from view.[17]

From the German side, *Von der Tann* is known to have opened fire at 15.49. An account by her gunnery officer, Korvettenkapitän (KK, the German equivalent of lieutenant-commander) Mahrholz, states that his target may have been initially hit by the earliest salvoes, but that the crippling blow came at 16.03 when the after part of the ship exploded. A further salvo struck forward and finished off the ship. But firing continued into the subsequent billowing smoke cloud to ensure the target was finished. The remarkably swift accurate fire by *Von der Tann* had sunk the *Indefatigable* in around a quarter of an hour by the expenditure of fifty-two 11-inch and thirty-eight 5.9-inch projectiles.[18]

Fig. 1.5 HMS Indefatigable *sinking by the stern before the reported final explosion, in contrast to Lovett-Cameron's assertion that the ship was intact until she exploded. (Picture: Windmill Books/ Getty Images)*

The only two survivors, Signaller C Falmer and Able Seaman Elliot (later rescued from the sea by the torpedo boat SMS *S16*), had been in the foretop and had been thrown sufficiently clear by the falling mast to have avoided being sucked down with the ship. Falmer later recounted:

> There was a terrific explosion aboard the ship – the magazines went. I saw the guns go up in the air just like matchsticks… bodies and everything. She was beginning to settle down. Within half a minute the ship turned right over and she was gone. I was 180 foot up and was thrown well clear of the ship… When I came up there was another fellow named Jimmy Green and we got a piece of wood… A couple of minutes afterwards some shells came over and Jim was minus his head.[19]

The few known eyewitness accounts differ, but when analysed a chronology of events seems to emerge. The accounts generally agree that the *Indefatigable* hauled out of line to starboard and then blew up as she sank. Two accounts claim she rolled over of which only Harper's account seems to state correctly that the ship was already sinking when struck a second time.

Photography

Remarkably, there is one photograph that depicts this incident. Other published photos claiming to show the *Indefatigable* sinking are most probably of the *Queen Mary* as will be explained in the next chapter.[20] Fig.1.5 was taken by Midshipman WP Carne from the after torpedo control station on the *New Zealand*. This photograph seems to clearly show the *Indefatigable* in her death throes, leaning very heavily to port and sinking by the stern. This fits with the Harper description and with what Oram claimed he saw.

The absence of the *New Zealand*'s wake in the photograph also seems to attest to eyewitness views that the *Indefatigable* hauled off to starboard, out of the correct line and was on the *New Zealand*'s starboard quarter at this time. The photograph must have been taken before the final conflagration in which the ship 'completely blew up' as stated by Lovett-Cameron and others. The noticeable shell splash to the right of the sinking ship either confirms that the *Indefatigable* was still under fire from *Von der Tann* at this time, or is possibly an 'over' aimed at the *New Zealand*. It can be surmised that the survivors from the foremast must already be in the sea as the mast is horizontal in this image. The continuing shell fire killed Jimmy Green in the water.

That a final explosion occurred after this photo was taken has been attested by several witnesses, notably Lovett-Cameron. However, its actual cause may never be known for certain; for example, it could have been down to shifting ammunition, as most likely in the case of HMS *Audacious* in 1914, which also exploded as she rolled over (as I've extensively investigated). It is also quite likely that it was a salvo from *Von der Tann*, as depicted by KK Mahrholz and others. The pall of smoke, drawn by King-Hall, was what the ship ultimately sank under and what drew the attention of several witnesses.

The wreck

One of the motivating factors for locating and examining this wreck was to see whether it was possible to ascertain if there had been a secondary explosion as the *Indefatigable* sank, or if she was largely intact as the Carne photograph seems to depict.

In 2000, I didn't know the position of this wreck. The Hydrographic Office record for the wreck, derived from the 75th Anniversary Expedition had proven to be a false lead. It later turned out to be 6.1 nautical miles away from the wreck.[21] So in 2001, I arranged to meet Gert Normann at his headquarters in Holstebro, Denmark. His knowledge of the shipwrecks off Denmark remains unsurpassed and a fascinating afternoon followed as we exchanged data. Gert had access to a database of trawler snags in the North Sea and shared the most promising positions (based on *Harper*) that he could find. In return, I shared my own positional information and videos of the wrecks I'd examined so far. This meeting directly led to me being the first to dive both the *Indefatigable* and *Defence* later that year.

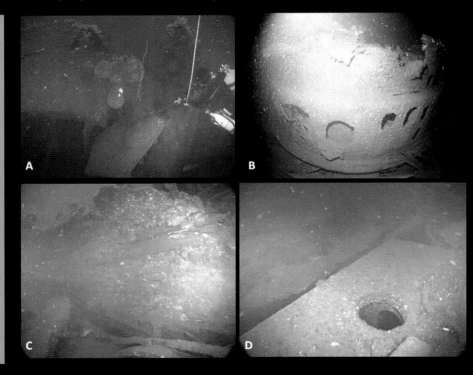

Fig. 1.6 *The scattered remains of the wreck of HMS* Indefatigable *as seen in 2001. A shows a diver tying our down line to the wreck on the first dive. A propeller from one of* Indefatigable's *tenders can be seen in the centre of the picture. B shows the upside-down remains of the lower portion of what is possibly 'P' turret. C depicts a portion of the deck seen lying on its side. The entire site is a jumble of twisted wreckage. D shows the open escape hatch on the underside of the counterbalance of what is possibly 'P' turret. (Picture B: Patricia McCartney)*

The site was first examined by diving on 17 May 2001. It was far from certain that this position would be the *Indefatigable* because of its distance from the *Harper* position (see Fig. 1.3). But when we looked at the site with *Loyal Watcher*'s bottom sounder, its sheer size made it worth examining by diving. And from the moment the dive team descended to the wreck, her identity was never in doubt. On that day the site was dived twice and the results were something of a surprise.

With underwater visibility on site being in excess of 25 metres and at a depth of 48 metres, it was easy to see that the wreck site was scattered over a very wide area. There was no part of the wreck standing much higher than five metres. Most of the wreck appeared to have been smashed into unrecognisable pieces of twisted metal. But among the wreckage was enough material to safely conclude that the wreck was the *Indefatigable* and that at least some portion of her was upside down. Figures 1.6 to 1.8 depict some of the items seen on the first dives in 2001.

After the dives in 2001 we concluded that in the wreckage were the remains of at least two of the 12-inch gun turrets, at least one 4-inch gun and some of the remains of the ship's 7-inch armour protection. The presence of these items clearly meant that this could not be any other wreck than the *Indefatigable* because the only similar type in the waters of the North Sea was HMS *Invincible* and her wreck had already been conclusively found elsewhere (see Chapter 5).

However, the real surprise was the extent to which the wreckage was broken down and scattered over a wide area, which was suggestive at the time of possible later salvage operations on the site, or even possible depth-charging in the Second World War. It was difficult to imagine that any other forces could have so completely destroyed such a large shipwreck. Four-inch guns were seen jumbled up with the crushed portions of the ship's Yarrow boilers, and few pieces of wreckage were much larger than a car. Swimming in any direction simply took the divers over a field of devastation. So after two dives, the hook was retrieved and *Loyal Watcher* moved on.

I briefly returned to the site on 17 August 2003 with the television documentary expedition. One evening, as MV *Gorm* was readied to move to the wreck of HMS *Queen Mary*, a few passes over the *Indefatigable* wreck site were made with the side scanning sonar system, in the hope that a clearer idea of what was actually present on the seabed might be established. By today's standards the system we had was primitive and the results did little more than confirm that the wreck site contained largely undecipherable wreckage.

The 2015 survey significantly changed the understanding of what this site represents. The main reason for this was multibeam. It represents a leap

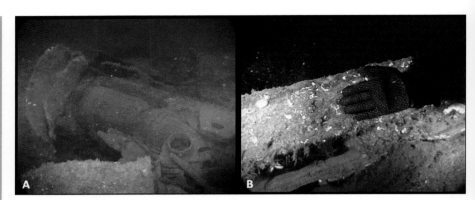

Fig. 1.7 *The scattered remains of the wreck of HMS* Indefatigable *as seen in 2001. A depicts a 12-inch gun on its side, lying completely separated from the remains of its turret. B shows my hand for scale on a portion of 7-inch armour plate as fitted to HMS* Indefatigable.

forward in shipwreck survey technology and its use on the Jutland wrecks has been very insightful in several cases, not least *Indefatigable's* wreck site. Finally the mystery of what actually happened to the *Indefatigable* when she sank could be unravelled and, despite the very damaged nature of the archaeology, the final moments of the ship are still clearly manifested in her remains.

Fig. 1.9 shows a plan view of the multibeam image of the site taken aboard *Vina* during the April 2015 survey. This image depicts the heavily damaged nature of the wreck site as seen in 2001. The colours, from violet to red, represent the height readings, with red being the highest points. But what was particularly surprising was the extent to which the seabed was pock-marked with pieces of wreckage hundreds of metres away from the main body of the ship. Comparisons with the video and positional data from 2001 and 2003 showed that the 2001 dives had been conducted on the large pile of wreckage in the northernmost portion of the wreck. It was in this pile that the turrets and other items I filmed are situated.

The navigational systems on *Vina* are all integrated, so once the multibeam image had been analysed it was possible to drop the ROV right on the wreckage to the south-west in order to ascertain whether it represented the bow or stern. Although the underwater visibility was poor, anchor chains were observed, with the double set shown indicating this was *Indefatigable's* bow. This southwest orientation of the wreck is consistent with the eyewitness accounts and the Carne photograph. From the bow the ROV was then piloted to explore some of the nearby wreckage, including the remains of 'A' turret (Fig.1.10).

Figure 1.11 shows another multibeam image of the wreck of *Indefatigable* with the location of the items identified in 2001 and 2015. The sleeve of what was probably 'A' turret is highlighted along with the 12-inch guns it probably

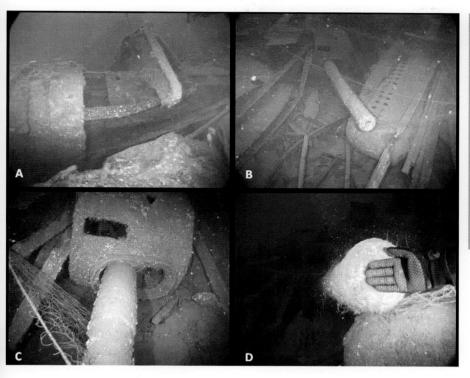

Fig. 1.8 *The scattered remains of the wreck of HMS* Indefatigable *as seen in 2001. A shows the crushed remains of a portion of the mainmast. B shows a 4-inch gun lying with its muzzle resting on the remains of a drum from one of the ship's Yarrow boilers. C shows a closer shot of the 4-inch gun with its shield. D shows my hand in the muzzle of the 4-inch gun for scale.*

held. The remains of two turrets, probably 'P' and 'Q' turrets, are also shown, along with the area dived in 2001. Assuming the wreckage is upside down, the turret to the west should be 'P' turret and is the one filmed in 2001, as seen in Figure 1.6.

The multibeam had allowed us to understand what the wreck site of *Indefatigable* represented. Clearly the final explosion as she rolled over was located in the fore part of the ship. It seems most likely that the explosion was attributable to the detonation of the magazine under 'A' turret. Even the magazines under 'P' and 'Q' may have exploded. What is more challenging to unravel is why the stern portion of the wreck is so damaged.

From measuring the dimensions of the multibeam image we know the length from the bow to the most north-easterly portion of the wreck to be 140 metres. HMS *Indefatigable* was actually 180 metres long, so some compression of the wreck seems to have occurred as she sank. It may be that the stern was already on the seabed when the second explosion occurred and the ship slipped back on to herself and concertinaed as she settled on the seabed. This would go some way to explaining why the site is so broken up and assumes that a

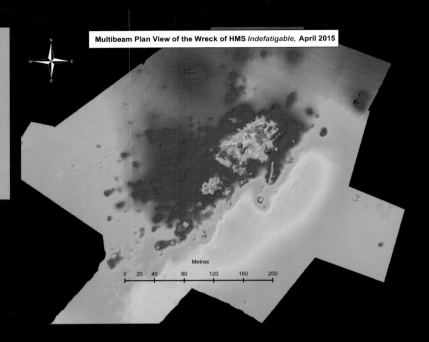

Fig. 1.9 *The plan view of the wreck of HMS* Indefatigable *as depicted on Vina's multibeam system. The wreck can be seen to be scattered over a large area, showing the devastating nature of the final explosion. (Picture: McCartney/JD-Contractor)*

Multibeam Plan View of the Wreck of HMS *Indefatigable*, April 2015

Metres
0 20 40 80 120 160 200

portion of the stern does not lie undiscovered somewhere to the north-east, in the path of the ship.

Alternatively, the extent of the damage can also be viewed as consistent with a wreck that has been literally pulled apart, which is symptomatic of a wreck that has undergone commercial salvage after she had sunk. In this regard it is noticeable just how similar the multibeam image of this site is to that of SMS *Pommern* (see Chapter 12), a site with a reputedly long history of salvage activity.

In this case, it is important to remember that Falmer's account describes how 'X' turret exploded first. That event must have extensively damaged the stern

Fig. 1.10 *Remains of the fore part of the wreck of HMS* Indefatigable *as recorded by the ROV in 2015. Anchor chains are visible in A, while B shows the barrel of what was probably once one of the guns of 'A' turret.*

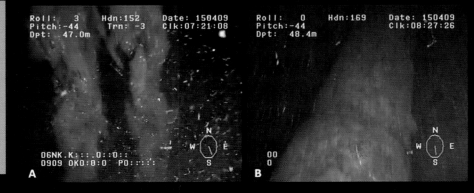

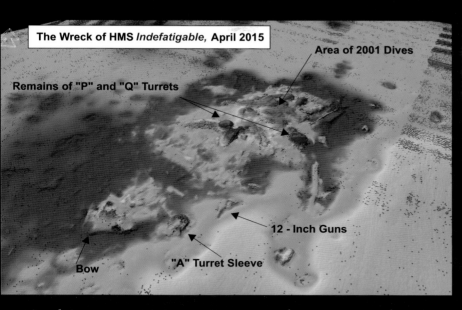

The Wreck of HMS *Indefatigable*, April 2015

Area of 2001 Dives

Remains of "P" and "Q" Turrets

12 - Inch Guns

"A" Turret Sleeve

Bow

Fig. 1.11 Multibeam image of the Indefatigable *wreck, with the location of the items identified in 2001 and 2015. (Picture: McCartney/JD-Contractor)*

area. So while it is currently impossible to say with any certainty what caused the stern of the wreck to be so degraded, a combination of salvage and trauma caused during the sinking process seems most likely.

Fig. 1.12 shows the layout of magazines, boilers and engines inside HMS *Indefatigable*. The detonation of the magazine situated under 'A' turret must have caused the final explosion witnessed by many. This clearly completely destroyed the forward portion of the ship, as seen on the multibeam images. It is possible that the magazines under the centre turrets also played a part in so heavily damaging the remaining portion of the ship.

I knew anecdotally that this wreck site had been salvaged in the past, although material evidence has been hard to find. Sadly there was no Hydrographic Office record pinpointed at the accurate position of the *Indefatigable* wreck until I reported it in 2001, meaning that no notices to mariners or other information has survived in its database relating to the wreck's position that might detail when salvage operations took place.

However, some material evidence of the commercial looting of this wreck does survive. The locking nut (Fig. 1.13) from the starboard inner propeller of HMS *Indefatigable* can be seen at the Terschelling Wreck Museum, alongside other items from the Jutland wrecks. Anecdotally the locking nut was liberated from its propeller after it had been landed in Holland, so it seems that at least one propeller from the wreck site has been salvaged for profit in the past few years.

Fig. 1.12 *The locations of the magazines, boilers and engines inside HMS* Indefatigable. *The detonation of the large magazine under 'A' turret probably destroyed the fore part of the ship. The stern was probably already on the seabed at that time. The stern portion of the wreck may well then have concertinaed as it fell back onto itself, leading to the foreshortened wreckage we see today.*

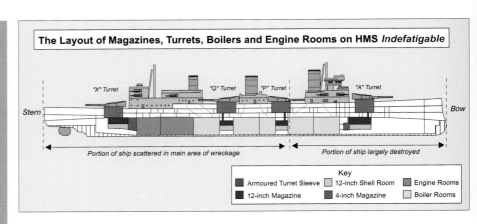

The Layout of Magazines, Turrets, Boilers and Engine Rooms on HMS *Indefatigable*

"X" Turret   "Q" Turret   "P" Turret   "A" Turret

Stern   Bow

Portion of ship scattered in main area of wreckage   Portion of ship largely destroyed

Key
Armoured Turret Sleeve | 12-inch Shell Room | Engine Rooms
12-inch Magazine | 4-inch Magazine | Boiler Rooms

HMS *Indefatigable*: in summary

The wreck of the *Indefatigable* was positively identified by me in 2001; its location was officially unknown in Britain up to that point. The dive surveys in 2001 and geophysics in 2003 and 2015 have finally built up a record of the characteristics of this site. Heavily damaged in battle, the results of the sinking are very evident in the remains today.

From a historical perspective, a sequence of events as to how the ship was sunk is now clear for the first time, although the positional discrepancy with the wreck of the *Queen Mary* continues to pose questions (see Chapter 15). Like so many other Jutland wrecks, this site has been subject to salvage for profit in the recent past. The violence of the ship's sinking and subsequent salvage works, in combination with the hostile environment of the North Sea and the passage of time, account for the wreck's condition today.

Fig. 1.13 *The locking nut from the starboard inner propeller of HMS* Indefatigable *saved by the Terschelling Wreck Museum after the propeller was salvaged. (Picture: Terschelling Wreck Museum)*

Notes

1 Roberts J. *Battlecruisers*. Annapolis: Naval Institute Press; 1997. p.28.

2 *Ibid.*, p.122.

3 Corbett JS. *History of the Great War based on Official Documents: Naval Operations, Vol. I.* London: Longmans, Green and Co.; 1920. pp.55–71.

4 *Ibid.*, p.89.

5 *Ibid.*, pp.362–64.

6 Burt RA. *British Battleships of World War One*. Barnsley: Seaforth; 2012. pp.112–16.

7 Harper JET. *Reproduction of the Record of the Battle of Jutland*. London: HMSO; 1927. p.20.

8 Campbell NJM. *Jutland: an Analysis of the Fighting*. London: Conway; 1986. pp.78,94.

9 National Archives (various dates). Groos O. *The Battle of Jutland: Official German Account.* Translated Bagot WT. ADM 186/626. London: Admiralty; 1926. p.60.

10 Harper JET. *Reproduction of the Record of the Battle of Jutland*. London: HMSO; 1927. p.117.

11 Fawcett HW, Hooper GWW. *The Fighting at Jutland*. Glasgow: Maclure, Macdonald & Co.; 1921. p.29.

12 Cave Papers, Liddle Collection, Leeds University.

13 Burroughs Papers, Liddle Collection, Leeds University.

14 Oram HK. *Ready for Sea*. London: Futura; 1976. p.153.

15 Harper JET. *Reproduction of the Record of the Battle of Jutland*. London: HMSO; 1927. p.21.

16 Campbell NJM. *Jutland: an Analysis of the Fighting*. London: Conway; 1986. p.60.

17 Fawcett HW, Hooper GWW. *The Fighting at Jutland*. Glasgow: Maclure, Macdonald & Co.; 1921. p.38.

18 Staff G. *German Battlecruisers of World War One*. Barnsley: Seaforth; 2014. p.45.

19 Steel N, Hart P. *Jutland 1916*. London: Cassell; 2003. pp.95–96.

20 Fawcett HW, Hooper GWW. *The Fighting at Jutland*. Glasgow: Maclure, Macdonald & Co.; 1921. p.28.

21 Hydrographics Department of the Admiralty. Record of Wreck No. 32354 HMS *Indefatigable*. Taunton: Hydrographics Office; 2000.

2
BATTLECRUISER HMS *QUEEN MARY*

Sunk by gunfire at 16.26 on 31 May 1916

Fig. 2.1 *HMS* Queen Mary. *Launched in 1913. Displacement 26,270 tons, length 660 ft, eight 13.5-inch guns, sixteen 4-inch guns. (Picture: Imperial War Museum Q21661A)*

Originally examined in 1991, the wreck site of HMS Queen Mary *was explored extensively by diving in 2000–03. It was found to be scattered over a wide area, with the fore section completely destroyed. The 2015 multibeam survey confirmed that the main portion of the wreck was oriented in reverse of her original course.*

HMS *Queen Mary* was the third ship of the 1909 Lion class and slightly improved over her predecessors, HMS *Lion* and *Princess Royal*. She was the last British battlecruiser built before the First World War. The sole battlecruiser of the 1910 building programme, *Queen Mary* was laid down at Palmers, Jarrow, in March 1911, launched the following March and handed over in August 1913. Industrial relations problems caused numerous delays during this time.[1]

The 'cats' were designed to have a speed in excess of 27 knots. This required seven boiler rooms holding 42 Yarrow boilers, six per room.[2] Compared with the Indefatigable class, the Lion class were huge ships, more than 100 feet longer (to permit the high speed specified) and therefore displaced an additional 8,270 tons. This made them the largest capital ships in the world at the time they were laid down.

The Lion class also represented the first battlecruisers fitted with 13.5-inch guns. They carried eight in four twin turrets. As Fig. 2.1 shows, *Queen Mary*, like her sisters, was a magnificent-looking ship with sleek lines and single pole masts.[3] Another major difference in design over the Indefatigable class were the two superfiring turrets forward ('A' and 'B'), with only one centre turret ('Q') and one aft turret ('X'). The trend towards turrets being mounted on the centreline was manifested in the most modern German battlecruisers too, notably SMS *Lützow* (see Chapter 10).

The heavy guns and high speed required armoured protection to be sacrificed, as in all the British battlecruisers. The Lion class was reported in the press as having protection on the 'battleship scale'. This was not the case; its protection was at least two to three inches thinner overall than the least armoured of the British battleships, the St Vincent class. In theory, at least, it was known that *Queen Mary* could be pierced at battle ranges by the 11-inch guns of the German battlecruisers.[3]

HMS *Queen Mary* was the only British warship at Jutland that had been part-fitted with the Pollen fire-control apparatus, which featured the Argo Clock Mark IV. In use, this supposedly caused *Queen Mary*'s gunnery to be regarded as the finest in the Battlecruiser Fleet, but its actual practical merits continue to be debated.[4]

Queen Mary's first commander was Captain Reginald Hall (later of Room 40 fame) and she was assigned to the First Battlecruiser Squadron, Home Fleet. A visit to Russia with the battlecruisers followed, with a great ball held aboard at the end of the visit. But as war broke out, HMS *Queen Mary*, in common with many of the more modern ships of the Grand Fleet, never again left the confines of the North Sea.

Under Hall the ship was much reformed, and fitted with a chapel, bookstall and cinema. Washing facilities were improved, including washing machines for petty officers and older seamen. The petty officers' messes were rebuilt and the ship's police force abolished.[1]

HMS *Queen Mary* first saw action at the Battle of Heligoland Bight on 28 August 1914, the first naval battle of the war. During this action five battlecruisers commanded by Admiral Beatty arrived late in the fight and effectively sealed a British victory by sinking two light cruisers.[5] The following months were characterised by regular patrolling, as far north as northern Norway.[6]

Now commanded by Captain CI Prowse (Hall's poor health had forced him to take a desk job at the Admiralty), HMS *Queen Mary* took part in Beatty's failed attempt to intercept the German battlecruisers that had shelled Hartlepool, Scarborough and Whitby on 16 December 1914. The following month saw *Queen Mary* dispatched to Portsmouth for refit, which meant she just missed participating in the Battle of Dogger Bank.[7] The refit continued into February 1915. Uneventful patrolling resumed until the eve of the Battle of Jutland.

Loss

It has been said *Queen Mary* was worth two ships of the Indefatigable class, perhaps as much as an entire army division and that her destruction at the Battle of Jutland was the German Navy's greatest single achievement of the First World War.[8] The second major British warship lost during the battle,

Fig. 2.2 Map showing the battle at the time when HMS Queen Mary *was sunk. Harper's position for the loss of the ship can be seen to be close to the wreck's actual position. HMS Lion's track is shown in solid red; this shows the turn towards the north twenty minutes after* Queen Mary *sank.*

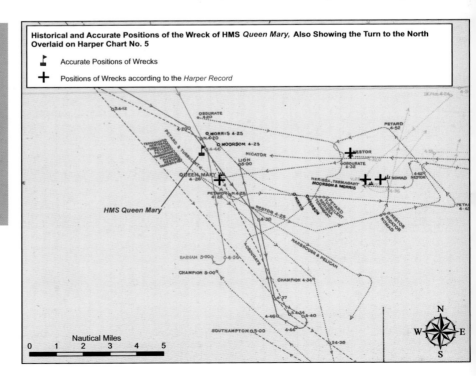

Historical and Accurate Positions of the Wreck of HMS *Queen Mary*, Also Showing the Turn to the North Overlaid on Harper Chart No. 5

Queen Mary was, according to Harper, sunk only 24 minutes after a similar catastrophe had claimed the *Indefatigable* (see Chapter 1).

For a quarter of an hour after the *Indefatigable* was sunk, the opposing lines of battlecruisers continued their fight as they ran south. Now with five ships each, a gunnery duel between single ships could be expected. But at around 16.23, *Queen Mary* came under fire from two enemy battlecruisers. Whereas the fighting had initially been only with SMS *Seydlitz*, now SMS *Derfflinger*'s salvos also began to fall on *Queen Mary*, since the *Derfflinger*'s previous target, HMS *Princess Royal*, had become lost in the smoke from the damaged *Lion* ahead of her.[9] This uneven duel was short-lived; within three minutes, at least two salvoes found their marks and *Queen Mary* blew up and sank. Fig. 2.2 depicts the situation at this time. According to Harper, the sinking of *Queen Mary* claimed 1,266 lives and only nine survivors were picked up.[10] The account of the senior ranking survivor, Midshipman JL Storey, differs in that he reported 18 survivors had been picked up from the sea.[11]

Eyewitness accounts

In contrast to the *Indefatigable*, there were many more eyewitnesses and survivor accounts to the destruction of *Queen Mary*. While there are naturally differences in what they depict, certain points do coalesce. This allows for a broader sequence of events to be compiled, which can be tested against the archaeological remains of the ship.

The salvoes that destroyed *Queen Mary* were witnessed by several crew on HMS *Tiger*, which was the ship astern, with a bridge-to-bridge distance of only 500 yards. Her torpedo officer reported:

> The *Queen Mary* *was the next ahead of us and I… saw one salvo straddle her. Three shells out of four hit and the impression one got of seeing the splinters fly and the dull red burst was if no damage was being done, but that the armour was keeping the shells out. The next salvo that I saw straddled her and two more shells hit her. As they hit, I saw a dull red glow amidships and then the ship seemed to open out like a puff ball… Then there was another dull red glow somewhere forward and the whole ship seemed to collapse inwards. The funnels and masts fell into the middle and the hull was blown outwards. The roofs of the turrets were blown 100 feet high, then everything was smoke and a bit of the stern was the only part of the ship above water.*[12]

Nearby, Lieutenant-Commander Edward Roynon-Jones, the *Tiger*'s navigator, related:

My impression at the time was that a full salvo fell on her centre turret ('Q' turret) which blew up and this detonated every other explosive on the ship. There were definitely two explosions with only a fraction of a second between them but the second one with its flame and smoke was much greater than the first.[13]

Observers on the German ships witnessed *Queen Mary* collapse from within as Comander Georg von Hase, the first gunnery office on *Derfflinger*, reported:

First of all a vivid red flame shot up from her forepart. Then came an explosion forward which was followed by a much heavier explosion amidships… A gigantic cloud of smoke arose, the masts collapsed inwards, the smoke cloud hid everything and rose higher and higher… At its base the smoke column only covered a small area, but it widened towards the summit and looked like a monstrous black pine.[14]

The evidence of the masts and funnels falling inwards is indicative of a ship breaking in half and the higher parts of the ship falling into the void created as the breaks in either half of the ship fill with water and begin to sink.

As he had with the *Indefatigable*, Chief Petty Officer William Cave, in the foremast of HMS *Dublin*, which was aft of HMS *Nottingham* (Second Light Cruiser Squadron to starboard of the battle line – her position at 16.25 is marked on Fig. 2.2 in the centre of the map as 'N.4·25') saw *Queen Mary* blow up and break in half:

*[A] terrific boom rent the air, for just abaft our port beam, the **Queen Mary** the biggest and nearest salvo, it shook our ship, & as we looked the whole of her abaft the fore tripod mast and funnel was enveloped in flame and smoke, but the forepart looked intact, we could see officers and men in the control-top, on the bridge, guns in the fore turret elevating, it was an uncanny sight, but this was only 2–3 seconds after the main explosion, for a delayed explosion in that turret's magazine entirely expended its force in the weakest direction, under water… This fore part suddenly shot ahead with a slight list to port & veered towards us, in so doing, we noticed the height of the bow-wave rising & our Navvy, sensing, maybe a collision, gave the order 'hard aport', but this sorry load of humanity, listing further, now slowing up, gently slid into the 'Deep' seemingly only a few feet from where we had been. Oh the sight of those poor fellows… I was to experience many many dreams, nightmares, more appropriate, for months afterwards. Those of us who witnessed this had similar symptoms.[15]*

As the *Dublin* raced onwards, it was the stern portion that now succumbed to the sea. There are at least three accounts of midshipmen who miraculously escaped from the foundering stern of the ship. John Lloyd Owen emerged from 'X' turret to see:

the ship lying on her side. She was broken amidships, her bows were sticking up in the air and the stern was also sticking out at an angle of about 45 degrees from the water. I was standing on the back of the turret which was practically level… the vessel lying on her port side… A few moments afterwards a tremendous explosion occurred in the fore part of the vessel, which must have blown the bows to atoms. The stern part gave a tremendous lurch, throwing me off into the water.[16]

The surviving petty officer from 'X' turret, Ernest Francis, wrote that he believed that it was a shell hitting the second ('B') turret and igniting the forward magazine that split the ship in half.[17]

Fig. 2.3 *King-Hall's sketch of the sinking stern of HMS Queen Mary. (Picture: King-Hall, Burroughs Papers, Liddle Collection)*

Midshipman JL Storey's report into the loss of *Queen Mary* is educative in a number of details. He was serving in 'Q' turret and stated:

At 5.20 a big shell hit 'Q' turret and put the right gun out of action but the left gun continued firing. At 5.24 a terrific explosion took place which smashed up 'Q' turret and started a big fire in the working chamber and the gun house was filled with smoke and gas. The officer of the turret Lt. Cmdr. Street gave the order to evacuate the turret. All the unwounded in the gun house got clear and as they did so another terrific explosion took place and all were thrown into the water. On coming to the surface nothing was visible except wreckage, but thirty persons appeared to be floating in the water.[11]

That 'X' turret was not hit seems fairly certain, only because it would have been easily visible from the *Tiger* and it is not reported. As with the *Indefatigable*, from the control station of HMS *Southampton* (the lead ship of the Second Light Cruiser Squadron), Sub-lieutenant Stephen King-Hall recorded:

*[A]t 4.23 in an almost similar manner the **Queen Mary** was obliterated by an 800 foot high mushroom of fiery smoke, in this case I remember seeing bits of her flying up. As I watched this fiery grave stone, it seemed to waver slightly at the base, and I caught a momentary but clear glimpse of the hull of **Queen Mary** sticking out of the water from the stern to the after funnel.*[18]

King-Hall also drew a simple sketch of what he saw (Fig. 2.3). The drawing shows the aft funnel of *Queen Mary* clearly, which seems to show that it broke in half no further aft than around 'Q' turret.

The eyewitness accounts depict a possible scenario that describes *Queen Mary*'s possible final moments. Either or both of the two salvoes were seen to hit, struck amidships on and around 'Q' turret. The following explosion broke the ship's back. Subsequently the forward magazines detonated (directly related to the explosion in 'Q' turret or caused by the next salvo striking forward) taking the fore part of the ship to the bottom. The stern rolled over, upended and then too slid into the deep, with Chief Petty Officer Cave later recalling the hiss of steam as 'X' turret's guns met the sea.[19]

Photography

There is one often published photograph of the main explosion on *Queen Mary* that predictably appears in any new literature on the battle. However, this comes from a sequence of 16 photographs of the earlier part of the battle taken under orders by Lieutenant HW Fawcett (later the co-author of *The Fighting at Jutland*) from the destroyer HMS *Lydiard* of the Ninth Destroyer Flotilla, which according to Harper was posted astern of the Battlecruiser Fleet,[20] although the photos seem to hint it was actually more on the port quarter aft. Certainly, the Ninth Destroyer Flotilla was close enough to *Queen Mary* for HMS *Laurel* to have been detailed to pick up her survivors.

Fig. 2.4 '*HMS* Lion *shots over*' *is how this photo was described by HMS* Lydiard's *commanding officer when it was submitted. Where it has been published in the past it is usually claimed that this photo shows the hit on the* Lion's '*Q' turret described in Chapter 1. (Picture: National Archives)*

Fig. 2.5 *Salvoes falling short of HMS* Lion. *(Picture: National Archives)*

Censorship after Jutland was initially lax, until Jellicoe intervened and the censor, Sir Douglas Brownrigg, had to silence the newspapers.[21] In this instance, the photographs were retained at the Admiralty and Fawcett's requests for publication in the *Illustrated News* were denied.[22] In 1921 some of this sequence, along with others, appeared in *The Fighting at Jutland*.

Five photos from this sequence are reproduced here, of which the first three (Fig. 2.4 and Fig. 2.5a and b) show the *Lion* under fire during the 'Run to the South' and give a good illustration of the 'forest of splashes' experienced by the Battlecruiser Fleet at this time.

The next two photographs (Fig. 2.6 and Fig. 2.7) show *Queen Mary* blowing up. They were the last taken by Fawcett during the battle. Interestingly, Fig. 2.6 is sometimes described as being of the *Indefatigable* blowing up, not least in *The Fighting at Jutland*.[23] But the original caption by *Lydiard*'s commanding officer after the battle clearly states that the picture shows the *New Zealand* passing by the explosion of *Queen Mary*.

The angle of the smoke cloud when compared with the famous Fig. 2.7 would seem to confirm that this is likely correct. Sadly, although possibly a rare photograph depicting *Queen Mary*'s end, it is not sufficiently detailed to add much to the story. Fig. 2.7 seems to have been taken shortly after Fig. 2.6 and shows either the development of the same cloud or a later detonation. In either case, it seems to show clearly the venting of smoke and gases upwards after they seemingly have passed through a confined space.

Fig. 2.7 has appeared in several different iterations made up of other photographs, in order to create a panoramic view of the scene, not least in *The Fighting at Jutland* where it is factually described as a composite image.[24] Although not very detailed, Fig. 2.7 is useful because it is a visual confirmation

Fig. 2.6 *This photograph was captioned by HMS* Lydiard's *commanding officer as 'New Zealand passing through explosion of HMS* Queen Mary' *and seems to depict the development of the familiar mushroom cloud seen in Fig. 2.7. (Picture: National Archives)*

Fig. 2.7 *The famous photograph of the explosion of one of the magazines on HMS* Queen Mary. *(Picture: National Archives)*

of the huge explosion that occurred. Its impact would surely be present in the remains of the ship on the seabed.

The wreck

The wreck of *Queen Mary* was examined by the 75th Anniversary Expedition in 1991. This was an expedition made up predominantly of armed services personnel. Plagued by bad weather and limited to a maximum diving depth of 50 metres, it nevertheless confirmed the presence of the *Queen Mary* and the *Invincible* by diving.[25] I used its positional data to relocate the wrecks in 2000. Of *Queen Mary*, the 1991 divers reported that they saw an upturned hull surrounded by debris,[26] although the seabed is at 60 metres, some 10 metres deeper than they could go because of the diving rules in force on the expedition. The wreck of *Queen Mary* is among the deepest of the Jutland wrecks.

I first examined the site by diving on 25 July 2000 and visited it on five subsequent expeditions. During the first dives on *Loyal Watcher*, the down line was dropped on the highest standing feature that could be seen using the boat's bottom sounder. It was challenging to work out the orientation of the hull, because so much of the keel had simply broken down and fallen into the wreck. This characteristically reveals the ship's collapsed internals and the first task was to ensure that the wreck was indeed *Queen Mary*.

This was achieved by locating a section of her 9-inch armour plate which was unique among the Jutland wrecks. Many other items, such as the 4-inch guns and the plethora of Yarrow boilers (*Queen Mary* was equipped with an unprecedented 42 of them, to deliver her high speed), were indicative that this could be no other shipwreck. Because of what is known of the sinking, we concluded that the largest piece of wreckage located on our bottom sounder had to be the stern section of the ship which was witnessed to be intact at the moment of sinking. Images of this stern portion can be seen in Fig. 2.8 and Fig. 2.9.

Fig. 2.8 *Features observed during the initial dives on the wreck of HMS* Queen Mary *in 2000. A shows the upturned hull of the wreck. B shows the water trough of one of* Queen Mary's *42 Yarrow boilers, with the locking bars for the inspection hatch. The wreck is upside down so the water troughs represent some of the highest points of the wreck today. C shows a section of the ship's 9-inch armour belt, with my hand for scale.*

Fig. 2.9 *Features observed during the initial dives on the wreck of HMS* Queen Mary *in 2000. A is another water trough standing proud of the wreck. Much of the surrounding structure has now collapsed well down into the wreck. B shows a porthole which has rotted out of the now collapsed superstructure. C depicts the barrel of one of* Queen Mary's *4-inch guns poking out from under a plate that has fallen on to it. (Pictures: Patricia McCartney)*

We quickly realised that the wreck of *Queen Mary* was vast and spread over a very wide area. Owing to the limited time divers had on the wreck, it was simply impossible to get an overview of the entire wreck site by diving. The big question was: what part of the wreck were we actually looking at?

The first clues came when I located a turret on the first day's diving, as depicted in Figure 2.10. This turret was not on the centreline of the wreck, but on the seabed to one side of the hull, similarly upside down. Its armoured sleeve can be seen lying next to the hull in images A and B. Right on the seabed was the entire turret, partially buried. At 62 metres' depth, a propeller from one of *Queen Mary*'s tenders was located. As no tenders were stowed anywhere nearby, it seems to suggest that they were most likely destroyed and scattered as *Queen Mary* sank. Right above the propeller was the upside-down roof of a turret, with the unmistakable 9-foot rangefinder clearly visible in the top right-hand corner of image C. In 2003, during the filming expedition, this area was examined with the ROV and it was seen that the entire counterbalance of a turret was projecting out from under the wreck, including the unmistakable sight of the opened escape hatch, similar to ones seen on *Indefatigable* and *Invincible*, as seen in image D. If this was 'X' turret, as seemed likely, then some survivors may have escaped through this hatch.

The most remarkable thing about this intact turret was its orientation: it was pointing in the direction of the enemy line, laterally across the ship. Although the turret looks to be offset from the centreline of the wreck and out of position, the once underlying magazine could be clearly seen in the collapsed hull plating, and on the centreline.

An interesting aspect of the images depicting the magazine was the apparently jumbled nature of the shells and the bronze 'Clarkson' cases which contained the cordite propellant (Fig. 2.11). The British magazine design of the time placed the shell room at the bottom, with the cordite magazine above.[27] The

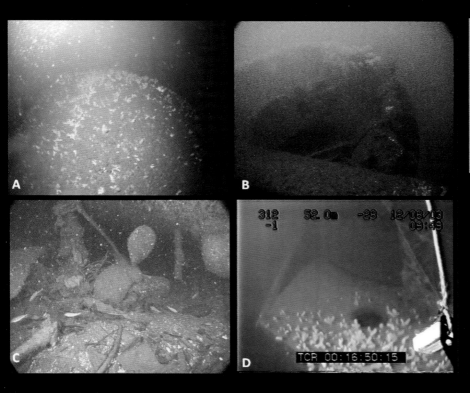

Fig. 2.10 The remains of 'X' turret on the wreck of HMS Queen Mary *as seen in 2000-03 (Pictures: A Patricia McCartney, B & C Innes McCartney, D Innes McCartney/ Ideal World Productions))*

fact that both shell and cordite cases are seen together here is further proof that this section of wreckage has collapsed over time.

Yet, the very presence of this seemingly intact magazine would appear to be proof that this section of the ship did not explode when *Queen Mary* sank, because almost inevitably, the cordite would have been responsible. The fact that the underlying turret still had its roof, which would almost certainly have been blown off in a magazine explosion, also supported this view.

Again, this suggested that the most likely identity of this magazine was the one below 'X' turret. Importantly, the fact that the turret sleeve is around 10 metres away but off to one side may indicate that as the wreck collapsed, it has slumped to one side, away from the barbette, instead of straight down on to it. In 2000 we concluded that this portion of the wreck was most likely the stern and subsequent diving mostly focused on other areas of the wreck.

During the 2015 expedition, the ROV was deployed to examine what was thought to be the extreme stern of the wreck. The propellers had reportedly been removed from the site,[28] but we hoped that some recognisable feature

Fig. 2.11 *Shell and cordite cases piled together in the large section of wreckage, as seen between 2000 and 2002. This is indicative of a magazine that has collapsed. (Picture B: Bradley Sheard)*

would be seen. In poor visibility, a propeller was seen half buried in the seabed. Visually it looked correct for *Queen Mary*'s port-side propeller. This discovery added to the view that the most intact portion of the wreck was the stern, with the other three propellers either buried or salvaged long ago.

One other, smaller area of wreckage to the west gave good height readings on *Loyal Watcher*'s fishfinder. This was first examined in May 2001 and found to be of an entirely different character than the larger section. The area itself was much smaller, with no substantial pieces of the ship's hull present, although items such as a number of boilers, mooring bollards and much twisted plating

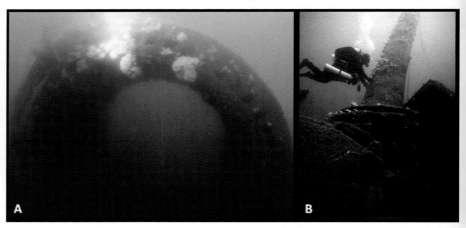

Fig. 2.12 *Features observed in the wreckage of the bow section of* Queen Mary *in 2001–02: A shows a turret sleeve on in its side, while B shows the remains of a 13.5-inch gun buried vertically in the seabed. (Picture B: Bradley Sheard)*

lay everywhere. We came across the strange sight of what appeared to be an armoured turret sleeve on its side, through which the divers could swim, but even more remarkable was the discovery of a 13.5-inch gun nearly vertical, like a huge industrial chimney, held in place by a combination of its breech being partially buried in the seabed and the surrounding wreckage (Fig. 2.12).

D-Contractor surveyed this area of the wreck by ROV in 2014 and the results are shown in Figs 2.13 and 2.14. The gun had fallen onto its right-hand side and broken out of its trunnion but was still held within the extremely shattered remains of its turret and sleeve. The impression you get is that the entire turret

Fig. 2.13 Features of the 13.5-inch gun turret as seen during the ROV survey of the wreck in 2014. The gun had fallen onto its right-hand side, with the mount clearly visible in A. B shows the gun broken out of its trunnion but still held within the extremely shattered remains of its turret and sleeve. The very distorted roller bearings that allowed the turret to rotate can also be seen. (Pictures: McCartney/JD-Contractor)

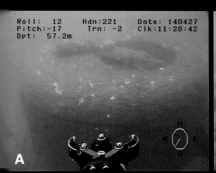

has exploded and the wreckage has fallen to the seabed, dragged down by the heavy weight of the gun breech which embedded itself in the seabed in a near vertical position.

To have survived for so long in this condition is remarkable as the images show that the gun barrel has snagged rope, net and chain in the past. This has precedent – similar has been reported by the salvage divers who scrapped the wreck of the major naval grave of HMS *Vanguard* (incredibly under MOD licence) in Scapa Flow during the 1970s.[29] In this case too, a magazine explosion sank a large Dreadnought. In both cases, the turrets have been blasted from the ship and the guns have pierced the seabed, breech first.

The 2014 ROV survey also revealed a number of new features unseen before (Fig. 2.14). Of particular note was the armoured conning tower, sitting upright

Fig. 2.14 Features observed during the ROV survey of the forward section of the wreck in 2014: A shows the armoured conning tower sitting upright on the seabed, seeming totally undamaged, but missing the range finder from its roof. B shows a 4-inch gun found in the extreme north-west of the wreckage area. C shows an entire Yarrow boiler lying isolated on the seabed. (Pictures: McCartney/JD-Contractor)

on the seabed, seeming totally undamaged, but missing the range finder from its roof. In the extreme north-west of the wreckage area, a 4-inch gun was found. This may well have been one of the first items to have been blown out of the ship and raises the possibility that the 4-inch guns and associated magazine aft of 'A' and 'B' turrets initiated the forward magazine detonation, as proposed by Burr.[30] This scenario has uncanny similarities to one of the theories behind the loss, in 1941, of HMS *Hood*, a ship with a number of design similarities to *Queen Mary*.[31] At present this theory is entirely speculative.

As the ROV made its way to the east, back to the large portion of the wreck, the seabed was seen to be strewn with wreckage in a widely scattered debris field, including the uncanny sight of an entire Yarrow boiler lying isolated on the seabed, as seen in Fig. 2.14.

By the end of the 2001 expeditions, a picture of the vast area of the *Queen Mary*'s wreckage had begun to emerge, using the bottom sounder to locate the wreck's larger parts and diving to examine them. What was required to extend our knowledge of the site was geophysics.

The wreck was very briefly surveyed by side scan sonar on 11 August 2003 (Fig. 2.15). With only time for a limited number of passes, the images seemed to fit in with the findings made by diving. One obvious, large section of wreckage can be seen and its shape and position fit in with what was thought to be the stern section. The area of damage right on the stern was thought to have been caused by post-depositional salvage activity. Similar damage is evident on the wreck of SMS *Wiesbaden* (see Chapter 6). The side scan also showed a large debris field in which the upright gun and other features were located. Although this seemed logical and matched with the positions of the diving, there was reason to be cautious.

This was because the path of the ship seemed to suggest that, once separated from the exploded bow, the stern section kept moving forward while turning and listing to port before it capsized and sank. This seemed incredible and more than a little implausible, so what was really needed was a more detailed survey of the site. Twelve long years passed before the truth was finally uncovered.

As was anticipated, the 2015 survey finally confirmed the layout of the wreck and demonstrated quite clearly that the ship's stern portion had carried on forward, passing over the already sunk bow, before rolling over to port and

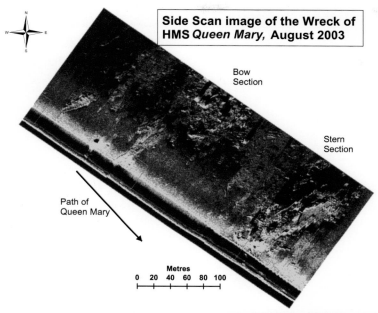

Side Scan image of the Wreck of HMS *Queen Mary*, August 2003

Bow Section

Stern Section

Path of Queen Mary

Metres
0 20 40 60 80 100

Fig. 2.15 The side scan sonar image of HMS Queen Mary taken in 2003. It seemed to reveal that the stern of the ship had continued forward to pass over the wreckage of the bow before it sank. Was this really the case?

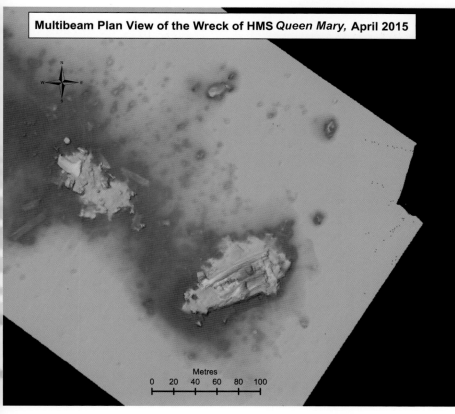

Multibeam Plan View of the Wreck of HMS *Queen Mary*, April 2015

Metres
0 20 40 60 80 100

Fig. 2.16 Plan view of the 2015 multibeam survey, finally revealing the entire wreck with her overall layout. Compare this with Fig. 2.15. (Picture: McCartney/JD-Contractor)

Fig. 2.17 *The wreck of HMS Queen Mary as depicted on Vina's multibeam showing the key features recorded by diving and ROV. (Picture: McCartney/JD-Contractor)*

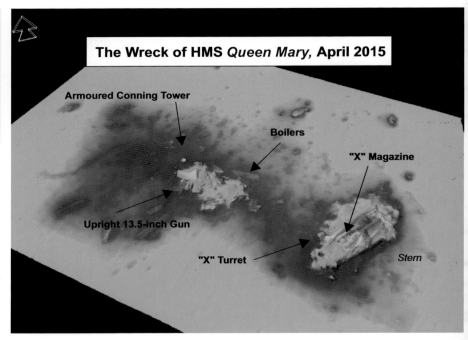

Fig. 2.17 *The wreck of HMS Queen Mary as depicted on Vina's multibeam showing the key features recorded by diving and ROV. (Picture: McCartney/JD-Contractor)*

sinking. Interestingly, the detailed account given by Cave in HMS *Dublin* partially fits this scenario. It may be that the 'rising bow wave' he saw was caused by the stern still moving ahead, although it turned away, leaning to port, not towards the *Dublin*, as Cave described; such are the memories of eyewitnesses.

Fig. 2.18 *The layout of magazines, boilers and engines of HMS Queen Mary. The combined magazines feeding 'A' and 'B' turrets clearly detonated, destroying the fore part of the ship. The surviving after portion seen upside down on the seabed today represents less than half of the ship. It seems likely that 'Q' turret magazine may also have exploded, causing the break in the wreck just aft of her location.*

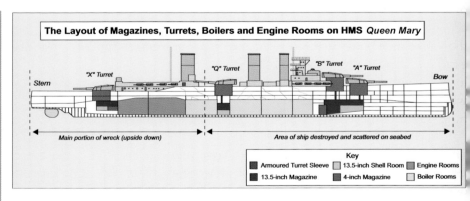

Fig. 2.16 shows the plan view of the multibeam results. The seabed around the forward section is very heavily pockmarked with pieces of wreckage, extending more than 100 metres to the west and north. A very distinct debris field can be seen between the two halves of the wreck, effectively showing

the path of the stern section as it sank. Fig. 2.17 shows the key features on the wreck that can be identified clearly on the multibeam scans. The highest point of the wreck is in the region of frame 212 and possibly represents the outer starboard-side high pressure ahead turbine.[32]

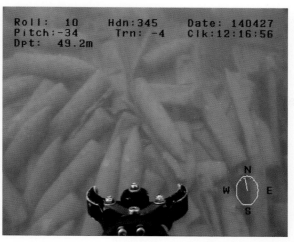

The stern section of the ship is approximately 90 metres long. *Queen Mary* was 201 metres long, so the stern represents less than half of the ship. Inspections of the makers' plans show that the break is in the region of frame 182, across the aftermost boiler rooms G and F. The layout of the magazines and boilers on HMS *Queen Mary* can be seen in Fig. 2.18.

Outstanding questions include: Where is 'Q' turret and did it explode? One explanation is that its remains lie in the area of the bow section, where at least one other turret and gun have been recorded in the past. Alternatively, some portions of it may one day be revealed at the area of the break in the stern section. The fact that the ship broke in half at the location of 'Q' magazine seems to suggest that this magazine exploded, breaking the ship in half, but this needs confirmation on the wreck to be certain.

Fig. 2.19 *The area of 'X' turret magazine, as seen in 2014. A much larger area is now exposed than was seen in 2000-03. Is this due to corrosion or the use of a grab or similar? (Picture: McCartney/JD-Contractor)*

One element of having video and geophysical data for this wreck going back over a 16-year period is that it can be used to see how much the wreck has changed over time. One area that has much altered since I first arrived on the wreck in 2000 is 'X' turret magazine. Looking back at Fig. 2.11, the area exposed on the early dives was fairly small. In fact, it took a great deal of locating with the ROV in 2003 for the cameramen to be able to dive it. So it was somewhat surprising that by 2014 the area of exposed ammunition was much larger, as depicted in Fig. 2.19.

That salvage has been undertaken on *Queen Mary* has been suspected since 1991, when it was observed that the propellers had gone, although we found one in 2015. The side scan and multibeam images show that the stern area is degraded in a way commensurate with the use of explosives or a grab on an upturned hull.

As I was writing this chapter, rumours and photographs were circulating of recent and presumably unlicensed salvage on this site when a condenser and other items were taken from the wreck. If this was the case the stern section, with its bronze engine room machinery, would obviously be a tempting target. The use of a grab or similar would also certainly cause the damage seen to the stern, and perhaps explains how 'X' magazine has been opened up. A noticeable hole can be seen in the multibeam images, roughly centred on frame 262, between the forward end of 'X' magazine and the after end of the engine rooms.[32] It is also interesting to note how the stern section appears more intact in the 2003 side scan image (Fig. 2.19) than in the multibeam, although it is difficult to be certain this is the case.

HMS *Queen Mary*: in summary

Many witnesses saw *Queen Mary* sink and she is, along with the *Invincible*, the most visited by divers of the Jutland wrecks. As the sleekest and most beautiful of warships that met such a catastrophic end, she has arguably become the most totemic and emotive of all the Jutland wrecks. Yet despite this, we still knew little of what was present until diving started. It took a geophysical survey to fully reveal what this wreck site contained. This is primarily because of the very large size of the ship, coupled with the extensive area over which the wreck is scattered.

It seems that *Queen Mary*'s stern stayed afloat long enough to pass over the already sunk bows. Some accounts state that her propellers could be seen slowly turning when she finally sank.[33] In Cave's account of the sinking, he noticed a 'rising bow wave'. Perhaps he actually saw the stern portion moving ahead of the already exploded bows? Some published accounts have claimed the stern exploded.[34] This may be because they witnessed clouds of papers blowing out of the quarterdeck hatches as the stern sank. This was most probably caused by the rising water forcing air out through the hatches. If the stern had in fact exploded it would not resemble what we see today.

Quite how the ship did break in half will probably never be known for certain. The remains are not in a condition to offer anything more than a broad indication of events. Detailed theories of what happened cannot be substantiated by the archaeological remains of the ship. But what is clear is that 'A' and 'B' magazines exploded (possibly initiated by the nearby 4-inch magazine), as most probably did 'Q' magazine, breaking the ship in half at the point now clearly shown on the wreck.

Notes

1 Parkes O. *British Battleships*. London: Seeley Service & Co.; 1970. p.536.

2 Roberts J. *Battlecruisers*. Annapolis: Naval Institute Press; 1997. p.75.

3 Parkes O. *British Battleships*. London: Seeley Service & Co.; 1970. pp.531–35.

4 Brooks J. *Dreadnought Gunnery and the Battle of Jutland*. London: Routledge; 2005. pp.286–87.

5 Corbett JS. *History of the Great War based on Official Documents: Naval Operations, Vol. I*. London: Longmans, Green and Co.; 1920. pp.117–20.

6 *Ibid.*, p.243.

7 Corbett JS. *History of the Great War based on Official Documents: Naval Operations, Vol. II*. London: Longmans, Green and Co.; 1921. p.82.

8 Gordon A. *The Rules of the Game*. London: John Murray; 1996. p.120.

9 National Archives (various dates). Groos O. *The Battle of Jutland: Official German Account*. Translated Bagot WT. ADM 186/626. London: Admiralty; 1926. p.66.

10 Harper JET. *Reproduction of the Record of the Battle of Jutland*. London: HMSO; 1927. p.117.

11 *Jutland: Reports of Flag and Commanding Officers*. ADM 137/302. National Archives (various dates), London.

12 Fawcett HW, Hooper GWW. *The Fighting at Jutland*. Glasgow: Maclure, Macdonald & Co.; 1921. p.42.

13 Gordon A. *The Rules of the Game*. London: John Murray; 1996. p.119.

14 von Hase G. *Kiel and Jutland*. London: Skeffington & Son; 1921. pp.160–61.

15 Cave Papers, Liddle Collection, Leeds University (various dates).

16 Steel N, Hart P. *Jutland 1916*. London: Cassell; 2003. p.107.

17 Fawcett HW, Hooper GWW. *The Fighting at Jutland*. Glasgow: Maclure, Macdonald & Co.; 1921. p.50.

18 Burroughs Papers, Liddle Collection, Leeds University (various dates).

19 Cave Papers, Liddle Collection, Leeds University (various dates).

20 Harper JET. *Reproduction of the Record of the Battle of Jutland*. London: HMSO; 1927. p.90.

21 Brownrigg D. *Indiscretions of the Naval Censor*. London: Cassell; 1920. pp.54–55.

22 Jutland: additional papers, 1916. ADM 137/1643. National Archives, London. pp.35–63.

23 Fawcett HW, Hooper GWW. *The Fighting at Jutland*. Glasgow: Maclure, Macdonald & Co.; 1921. facing p.28.

24 *Ibid.*, facing p.35.

25 Moor G. *Battle of Jutland 1916. 75th Anniversary 1991: the Expedition Report*. 1991. Unpublished copy in author's collection.

26 *Ibid.*, p.27.

27 Brown DK. *The Grand Fleet*. London: Chatham; 1999. p.56.

28 Gordon A. *The Rules of the Game*. London: John Murray; 1996. p.601.

29 *ScapaMAP 2000–2002: Report Compiled for Historic Scotland on the Mapping and Management of the Submerged Archaeological Resource in Scapa Flow, Orkney*. Orkney: Scapa Flow Marine Archaeology Project; 2003. appendix III.

30 Burr L. *British Battlecruisers 1914–18*. Oxford: Osprey; 2006. p.43.

31 Roberts J. *Battlecruisers*. Annapolis: Naval Institute Press; 1997. p.67.

32 Constructor's plans of HMS *Queen Mary*. Ship's plans collection. National Maritime Museum (various dates) Controller's Department, Admiralty (undated), London.

33 Roberts J. *Battlecruisers*. Annapolis: Naval Institute Press; 1997. p.116.

34 Campbell NJM. *Jutland: an Analysis of the Fighting*. London: Conway; 1986. p.63.

3
DESTROYER WRECKS OF THE BATTLECRUISER ACTION

SMS V27, SMS V29, HMS Nomad *and HMS* Nestor *sunk by combinations of gunfire and torpedo between around 16.30 and 17.30 on 31 May 1916*

Fig. 3.1 *The torpedo boat SMS V27, as seen at sea. Length 257 ft, displacement 812 tons, three 3.46-inch (88 mm) guns of 45 calibre mounted singly fore, central and aft and six 19.7-inch torpedo tubes, single tube each side at the bow and two double mounts central and aft. (Picture: Archiv Deutscher Marinebund)*

At around 16.26 when Queen Mary *blew up, the two opposing forces of destroyers and torpedo boats attempted attack runs on the opposing lines of battlecruisers. They met in 'no man's land' and a confused action followed, by the end of which four had been sunk. During the close of this engagement, Scheer arrived on the scene and the 'Run to the North' soon ensued. Commander Bingham of HMS* Nestor *was awarded the Victoria Cross in this action for pressing home a close range torpedo attack on the encroaching German battle fleet while under heavy fire. All four of the wrecks have been located and surveyed and their identities investigated.*

As the German official historian noted, the specific details of the engagement between elements of the British Ninth, Tenth and Thirteenth Destroyer Flotillas and the German Ninth Torpedo Boat Flotilla during the height of the Battlecruiser Action and how they fit into the broader chronology of the battle are 'difficult to record accurately'.[1] There are conflicting details in the *Harper Record*, the German official history and in more recent analyses.

Nevertheless, we examined the original battle reports and the known positions of four smaller warship wrecks in the area to review the action and attempt to identify the wrecks. The typology developed to help identify the destroyer wrecks (see page 24) was tested for the first time on the wrecks in this chapter. After a brief description of the action, we will look at the losses and wrecks in chronological order.

The action

At around 16.00, HMS *Champion*, the light cruiser in command of the Thirteenth Destroyer Flotilla, operating in accordance with standing orders to attack the enemy when opportunity arose, ordered the Thirteenth Destroyer Flotilla to attack First Scouting Group. The attack also drew in HMS *Morris* and *Moorsom* of Tenth Destroyer Flotilla, which were attached to Ninth Destroyer Flotilla at the time. Fig. 3.2 shows the Harper depiction of this action and the actual position of the wrecks today.

The British attack line was broken during deployment by having to cross the path of the Battlecruiser Fleet and HMS *Nottingham*. In effect, it became three different lines: *Nestor*, *Nicator* and *Nomad* to the south: followed by *Petard*, *Turbulent*, *Nerissa*, *Termagant*, *Moorsom* and *Morris*; further north, *Obdurate* closed on the German flank.[2] At the time of deployment, the light cruiser SMS *Regensburg*, locally in command of the German torpedo boats, ordered the

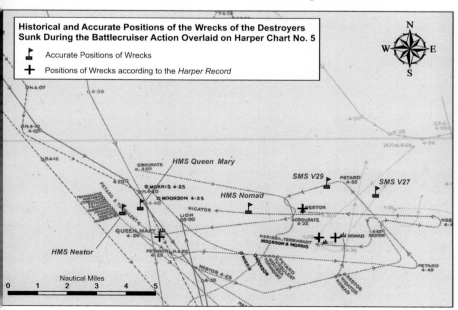

Fig 3.2 *Harper Chart No. 5, showing the Thirteenth Destroyer Flotilla's attack on First Scouting Group and the concurrent destroyer action between 16.00 and 17.00, and the accurate positions of the destroyers and torpedo boats sunk in this action.*

Ninth Torpedo Boat Flotilla to attack the Battlecruiser Fleet and by the time the German boats got clear of their own lines the British destroyers could be seen closing. The German lines consisted of *V28*, followed by *V26*, *V52*, *V27*, *S36*, *S51*, *V29*, *S35*, *V30*, *S34* and *S33*.[1]

A violent action now ensued in which the opposing destroyers sought to prevent their opponents from reaching their quarry, while attempting to reach their own. Aside from their gunfire and torpedoes, the secondary armament of both the First Scouting Group and the Battlecruiser Fleet added to the ferocity of the fighting. The speed of closure between the Thirteenth Destroyer Flotilla and the Ninth Torpedo Boat Flotilla was around one mile a minute, with *Nestor* reporting that fire was opened at the maximum range of 10,000 yards.[3]

The range rapidly closed until it effectively became point-blank. Inevitably some of these lightly protected ships were soon in trouble. HMS *Nomad* appears to have been the first to receive a hit in a vital spot when struck in the engine room from fire attributed to *S51*.[1] Although disabled, *Nomad* continued to fire. A torpedo fired by the line led by *Petard* then struck *V29*. Heavily damaged, *V29* nonetheless managed to fire four torpedoes before foundering under gunfire.

The Germans pressed on and managed to get to within 9,000 yards of the Battlecruiser Fleet before firing ten torpedoes, reversing course and heading back to the cover of the First Scouting Group. The more powerful British destroyers had in effect forced the Ninth Torpedo Boat Flotilla to fire its torpedoes prematurely and hurry back to safety. On the return run, *V27* was hit twice in the forward engine room, destroying the main steam pipe and disabling her. *V26* came alongside under heavy fire, rescued the crew and finished off *V27*, ensuring she sank. Meanwhile, *S35* rescued crew from *V29* at this time.[4]

On the British side, *Obdurate* was now too far astern of the other destroyers to proceed with a torpedo attack and turned back, while the other two lines pressed home their attack, driving the German torpedo boats ahead of them. Those heading for the rear of the First Scouting Group (still heading southward at this time) were chased by *Petard*'s line, while the remainder headed for the van of the First Scouting Group, chased by *Nestor*'s line. Once driven off, *Petard*'s line attacked the First Scouting Group with torpedoes at a range of around 7,000 yards; one of them struck the *Seydlitz*, causing localised flooding, but not affecting her speed.[5] *Petard*'s line then turned to rejoin HMS *Champion* on the Battlecruiser Fleet's disengaged side.[6]

Closer to the enemy, *Nestor* and *Nicator* pressed onwards. As they did so, the First Scouting Group reversed course, and the 'Run to the North' began. Now with the German battle fleet in sight to the south, hot fire was poured on the two destroyers. Led by Commander Bingham in *Nestor*, *Nestor* and *Nicator* determinedly closed the van of the battle fleet to around 3,000 yards, discharged their torpedoes and attempted to withdraw.[7] Campbell's analysis of this action suggests that *Nestor* and *Nicator* were actually attacking SMS *Lützow* of the First Scouting Group at this time, but he admits 'it is impossible to be certain over the details'.[8]

It seems that at this time SMS *Regensburg* appeared from the disengaged rear of the First Scouting Group and took *Nestor* under accurate fire. At around 17.00 *Nestor* was hit for the first time when a round hit No. 1 boiler room. Six minutes later, No. 2 boiler room suffered the same fate and *Nestor* suffered a diminution in speed. Offered a tow by *Petard*, Bingham declined, not wanting to risk two ships being lost during the recovery. At some point after this, *Nestor* gradually slowed to a stop westward but in sight of the *Nomad*.[9] Isolated, as the Battlecruiser Fleet was now heading north with her attendant squadrons and flotillas, the two disabled ships awaited their fate.

First *Nomad* and then *Nestor* were sunk by shellfire from the light cruiser SMS *Rostock* and the battle fleet, with their crews abandoning ship when the inevitable was about to happen. The survivors from both ships were picked up and became prisoners of war. They were later joined by two crew from the *Indefatigable,* also plucked from the sea. Someone aboard the *Nomad* revealed to his captors that the Battlecruiser Fleet was not alone and that Jellicoe was about. However, by the time this was relayed to Scheer, the Fleet Action was already developing (see Chapter 4).

The wrecks

SMS *V29*

V29 of the V25 class of torpedo boats was designed just before the outbreak of war; the last of the 71 in this class were built in 1916.[10] The nomenclature for torpedo boats was in part based on which shipyard constructed them. In this case, *V29* was built by the Vulcan yard at Stettin, hence the 'V' in front of her order number. While slight differences existed between builds, the overall characteristics are broadly similar (Fig. 3.3).

Fig. 3.3 *The torpedo boat SMS V29, as seen underway. Length 257 ft, displacement 812 tons, three 3.46-inch (88 mm) guns of 45 calibre mounted singly fore, central and aft and six 19.7-inch torpedo tubes, single tube each side at the bow and two double mounts central and aft. (Picture: Archiv Deutscher Marinebund)*

When sunk at Jutland, *V29* was part of the Eighteenth Half Torpedo Boat Flotilla, which formed half of the Ninth Torpedo Boat Flotilla. *V29* appears to have been the first of the four ships to sink. The German official account of the action gives only a cursory description of what actually happened. *V29* was believed to have been hit by a torpedo, probably from the *Petard* or *Turbulent*. This disabled *V29*, which fired four torpedoes before sinking.[1 4] It seems that *V29* was hit by the torpedo in the region of the stern, which was soon underwater. But the fore part stayed afloat for around 30 minutes, allowing torpedoes to be fired and most of the crew to be saved by *V26* and *S35*.[11]

Quite when the wreck at the position shown on Fig. 3.2, now thought to be *V29*, was first found is not known. However, she was subject to an ROV survey by JD-Contractor in 2014 and the 2015 multibeam survey in which I participated. Since her wreck is in an area close to three other small warship wrecks, the challenge is to tell them apart.

The task of examining the small warship wrecks is particularly challenging because of their heavily degraded condition. These vessels were not armoured and their thin hulls have in most cases completely corroded away, leaving only heavier and more robust items such as machinery and guns, which are often scattered seemingly randomly on the seabed. This is clearly visible in the 2015 multibeam plan views of all these wrecks, for example Fig. 3.4. While the shape of what is present and the overall length are consistent with this being a destroyer or torpedo boat, a closer examination was required.

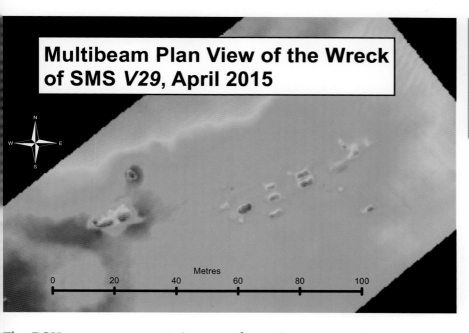

Multibeam Plan View of the Wreck of SMS *V29*, April 2015

Fig. 3.4 Multibeam plan view of the SMS V29 wreck, as seen on Vina's multibeam system in April 2015. (Picture: McCartney/ JD-Contractor)

The ROV survey was carried out in the early evening of 26 April 2014. Conditions on the wreck site were dark, but enough was seen to be certain that the wreck was definitely German (Fig. 3.5).

The survey began on the westerly portion of the wreck, which (image A) turned out to be her stern (the starboard-side 'A' bracket with its sacrificial anode was found partially buried in the seabed). The rudder post was seen to be upright; this is most probably the highest part of the wreck showing above the seabed. The first clue to this wreck being German was the presence of at least two of the 3.46-inch (or 88 mm) guns on the wreck. Image B shows one gun lying on its side on the seabed; the design and mount are consistent with German guns of the period. C shows one torpedo tube on the seabed with the rotten remains of a torpedo inside it. D shows the corner of the top of one of *V29*'s turbines. At this location would have been the cover that collected steam for the condenser alongside (see the typology of destroyer layouts on page 25). E shows the tubes of the water troughs of *V29*'s boilers pointing upwards from the seabed. Here there would have been the main steam drum of the Schulz-Thornycroft boiler type as fitted to German warships, but it has long since corroded, leaving just the remains of the tubes. The join where the main steam pipe would have connected to the boilers survives, but the boilers have rotted and collapsed.

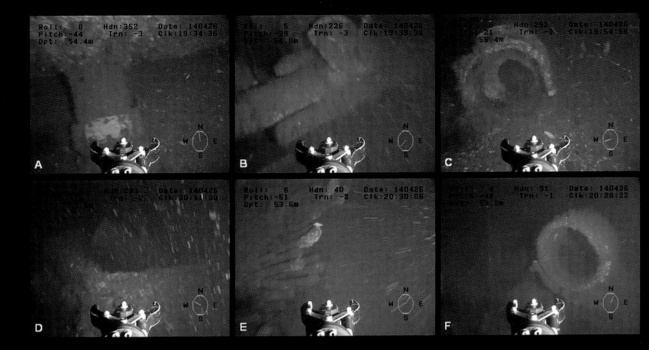

Fig. 3.5 *Key features identifying this wreck, now known as SMS V29, to be of German build. (Pictures: McCartney/JD-Contractor)*

So it seemed that the wreck was one of the German losses. We then overlaid the hull form and machinery layout drawing for *V29* on the multibeam plan view to see whether the remains of the wreck coincided with the hull form and known distribution of the machinery in the ship (Fig. 3.6). It can be seen straight away that the machinery plan coincides with the multibeam image. Of particular note is the way the boilers appear on the multibeam. In the ROV survey, the upper main steam drum looks to have possibly corroded away (or exploded in action), leaving just the water troughs and partial remains of the tubes as the highest points. The same is seen on the multibeam image. Interestingly, the forward boiler room appears to have been destroyed, probably as the ship was sinking.

At least one whole turbine can be seen on the multibeam and this is probably the one seen on the ROV survey (Fig. 3.5D). It is evident on both the multibeam and the ROV tape that the condensers have been removed from this wreck, as there are distinctive voids where they would have been expected. I have seen video of the wreck shot in 2002 showing them to be present, so it seems that at some point after that this wreck has been subject to opportunistic salvage for profit. Sadly, this is far from uncommon on even the smallest of the Jutland wrecks and can be clearly seen on several other sites.

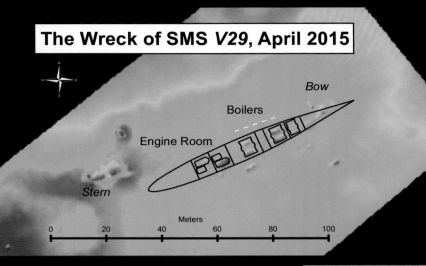

The Wreck of SMS *V29*, April 2015

Bow

Boilers

Engine Room

Stern

Meters
0   20   40   60   80   100

Fig. 3.6 *The hull form and machinery distribution plan for SMS V29 overlaid on the plan view of the multibeam image reveals that the wreck is definitely of German type. (Picture: McCartney/JD Contractor)*

The stern portion can be seen to the west, separated from the rest of the ship. This is the best indicator we currently have that this is the wreck of *V29* and not *V27*: *V29* was struck by a torpedo in the stern region, which then submerged before the rest of the ship sank. By comparison, *V27* is thought to have gone down in one piece.

SMS *V27*

V27 was in effect *V29*'s sister ship and most likely identical in nearly every feature. Fig. 3.1 (page 66) shows a photograph of her at sea, showing the location of the three guns and the centrally mounted pair of torpedo tubes.

When sunk at Jutland, SMS *V27* was the commanding ship of the Seventeenth Half Torpedo Boat Flotilla, which formed half of the Ninth Torpedo Boat Flotilla. According to the German official history, *V27* was disabled by shellfire very shortly after *V29* had been hit by a torpedo. She was at that time retiring and attempting to break through the British lines of destroyers, having fired her torpedoes. She was hit in the starboard side alongside the forward engine room, destroying the main steam pipe. SMS *V26* came alongside, under fire, rescued the crew and then sank *V27* with gunfire.[14]

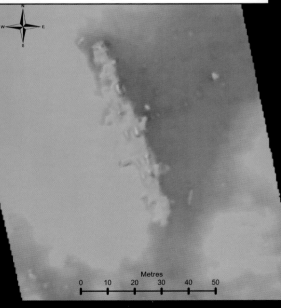

Multibeam Plan View of the Wreck of SMS *V27*, April 2015

Metres
0   10   20   30   40   50

Fig. 3.7 *Multibeam plan view of the wreck of SMS V27, as seen on Vina's multibeam system in April 2015. (Picture: McCartney/JD Contractor)*

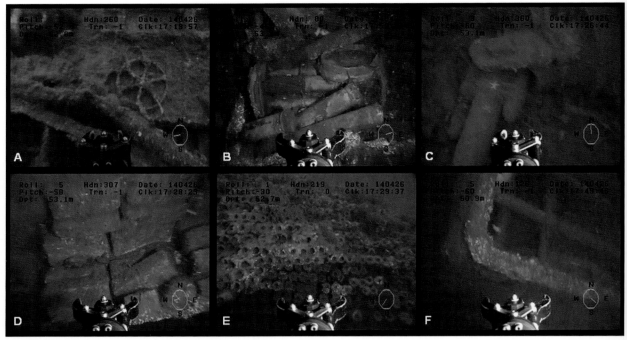

Fig. 3.8 Key features identifying this wreck, now known as SMS V27, to be of German build. and similar to V29. (Pictures: McCartney/JD-Contractor)

Similar to the wreck of *V29*, it is not known when this wreck was first found, but it was surveyed by ROV in 2014 and with multibeam in 2015. The results of the multibeam survey are shown in Fig. 3.7. Again, in common with other similar wreck sites, the entire structure is very broken down, with mainly only the more substantial portions of the ship remaining. In this case, it seemed as if the ship had sunk in one piece, as her overall length was a close match to the length of *V27*.

We next examined the tape of the ROV inspection of 26 April 2014 and identified several key identifying features (Fig. 3.8). One of the first items seen by the ROV was the ubiquitous circular 'carrying handle' as seen on the German wrecks at Jutland (see Chapter 10 for more detail). Its presence meant that the nationality of this site was not in question. Image B shows one of the magazines for the ships ammunition. The gun seen in C was identical to the similar one seen on the wreck of *V29*. D shows the base of one of the ship's boilers with the familiar white fire bricks seen on German naval vessels.

Identical to *V29*, the highest surviving point of the boilers were the pipes rising out of the water troughs to join the upper steam drum of the Schulz-Thornycroft boiler, which has either corroded or exploded in action, as seen in E. Also similar to *V29*, the tops of both turbines had the combing attaching them to their condensers removed, revealing the internals of the turbines, as seen in F.

The multibeam and ROV survey in conjunction reveal that the wreck was German and therefore had to be either *V27* or *V29*. In order to confirm this and to see what else could be learned from the wreck, we again overlaid the hull form and machinery distribution schematic for *V27* on the multibeam plan (Fig. 3.9).

In this instance, the match was even better than in the case of *V29*. All three of the ship's boilers have degraded in a consistently similar way, with the top steam drums the first to disappear. All steam drums have gone. Both turbines are present, as was observed on the ROV survey. But again, as with *V29*, both condensers are conspicuous by their absence. It must be concluded that they have been salvaged for profit at some time in the past.

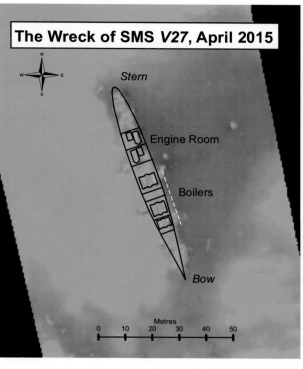

Fig. 3.9 *The hull form and machinery distribution plan for SMS* V27 *overlaid on the plan view of the multibeam image reveals that the wreck is definitely of German type and most probably* V27. *(Picture: McCartney/JD-Contractor)*

Supporting the view that this is *V27* is the fact that the wreck appears to have sunk in one piece. It is known that all of the damage she sustained was by gunfire, so this seems possible – unlike *V29*, which has her stern laying away from the rest of the wreck because of much more devastating torpedo damage.

Of course, the identification of both these wrecks is based on circumstantial evidence and currently no absolute proof can be found. This could emerge in the future with a close study of both wrecks. This is not a problem faced when examining the two British wrecks, because divers have conclusively identified one of them.

HMS *Nomad*

The destroyer HMS *Nomad* was built to the Admiralty M class design, as part of the third emergency war programme order placed for this type. She was launched in February 1916, just in time to see action at Jutland. Her short life is probably the reason why no photograph seems to have survived. Fortunately, a photograph of HMS *Nestor*, which was part of the same order, has been found and can be seen on page 80.

The M class were 273 ft long, displacing around 918 tons. They were more heavily armed that their German opponents, with three 4-inch guns and a pompom gun. The greater firepower of the British destroyers was said to be one reason why the German torpedo attack on the Battlecruiser Fleet was carried out prematurely; the German ships lacked the fighting power for a prolonged engagement.[4] The M class ships also carried four torpedo tubes in two double mounts abaft the after funnel. Top speed was around 34 knots, comparable with the enemy.

During the battle both HMS *Nestor* and *Nomad* were attached to the Thirteenth Destroyer Flotilla. The *Nomad* was disabled during the fight with Ninth Torpedo Boat Flotilla. The circumstances that led to the *Nomad* being disabled and what happened afterwards were reported by Lieutenant-Commander Paul Whitfield as a prisoner of war in Wilhelmshaven:

> *Our misfortune lay in getting a shell from one of their light cruisers clean through our main steam pipe, killing instantly the Engineer Officer… At the same time from two boilers came the report that they could not get water. We then shut off burners… The ship finally stopped though steam continued to pour from the ER [Engine Room] obliterating everything… I noticed that we had listed to port considerably and so I thought rather than let the torpedoes go down with the ship and before the list got too bad, I would give them a run for their money and fired all four at the enemy's battleships who were on the starboard beam… Having no one within gun range, we set to work putting out small fires etc. and I also prepared for being towed, in case a friendly destroyer came along. Just about this time the 1st High Sea Fleet [sic] spotted us and started a 'battle practice' at us with 6" or bigger guns. Salvo after salvo shook us and wounded a few. The ship sinking fast I gave the order to abandon her and pull clear, and about 3 minutes after she went down vertically by the stern. Three German torpedo boats picked us up.[12]*

According to Harper, only eight crew had died and 72 were made prisoners of war, joining their compatriots from *Nestor*, *Tipperary*, *Queen Mary*, *Indefatigable* and *Turbulent*.[13]

It is not known when the wreck was first found, but it seems likely that I was among the first team to dive it. On 23 May 2001 *Loyal Watcher* arrived at the wreck site of HMS *Queen Mary*, only to be confronted by the sight of a Danish trawler in the process of netting the wreck; an all too frequent occurrence on the larger wrecks. A radio conversation revealed his intention to be on the site for 24 hours. However, the trawler captain gave us a GPS position for a nearby wreck. This site was investigated by diving on the same day and, on examination, turned out to be the remains of a British destroyer.

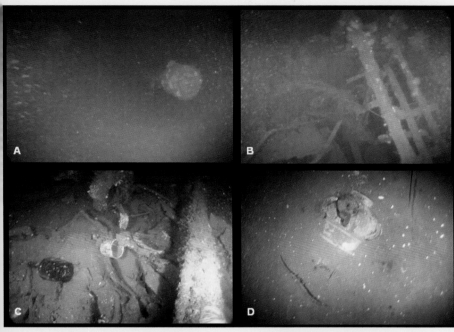

Fig. 3.10 Images from the wreck of HMS Nomad *taken in 2001 on the day it was first dived.*

The wreck lay in a depth of 57 metres and the visibility on site was poor, no more than 5 metres. In all likelihood this was because of the fishing activity nearby, which can greatly reduce visibility by stirring up sediment on the seabed. Fig. 3.10 shows what the conditions were like and depicts some of the few recognisable items lying in the wreckage.

The dive turned out to have taken place on a small piece of the wreck. Initially both propeller shafts were seen jutting a few metres out of the wreck, around half a metre above the seabed. One can be seen in Image A. This obviously indicated the portion of the wreck was somewhere aft of the engine room. However, having swum up to the other end of the wreckage and seen the curved stern, we could see that the shafts at the other end of the wreck were actually pointing towards the engine room. Swimming out in that direction revealed no other wreckage. If this was correct, it meant that the portion of the wreck was around only 10 metres or so of the stern of a destroyer.

Interestingly, the wreckage actually contained some still standing frames, as seen in image B, which give the indication that she was leaning around 40 degrees to the port side. Portable items such as bottles, plates and cups were seen in the stern and were of the period's Royal Navy design (C). Finally, at the end of the dive, we discovered what seemed to be a magnetic compass housing nearly completely buried in the muddy seabed (D).

Fig 3.11 *HMS* Nomad's bell, now at the Strandingsmuseum in Thorsminde, Denmark.

At the conclusion of the two dives carried out on the site in 2001, the British identity of the wreck was known without doubt, thanks to the presence of Royal Navy pattern crockery on board. However, her specific identity was not known. The nearest position given in *Harper* (as seen in Fig. 3.2) suggested that this destroyer wreck was most likely HMS *Nestor*.

However, in 2002 another group of divers visited the site, dived the other piece of the wreck and located and recovered the ship's bell, which confirmed the wreck without doubt to be HMS *Nomad*. The bell was donated to the Strandingsmuseum at Thorsminde, Denmark. I visited the museum in 2003 and photographed a number of Jutland items, including the *Nomad* bell (Fig. 3.11). It is to the credit of the divers that this artefact was recovered for the purposes of public education and not for profit.

The fact that the stern section seems to lean to port supports the description that HMS *Nomad* was listing that way after being disabled. It seems most likely that the stern portion broke off when it hit the seabed. The ship in the vertical position would have stuck out of the sea by around 11 metres, being longer than the depth of water on the wreck site. It is known from Whitfield's description that the ship had been weakened in the area of the engine room.

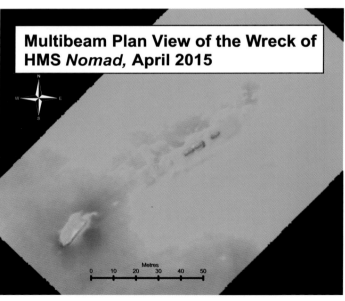

Multibeam Plan View of the Wreck of HMS *Nomad*, April 2015

Fig. 3.12 *Plan view of the wreck of HMS* Nomad, *as seen on Vina's multibeam system in April 2015. (Picture: McCartney/JD-Contractor)*

Once again, we overlaid the hull form and machinery schematic for HMS *Nomad* on the multibeam image (Fig. 3.13). This matched exactly. As seen on the wrecks of both the torpedo boats above, the condensers appear to have been salvaged for profit by scavengers.

One interesting additional element to the story of the *Nomad*'s sinking comes from Whitfield's report to Commander Bingham of HMS *Nestor* while both men were prisoners of war. It contains more detail on a number of counts and is interesting because it describes how the fore magazine exploded as the ship was being abandoned.[14] This magazine detonation would likely show on a multibeam survey, but it is not obvious. Perhaps Whitfield saw the flaring of several cordite containers rather than an explosion per se. Based on the evidence on other sites where magazine explosions have taken place, an explosion would have most likely caused the bows to have been blown off entirely.

HMS *Nestor*

HMS *Nestor* (Fig. 3.14) was ordered at the same time as HMS *Nomad*. She was the same in nearly all regards, except that she was one of the first to be fitted with geared cruising turbines and that she had been built at Swan Hunter, as opposed to A Stephen.

HMS *Nestor* was hit in the boilers while attacking the German line and was able to run west for a while before coming to a standstill. As in the case of the *Nomad*, she then awaited her fate. Commander Bingham of HMS *Nestor* wrote an account of the ship's last minutes while a prisoner of war:

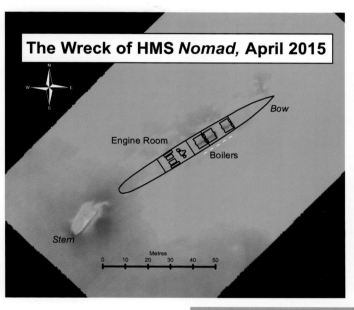

Fig. 3.13 The hull form and machinery distribution plan for HMS Nomad overlaid on the plan view of the multibeam image revealed that the wreck is a British destroyer of the M class. (Picture: McCartney/JD-Contractor)

> No sooner had the two B.C. [battlecruiser] lines disappeared to the N.W. hotly engaged, than the German High Sea Fleet was observed approaching from the S.E… At this time Nomad *was lying stopped E.S.E one and a half nautical miles from* Nestor… *From the time we realised our destruction was iminent [sic] all preparations were made with a view to saving as many lives as possible… The High Sea Fleet drew up and we were very soon straddled, not before we had fired our fourth and remaining torpedo. The* Nestor… *was hit in many places principally aft and rapidly commenced sinking by the stern. Immediately I saw that she was doomed I gave my last order 'ABANDON SHIP'… a few minutes afterwards she reared up in a perpendicular position and sank by the stern… a division of enemy T.B.Ds were detached from the H.S. Fleet… and picked up all the survivors and hoisted our motor boat on board. At 8.30pm two stokers from the* Indefatigable, *unconscious and covered in oil, were picked up and treated by Surgeon probationer A. Joe of* Nestor.[15]

Of particular note in this account are the relative positions of the *Nestor* and the *Nomad* at the time when the end came. Bingham clearly states that *Nestor* is to the west of *Nomad* by 1.5 nautical miles (by the time Bingham wrote his autobiography this had grown to two nautical miles)[16] and it is this positional information that must have been used by Harper when drawing up Chart No.5 (Fig. 3.2). Without power, the *Nestor* would almost

certainly have not had a functioning repeater compass and therefore such a bearing was probably taken by magnetic compass. The variation in the North Sea at the time of Jutland was +13.25 degrees, which would have given a true reading of 99.25 degrees.[17] This is much closer to the relative bearings of the two wrecks, although the distance between them is closer to 4.5 nautical miles.

The Surgeon A Joe mentioned in Bingham's account was seen by a British liaison officer on 22 June 1916 while Joe was a prisoner of war and related details of Nestor's last moments after she was disabled:

> By this time the German fire was a bit hot, and before I knew where I was someone pushed a life belt over my head and shoved me in a boat. I was no sooner in and we were about to shove off when someone shouted 'What about Freeman?' This man had been left on the bridge with his leg half shot away, so I rushed up on top only to find poor Freeman dead. In about 30 seconds or so I was back in the boat again. There was a frightful shriek and the whole bridge crashed over the side. If Freeman had been alive and it had been necessary for me to carry him down I would have assuredly have gone at that time, for he was a heavy man… We were now out of the frying pan and into the fire, as we had no oars and couldn't shove off from Nestor, while the wash from the shells dropping into the sea close to us nearly swamped us, not to mention that it half drowned us with spray. At last we got away… paddling with our hands… and I saw Nestor about 30 or 50 yards away badly down astern; then she sank, gradually and with dignity until her bow remained projecting out of the sea.[18]

Both Joe's and Bingham's accounts describe how the ship sank by the stern and how she went perpendicular. In his autobiography Bingham also states

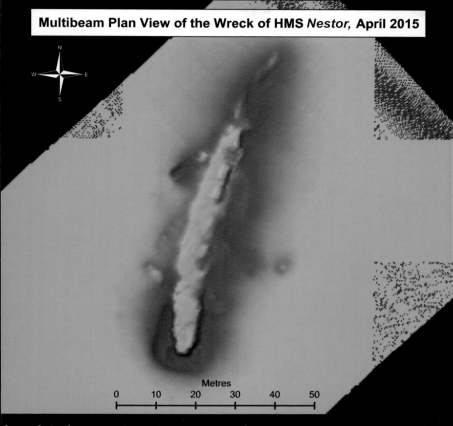

Multibeam Plan View of the Wreck of HMS *Nestor*, April 2015

Metres

0   10   20   30   40   50

Fig. 3.15 Plan view of the wreck of HMS Nestor, *as seen on* Vina's *multibeam system in April 2015. (Picture: McCartney/JD-Contractor)*

that while the stern slipped underwater, the German gunners were still firing at the forecastle.[19] Another survivor, Able Seaman Ernest Sheard, also reported that the ship sank by the stern, with the bows hanging on above water for a few minutes.[20] Both of these points are notable in the light of how the wreck looks today on the multibeam survey.

It is not known when this wreck was first found, but in 2000 the Hydrographic Office database gave a position that plots 0.13 nautical miles north of the actual wreck. The satnav position came from the 75th Anniversary Expedition and was reported as a mark regularly fished.[21] In 2000 we were unable to locate enough wreckage on *Loyal Watcher*'s fishfinder to make a dive worthwhile (we thought at the time that it was probably only pieces of the *Queen Mary* which is very nearby). Several other of the Hydrographic Office records had also proven false. On the first expedition in 2000, we tended to focus on sites we knew to be Jutland wrecks.

Fig. 3.16 *The hull form and machinery distribution plan for HMS* Nestor *overlaid on the plan view of the multibeam image reveals that the wreck is correct for a British destroyer of the M class. (Picture: McCartney/JD-Contractor)*

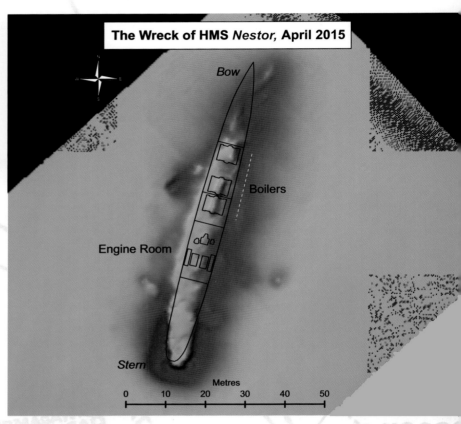

However, in April 2015 the site was scanned by *Vina*'s multibeam system and the obvious remains of a small warship were seen (Fig. 3.15). It was immediately apparent that the configuration of the wreck's high points looked similar to those on the wreck of HMS *Nomad*, except in this case it looked as if the entire wreck was whole and the stern had not parted company with the rest of the ship as she sank. We overlaid the hull form and machinery schematic for HMS *Nestor* on the multibeam and a good match resulted (Fig. 3.16).

The fore section of the ship is seen to be quite damaged and collapsed, including the No. 1 boiler room. The next two boilers are intact and, unlike the German Schulz-Thornycroft three-drum boilers, the British Yarrow type seems sufficiently strong for the upper central steam drum to still be in place, boiler explosions notwithstanding. This was later confirmed to be a consistent feature seen on all of the British destroyers at Jutland and made lining up the schematics with the multibeam images a simple process. The stern of the wreck appears to be slightly distorted, as it gave way when the ship was in the perpendicular position. Again, the condensers seem to have

been illegally recovered by scavengers, although the engine room is not well defined on the multibeam scan.

A further piece of evidence that points to this being the wreck of HMS *Nestor* comes from the narrative of HMS *Petard*. The *Petard* had offered a tow to the *Nestor*, but Bingham declined, not wanting to risk the loss of the *Petard* to the encroaching enemy. On leaving *Nestor,* the *Petard* came across a 'huge patch of oil fuel' from which it plucked Petty Officer Ernest Frances of the *Queen Mary*. The proximity of *Nestor'*s wreck to that of the *Queen Mary* as seen in Fig. 3.2 is worthy of note in this regard.[22]

Destroyer wrecks of the Battlecruiser Action: in summary

With all four of the destroyers and torpedo boats lost during the Battlecruiser Action now found and seemingly identified, a sharper picture of this pell-mell battle has emerged. There can be little doubt about the identities of the two destroyers because the bell was recovered from one of them, thereby eliminating her as a candidate for being the other. In relative positional terms, they match with Bingham's account.

However, it is possible that the torpedo boats' identities could be reversed in the future if closer archaeological studies are made of the wrecks, because the current identification is based on best circumstantial evidence only. Harper was unable to say which was sunk where and gave the same position for both of them (Fig. 3.2).

The confused nature of this engagement means that it is not known for certain which portion of the German fleet the *Nestor* and *Nicator* actually attacked on their final run. If anything, the distribution of the actual wrecks has a northerly bias over where Harper had calculated they would be. This possibly supports Campbell's view that the *Nestor* and *Nicator* actually attacked SMS *Lützow* of the First Scouting Group and not the battle fleet, with *Nestor* being disabled by fire from SMS *Regensburg*, which was in company with the First Scouting Group, but this cannot be known for certain.[23]

The multibeam scans of each site, in conjunction with diving and ROV, have revealed that the small warships are now much degraded. The distribution of their heavier pieces of machinery used in conjunction with the hull form and machinery schematics has proven a useful tool. Closer inspections using this methodology seem to suggest strongly that illegal salvage of non-ferrous components has been a problem on these smaller wrecks, as well as on the larger ones. This was something of a surprise and shows just how vulnerable all of the Jutland wrecks have become in recent years.

Notes

National Archives (various dates). Groos O. *The Battle of Jutland: Official German Account*. Translated Bagot WT. ADM 186/626. London: Admiralty; 1926. p.69.

Harper JET. *Reproduction of the Record of the Battle of Jutland*. London: HMSO; 1927. p.97.

Jutland: additional papers, 1916. ADM 137/1643. National Archives, London. p.239.

National Archives (various dates). Groos O. *The Battle of Jutland: Official German Account*. Translated Bagot WT. ADM 186/626. London: Admiralty; 1926. p.70.

Campbell NJM. *Jutland: an Analysis of the Fighting*. London: Conway; 1986. pp.80–85.

Harper JET. *Reproduction of the Record of the Battle of Jutland*. London: HMSO; 1927. p.98.

Battle of Jutland: extracts from reports, logs and signal logs from the Fleet. ADM 137/4825. National Archives (various dates), London.

Campbell NJM. *Jutland: an Analysis of the Fighting*. London: Conway; 1986. pp.55–56.

Jutland: additional papers, 1916. ADM 137/1643. National Archives, London. p.240.

10 Gröner E. *German Warships 1815–1945. Vol. I*. London: Conway; 1990. pp.178–79.

11 Campbell NJM. *Jutland: an Analysis of the Fighting*. London: Conway; 1986. p.50.

12 National Archives (various dates). Battle of Jutland, press and survivors' reports, press cuttings, extracts from letters etc: Vol I. ADM 137/4808. London.

13 Harper JET. *Reproduction of the Record of the Battle of Jutland*. London: HMSO; 1927. p.117.

14 Jutland: additional papers, 1916. ADM 137/1643. National Archives, London. pp.243–44.

15 *Ibid.*, p.242.

16 Bingham B. *Falklands, Jutland and the Bight*. London: John Murray: 1919. p.142.

17 Gordon A. *The Rules of the Game*. London: John Murray; 1996. p.605.

18 Battle of Jutland: press and survivors' reports, press cuttings, extracts from letters etc. Vol II. ADM 137/4809. National Archives (various dates), London.

19 Bingham B. *Falklands, Jutland and the Bight*. London: John Murray: 1919. p.146.

20 Church Papers Misc 1010. E Sheard correspondence. Imperial War Museum (various dates), London.

21 Hydrographics Department of the Admiralty. *Record of Wreck No. 32352 HMS* Nestor [Probably]. Taunton: Hydrographics Office; 2000.

22 Fawcett HW, Hooper GWW. *The Fighting at Jutland*. Glasgow: Maclure, Macdonald & Co.; 1921. p.50.

23 Campbell NJM. *Jutland: an Analysis of the Fighting*. London: Conway; 1986. pp.55–56.

Admiral Jellicoe alongside HMS Iron Duke's *formidable 13.5-inch guns. Jellicoe's timely deployment of the battle fleet placed the German High Seas Fleet in a perilous position and gave the British a distinct advantage as the Fleet Action unfolded. The Fleet Action lasted a matter of minutes before the German High Seas Fleet retired. British gunnery at this time is noted to have been markedly more accurate than during the Battlecruiser Action. However, critics later claimed that Jellicoe did not aggressively pursue a fleeing enemy, leading to controversy in later years. (Picture: Nick Jellicoe)*

PART TWO

THE FLEET ACTION

4
ARMOURED CRUISER HMS *DEFENCE*

Sunk by gunfire at 18.19 on 31 May 1916

Fig. 4.1 Admiral Arbuthnot's flagship, HMS Defence, launched in 1907. Displacement 14,600 tons, length 520 ft, four 9.2-inch guns, ten 7.5-inch guns. The twelve gun turrets make her class unmistakable. (Picture: Imperial War Museum Q21149)

The first dives on this awe-inspiring shipwreck in 2001 revealed an upright and comparatively intact wreck, belying accounts of her obliteration in battle. In the subsequent years the site has become better known and in 2015 was finally mapped with accuracy. Witnesses reported that the ship foundered in seconds and the evidence seen today tends to support such a scenario.

HMS *Defence* (Fig. 4.1) was a Minotaur class armoured cruiser and the last of this type of ship to be built for the Royal Navy. The armoured cruiser was in effect the pre-Dreadnought version of the battlecruiser. Whereas the battlecruisers were powered by turbine technology and equipped with all big-gun armament, the armoured cruisers were equipped with mixed armament and less durable triple expansion steam engines.

Both types of ship were built primarily to be able to easily dispatch any ship afloat apart from battleships. They were intended to be used globally to chase down the weaker ships of lesser naval powers. Speed and firepower were the key components of this concept. The launch of the battlecruiser HMS *Invincible* in the same year as HMS *Defence* effectively rendered her obsolete as a frontline ship, especially on a fast wing of a battle fleet where heavily gunned enemy ships may be faced, as at Jutland. The inception of the Battlecruiser Fleet as a separate force effectively compelled the Royal Navy to use her old armoured cruisers in this unsuitable role.

HMS *Defence* was ordered as part of the 1905 construction programme and laid down at the Royal Dockyard, Pembroke. She was launched on 13 April 1907 (two weeks after the *Invincible*) and completed a year later. Initially assigned to the Home Fleet, she served as escort for a royal visit to India in June 1909 and then on the China Station until the end of 1912. She was subsequently assigned to the Mediterranean Fleet and was serving there when war broke out.[1]

Fig. 4.2 *The commander of the First Cruiser Squadron, Admiral Sir Robert Arbuthnot, was killed when HMS* Defence *sank with all hands during the Battle of Jutland. (Picture: Crown Copyright)*

HMS *Defence* served as Admiral Troubridge's flagship during the pursuit of the German battlecruiser *Goeben* in August 1914 and was, with HMS *Indefatigable,* part of the initial Dardanelles blockading force.[2] In September that year she was ordered to the South Atlantic to join the hunt for von Spee's squadron. This order was cancelled by the time the *Defence* had reached Malta and she returned to the Dardanelles.[3]

In October 1914, the *Defence* was again ordered south to join the search for von Spee and latterly to join Admiral Cradock's ill-fated squadron. Arriving in Montevideo on 3 November the *Defence* crew learnt that Cradock was dead and his squadron destroyed at the Battle of Coronel two days earlier.[4] The *Defence* remained on station until Admiral Sturdee's battlecruisers, the *Invincible* and *Inflexible,* arrived, having been sent out to deal with von Spee once and for all. HMS *Defence* then transferred her Poulsen long-range radio gear to the *Invincible* and was dispatched to join the Cape Squadron, to escort a convoy from Cape Town to Britain. Once back in the UK, she joined the Grand Fleet in January 1915.[5] A seemingly uneventful period then followed before the Battle of Jutland.

Loss

Despite their near obsolescence, armoured cruisers were employed by the Grand Fleet in a screening role. HMS *Defence,* under the command of Admiral Sir Robert Arbuthnot, was the lead ship of the First Cruiser Squadron, which was made up of the armoured cruisers *Warrior*, *Black Prince* and *Duke of Edinburgh*. Only the *Duke of Edinburgh* was to survive Jutland. *Warrior* foundered while being towed back to Britain and *Black Prince* was sunk shortly after midnight.

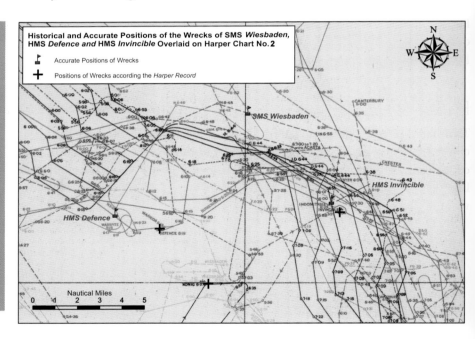

Fig. 4.3 *Harper chart No.2, adapted to show the positions of the wrecks of HMS* Defence, SMS Wiesbaden *and HMS* Invincible. *The First Cruiser Squadron (green track) steamed into the way of the approaching Battlecruiser Fleet and Fifth Battle Squadron (orange track), nearly causing a series of collisions and ultimately paid for this decision by coming under fire from the approaching First Scouting Group and the van of the German battle fleet.*

Historical and Accurate Positions of the Wrecks of SMS *Wiesbaden,* HMS *Defence* and HMS *Invincible* Overlaid on Harper Chart No. 2

Accurate Positions of Wrecks

Positions of Wrecks according the *Harper Record*

Shortly after the loss of *Queen Mary*, the Battlecruiser Fleet had sighted the main body of the High Seas Fleet and had swung north towards Jellicoe, drawing the Germans on to the guns of the Grand Fleet – the so-called 'Run to the North'. The battlecruisers, now supported by the fast battleships of the Fifth Battle Squadron, duly delivered their prize. As the Grand Fleet deployed and the battlecruisers sped towards the van of the fleet, the First Cruiser Squadron was caught in a dangerous situation between several lines of ships redeploying at high speed in what has become known as 'Windy Corner' (Fig. 4.3).

This danger was partly of Arbuthnot's own making, because, being on the starboard wing of the fleet as it deployed to port, he would have naturally deployed astern of the battle line. However, the eccentric Arbuthnot seems to have had his eye on the disabled German light cruiser SMS *Wiesbaden*, aiming to sink her as she could still fire torpedoes at the long line of British battleships deploying to the north of her. So the First Cruiser Squadron steamed into the way of the approaching Battlecruiser Fleet and the Fifth Battle Squadron, nearly causing a series of collisions and ultimately paid for this decision by coming under fire from the approaching First Scouting Group and the van of the German battle fleet.[6] Rapidly surrounded by shell splashes, the inevitable happened when the *Defence* blew up and rapidly foundered with all 903 hands on board.[7]

Fig. 4.3 shows the wreck of the *Defence* to be two nautical miles to the west of Harper's position. Harper's estimated range between the *Wiesbaden* and *Defence* was around three nautical miles.

Eyewitness accounts

The destruction of the *Defence* was seen by many witnesses during this chaotic ballet of ships manoeuvring at high speed. Interestingly, there is little controversy among the various surviving testimonies. The ship that most likely sank the *Defence* was Hipper's *Lützow*, because behind her the *Derfflinger* was about to open fire when:

> [S]omething terrific happened: the English ship, which I had meanwhile identified as an old English armoured cruiser, broke in half with a tremendous explosion. Black smoke and debris shot into the air, a flame enveloped the whole ship and she sank before our eyes. There was nothing but a gigantic smoke cloud to mark the place where just before a proud ship had been fighting. I think she was destroyed by the fire of our next ahead… the Lützow.[8]

From the nearby Fifth Battle Squadron, the merciless exposure of the *Defence* and *Warrior* to heavy fire was witnessed at close range. Captain Poland of HMS *Warspite* reported:

> I saw three salvoes fall across her in quick succession, beauties. A flicker of flame ran aft along her forecastle head and up her fore turret, which seemed to melt. Then –

whoof, up she went, a single huge sheet of flame, 500 feet high, mixed up with smoke and fragments. As it died down I saw her crumpled bow, red hot, at an angle of sixty degrees, and then she sank. I nearly vomited – God it was an awful sight. I couldn't get to sleep that night for thinking of it.[9]

Among the battle fleet witnesses, an officer in the foretop aboard the battleship *Neptune*, which was deploying towards the rear of the British battle line, witnessed:

[The Defence *and* Warrior *were] practically continuously hidden by splashes, they were being repeatedly hit by heavy shell and must have been going through hell on earth. The* Defence *which was leading was just about abeam of the* Neptune, *and barely a mile away, when she was hit heavily and blew up in one fearful cloud of smoke and debris. The foretop fell with a sickening splash into the water, and the* Warrior… *raced over the spot where the* Defence *had been, through the smoke cloud of her flagship's explosion.*[10]

In the narrative of the battleship *Colossus* (two ships ahead of the *Neptune*) the following was recorded:

We thought she [Defence] had gone about a minute before she finally blew up, as she completely disappeared in a mass of spray smoke and flame. But she came through it apparently still intact, only to disappear a few seconds later in a tremendous belch of vivid flame and dense black smoke, from which some dark object, possibly a boat or a funnel, was hurled through space, twirling like a gigantic Catherine-wheel.[11]

Another interesting, yet unattributed, description was published in 1919:

Defence *was hit by two salvoes fired in quick succession. The effect was instantaneous. Her magazine exploded with tremendous violence… Fire seemed to run along from the explosion in each end of the ship and to meet in the middle. In a moment she simply disappeared.*[12]

Ernest Amos, telegraphist on HMS *Faulknor* (of the Twelfth Destroyer Flotilla), saw the *Defence* when she passed abreast:

The Defence *passed first with salvoes falling all around her & a shot or two perhaps striking her. I was intently watching her & when she arrived at our starboard quarter, a salvo evidently struck her, as a great flame leaped up forward & an instant later she blew up with no sound whatever. I almost went sick at the sight but I still kept my eyes glued at the spot. When the smoke had cleared away not a sign of a ship was to be seen.*[13]

Midshipman T Haldane was in the conning tower of HMS *Valiant* (of Fifth Battle Squadron) and witnessed the scene in a slightly different way:

> [Defence] *steamed through the line on the engaged side. Hardly had she done so when she received a salvo aft, which wrecked her after part. Thirty seconds or so afterwards and before the smoke had cleared away, she must have been hit forward, as flames appeared out of the sighting hoods of her fore turret and almost immediately there was a terrific explosion in the fore part and the whole ship disappeared in a cloud of smoke and flames. This occurred at 7.20 P.M.*[14]

All of these descriptions depict a horrible and almost instantaneous end to Admiral Arbuthnot, the *Defence* and her crew. The Poland and Haldane accounts suggest she was hit aft first, and then the fore part also blew up. Amos appears to have seen only the fore part explode. But there can be no doubt that the memory of this event by those who saw it was of a cataclysmic explosion, a fireball, smoke and then nothing. Certainly, from these accounts you'd expect to find a largely exploded ship on the wreck site. My discovery of the *Defence* wreck in 2001 showed that this was not the case at all.

Photography

While there are no photographs of the *Defence* sinking, there is a photograph of her supposedly five minutes before she was destroyed (Fig. 4.4). This photograph appears to have been published for the first time in *The Sailor's War* in 1985.[9] It was captioned as being an image of the *Defence* five minutes

Fig. 4.4 The photograph described by Liddle as being HMS Defence *five minutes before destruction. Its provenance has subsequently fallen into question.*
(Picture: Mrs N Hoare)

before being destroyed at Jutland; the nearby ship was described as being the burning *Wiesbaden*. However, this is probably unlikely because the burning vessel is by most accounts far too near the *Defence*. On close inspection, this warship is revealed to be akin to the visually different Warrior class type of armoured cruiser. Therefore the provenance of the photograph must be considered suspect. This is not the first nor the last time that Jutland photographs fall under suspicion in this book. With the passage of time (and now outside of human memory), this is hardly surprising.

The wreck

The whereabouts of the HMS *Defence* wreck remained unknown to the Hydrographics Office in the UK and was presumed to be undiscovered until 6 June 2001 when it was located and dived by me from *Loyal Watcher*. The position where the wreck was found was provided to me by Gert Normann Andersen as a known fishing snag, in the same information exchange that yielded the position of the *Indefatigable*. The proximity of this snag to the Harper position for the loss of the *Defence* made it a natural target. And so it was that the *Defence* emerged from the pages of history books to become an important archaeological site from the First World War on the bottom of the North Sea.

The quite startling discovery was made that the wreck itself was largely intact, although there was not time to explore it all. Only two dives were possible before poor weather drove the team back to Esbjerg. It was not until 2003 on the documentary filming project that the site was examined in any detail. The project team was equipped with an ROV and, whenever time allowed, it was lowered to the wreck and used to explore the entire site and get a unique and unprecedented overview of what is there.

The intact and undisturbed nature of this wreck, in comparison to the scattered remains of *Queen Mary* and *Indefatigable*, considerably simplified the task of recording what was present and proved more productive than the mixed results gathered by side scan sonar in rough sea conditions. The results of the diving and ROV surveys of 2001–03 were detailed enough to produce a tentative site plan and to attempt a description of what actually happened when the *Defence* sank.[15]

One of the features of the Minotaur class is the five turrets situated along each side of the hull. Each turret contained a single 7.5-inch gun. When I first dived the site, these turrets were the key identifying feature confirming the wreck

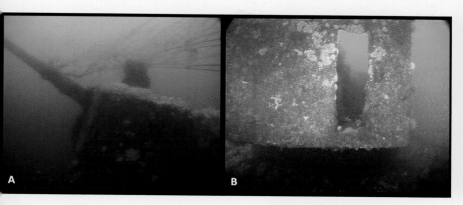

B

Fig. 4.5 *Turret S2, as first seen in 2001. A shows its gun slightly elevated. The mount for the Defence's 12-pounder gun is visible on the roof. B shows that the rear door to turret S3 was blown off as was half of its roof. None of the wreck's side turrets retains its doors.*

to be HMS *Defence*. Fig. 4.5A shows the first turret I saw during my first dive on the wreck in 2001. It turned out to be the second one from the bow on the starboard side (S2). It had its rear door blown off, which was the case with all the side turrets. The turrets were found in varying states of destruction. Eight of these turrets were discovered still in place and their condition and orientation were recorded by the ROV in 2003.

Other areas inspected by diving in 2001 and 2003 are depicted in Fig. 4.6. They included the barbette and ammunition hoist that fed 'A' turret, as

Fig. 4.6 *Items observed on the wreck of HMS Defence in 2003 as described in the text. (Pictures: McCartney/Ideal World Productions)*

seen in image A. The exposed hoist of 'A' barbette was an area of particular interest, because it offered the possibility to see if the flash arrangements in the turret system were being used or had been left open for rapid loading, as suggested by Lambert and others.[16] A thorough examination of the hoist revealed that it had collapsed internally at the point where the upper doors to the hoist might be seen and therefore it was not possible to draw any conclusions in this regard.

The *Defence* was fitted with a pair of four-cylinder triple-expansion engines. The engines were found to be exposed, with the decking collapsed around them. Image B shows the top of the widest cylinder at the stern end of the starboard-side engine. The remains of the magazine under 'X' turret had also collapsed into a jumble of cordite cases and rounds, as seen in C. This was interesting in the light of the discovery in 2015 that some portion of this magazine must have exploded. The wreck was a time capsule in 2001, clearly untouched, with portable artefacts visible everywhere, including reminders that this wreck is the grave of 903 sailors, as seen in D.

Fig. 4.3 shows that the *Wiesbaden* was to port of the *Defence* when the latter sank. The orientation of the 7.5-inch gun turrets along the port side of the wreck (P1–5) indicated that the *Defence* had been engaging a target on that side. Initially 'X' turret was thought to point aft, but it is now established that it too points to port, as would be expected. Also of note is the complete absence of turrets S1 and P1. The ROV survey did not encounter any easily recognisable parts of these turrets. However, during the diving operations in 2003, a possible portion of S1 was seen lying to starboard and aft of the wreck. Its exact location was identified in 2015 (Fig. 4.8F).

The 2003 ROV survey was conducted over a total period of four hours, during which the entire wreck was filmed and all of the main features captured on tape. The wreck lies at a maximum depth of 50 metres and the visibility on site was excellent. The wreck was filmed in ambient light conditions. The ROV survey was useful in building up a picture of what the site actually contains. However, the major drawback with the ROV was that it was very challenging to assess the scale and spatial relationship of the items seen through a television monitor. Neither was any telemetry then available to show where the ROV had actually been; a feature much more common today and in use on *Vina* in 2015. Nevertheless the site plan compiled in 2003 proved to be accurate on nearly all counts, with only the extent of the stern damage having been underestimated. In April 2015

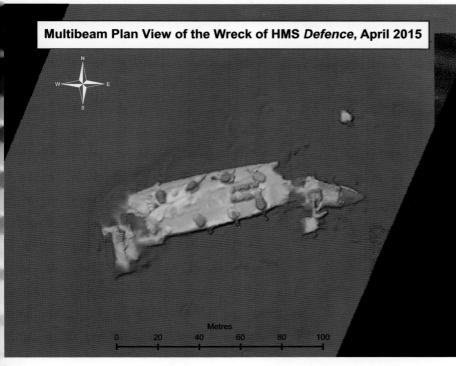

Multibeam Plan View of the Wreck of HMS *Defence*, April 2015

Metres

0   20   40   60   80   100

Fig. 4.7 *Plan view of the wreck of HMS* Defence *as recorded by* Vina *on multibeam in April 2015. (Picture: McCartney/JD-Contractor)*

Vina's multibeam system recorded the wreck site and confirmed much of the findings from the previous two expeditions. Fig. 4.7 shows a plan view of how the *Defence* wreck looks today as seen on multibeam. The bow is broken away, lying on its port side. 'A' turret and turrets S1 and P1 were either completely destroyed or blown out of the wreck. The stern was seen to have broken away when the area around 'X' turret exploded, the single remaining gun pointing to port. The area of seabed littered with wreckage from the explosion that sank the *Defence* was found to be far more limited than was the case with the *Indefatigable* and *Queen Mary*.

Using the 2015 multibeam data in combination with the hours of video of this wreck shot previously, we compiled an illustrated site map showing some of the highlights of the wreck (Fig. 4.8). Image A shows that the bow section has broken away from the main body of the wreck and lies on its port side. The planking has been well preserved in this area. The bow section sheared off forward of 'A' turret, leaving the armoured sleeve with the remains of the barbette lying on its side in the space between the bows and the main part of the wreck.

Image B shows the central part of the barbette, snapped open, revealing the ammunition hoist. C shows the 7.5-inch turret S2. Its gun points skyward,

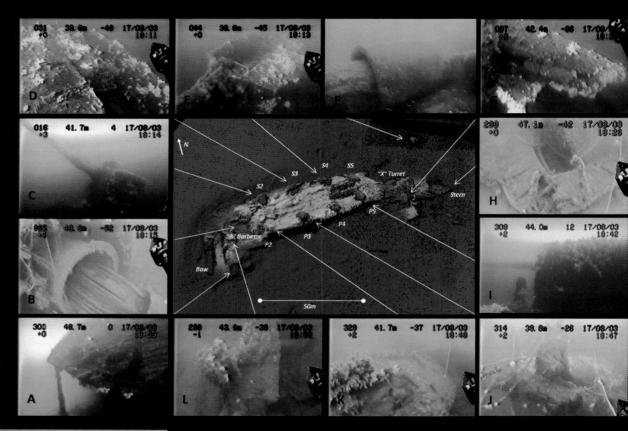

Fig. 4.8 How HMS Defence looks today, using the multibeam record as a basis for a visual tour of some of the wreck's features. (Pictures: McCartney/JD-Contractor/Ideal World Productions)

not as it was aimed, but because the turret is tilted backwards into the collapsed boiler space behind it. The roof of this turret is complete. D shows that the roof of turret S3 has been partially blown off, revealing the breech of the gun inside. E shows turret S4 has also had its roof partially blown off. The roof of turret S5 (not shown) was intact. F shows the lower portion of the barbette of what seems to be S1 turret. This was examined by divers in 2003 and is now accurately pinpointed. G shows the single remaining 9.2-inch gun (port side) of 'X' turret pointing to port and now downward to the seabed. H shows the extreme stern of the wreck where the remains of the Admiral's sternwalk is now collapsed onto the seabed. I shows turret P5 pointing out to port. The roof of this turret is intact. Turret P4 (not shown) had its roof blown off. J shows the roof of turret P3, with the gun mount for its 12-pounder in place, as was also seen of turret S2. K shows that all that remains of turret P2 is the base. It has been almost completely destroyed. Finally, back at the bow, the windlass of the bow section is hanging out of the foredeck with its shaft distorted by the blast

hat blew the bows off. This marks the exact area where the bow section
;eparated from the rest of the ship.

[he extent to which the 7.5-inch turrets were involved in the explosion that
;ank the *Defence* has been attested in several ways. The roofs of four of the
'emaining eight turrets (if the blasted remains of P2 are included) have been
)lown off, showing that whatever propellant was present in the turrets
:ertainly burned. There are some heavily damaged and corroded cordite
:ontainers in some of the turrets, as well as unexploded rounds. It seems that
he cordite was ignited in some way, although the consequent explosions
/aried in power from turret to turret; they were less powerful in the turrets
:hat still have their roofs.

[he complete absence on the main body of the wreck of turrets S1 and P1 means
:hat they were inevitably involved in the detonation of the forward section.
Moreover, the extremely damaged nature of the remains of turret P2 in contrast
:o the intact turret S2 is evidence that the explosion in the fore section of the ship
was more violent on the port side, where the ship faced the enemy.

[here appears to have been one major detonation that ignited the magazine
_nderneath 'A' turret and also detonated the contents of both P1 and S1
:urrets. This tore off the forward portion of the ship along a line roughly in
:he location of watertight bulkhead 67½. A study of the surviving plans of
HMS *Minotaur* (*Defence*'s sister ship) reveals that this forward section, which
is now seen to be nearly completely destroyed, contained not only the 9.2-
inch magazines and shell rooms, but in the hold deck was the forward 7.5-
inch magazine, the 12-pounder magazine, a black powder magazine and the
mine store (Fig. 4.9). The platform deck housed the 9.2-inch magazines (the
shell rooms were underneath, in the hold), two lateral torpedo tubes and
a store of torpedoes. It can only be imagined that a significant proportion
of this vast assemblage of explosive materials detonated almost at once,
finishing off the ship.[17]

Similarly the damage to the stern portion of the wreck lies mainly in the region
between watertight bulkheads 164 and 184. This area of the ship housed not only
the aft 9.2-inch shell room, but also the aft 12-pounder and 7.5-inch magazines,
the torpedo head magazine and the small arms magazine (Fig. 4.9). Also the
platform deck housed the aft 9.2-inch magazine and lateral torpedo tubes with
torpedo store. Again, it can only be imagined that a significant proportion of
this collection of explosive materials detonated, blowing off the stern portion of

the wreck. Interestingly, surviving munitions under 'X' turret seem to suggest that the main explosion was probably centred slightly further forward.

There is no doubt that explosions occurred at each end of the ship. It is possible that the *Defence* was hit around both 'A' and 'X' turrets, causing a subsequent detonation at each end's magazines and surrounding torpedo tubes and stores.

However, another, more likely explanation is that an explosion at the forward part propagated its way through the ship. This 'A' explosion tore off the bow section and the ship rapidly foundered, bow first. This explains the somewhat compressed remains of the fore section. Almost simultaneously the shock wave and then flame from this magazine detonation then ran aft through the ship, along the ammunition passages seen on Fig. 4.9, igniting

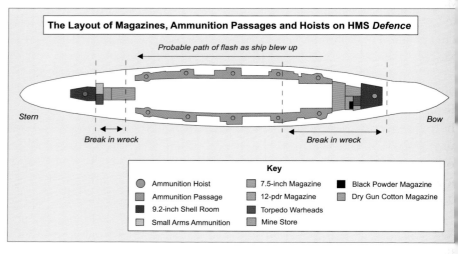

Fig. 4.9 *The layout of magazines, ammunition passages and hoists on HMS Defence (drawing based on plans of her sister ship, HMS Minotaur). The magazines shown are on the hold deck. The ammunition passages ran along the ship one deck above the hold, on the platform deck, which also housed the 9.2-inch cordite magazines, directly above the 9.2-inch shell rooms shown on the diagram. See Fig. 9.14 for a notionally similar arrangement seen in elevation on HMS Black Prince.*

The Layout of Magazines, Ammunition Passages and Hoists on HMS *Defence*

Probable path of flash as ship blew up

Stern

Break in wreck

Bow

Break in wreck

Key

- Ammunition Hoist
- Ammunition Passage
- 9.2-inch Shell Room
- Small Arms Ammunition
- 7.5-inch Magazine
- 12-pdr Magazine
- Torpedo Warheads
- Mine Store
- Black Powder Magazine
- Dry Gun Cotton Magazine

the propellant in each of the eight surviving 7.5-inch hoists, barbettes, side turrets and 'X' turret, giving the impression of flames running along the ship as depicted in Wyllie[12] and by the flicker seen by Captain Poland.[9] The image of the ship breaking in half was seen by several of the witnesses. Equally plausibly the initial explosion may have been aft, as witnesses reported, and spread forward.

It seems that all of the 7.5-inch turrets were fed from below from the two 7.5-inch magazines, one forward and one aft. HMS *Minotaur's* plans show that on the platform deck an ammunition passage ran down each side of the ship, under the turrets.[17] Such a passage in action would, presumably, have had ammunition continually carried through it, aside from what was stored in the acks alongside each ammunition hoist. This would have provided a ready means through which the flash was propagated through the ship.

As the historian DK Brown has shown, a magazine detonation creates a devastating supersonic shock wave that travels within the ship, destroying everything in its path. In the case of the *Defence*, these ammunition passageways provided the perfect, unhindered route.[18] The possibility cannot be ruled out that this also ruptured the keel and thus contributed to the ship's very rapid foundering, although this is speculation.

The propagation of flame from burning ammunition cartridges on an armoured cruiser has a historic precedent from 1914. At the Battle of the Falklands, HMS *Kent* was hit by a round from SMS *Nürnberg*, and this ignited some cordite charges in an ammunition passage. Disaster was averted only by Sergeant Mayes of the Marines who threw the cartridges away from other charges and then flooded the compartment, thus preventing the spread of flames to a magazine. The award to Mayes of the Conspicuous Gallantry Medal and a parliamentary annuity says much about how high the risk of disaster was.[19]

Only one armoured cruiser exists today: the *Georgios Averof*, which is on display in Athens (Fig. 4.11). Although similar in only some areas (such as the twin 9.2-inch turrets), a visit to this ship in 2006 showed that its side turrets were in fact fed from an ammunition passage, notionally similar to *Defence*. Visiting this ship was very useful in coming to understand just how such a system worked in practice and how it may have contributed to *Defence*'s destruction.

Two questions remain: Why is the *Defence* upright on the seabed? And why did she sink so rapidly? The evidence from every other heavy warship sunk at Jutland (except the stern half of the *Invincible* for which there is an explanation) is upside down. In the cases studied in the most detail, *Invincible* and *Queen Mary*, the ship's momentum drove them forward as they broke up, scattering wreckage along a path on the seabed behind the wreck. This phenomenon is limited on the *Defence*; it is clear that she sank fast, which may explain why she is upright. The rapidity of her sinking was probably caused by the sheer magnitude of the magazine detonations, allowing for immediate flooding of the entire vessel.

Being able to pinpoint the location of what appears to be S1 turret at a distance of around 120 metres away from where it would have been on the ship makes it possible to work out how quickly the ship sank. HMS *Minotaur* (*Defence*' sister ship) was able to make 20 knots at Jutland and it can be assumed that the *Defence* was travelling at least that speed.[20] This means that, assuming the *Defence* was close to stationary when she foundered, the whole process took no less than 12 seconds from when turret S1 was blasted out of the ship. This does not take into account the fact that the *Defence* probably began to slow down, but gives an indication of the rapidity of events. The ship sank very rapidly and this would appear to be supported by the eyewitness account which record that nothing was left of her when the smoke cleared.

HMS *Defence*: in summary

The largely intact remains of HMS *Defence,* as seen in 2001, initially seemed to contradict the eyewitness reports of the ship largely atomising in one big explosion and caused a ripple of surprise in the world of the Jutland historian as evidenced by the following:

'Contemporary descriptions of the demise of the *Defence* have been slightly undermined by divers and marine archaeologists, who recently discovered the wreck to be in remarkably good condition for a ship reported to have been blown to smithereens.'[21]

There is no definite evidence of commercial salvage on this wreck site. Because the ship is upright, traditionally salvagers may have found the armoured deck an obstruction too far in the path to the valuable bronze below it.

Because of the intact nature of this shipwreck and her condition, the boundaries of the site itself were easy to identify early on. This was confirmed in 2015 by the multibeam survey that shows the debris field is mainly confined to an area close to the wreck. The 2015 survey has increased the accuracy of the plan of the entire wreck site and has led to a clearer appraisal of how the ship may have rapidly sunk, killing all on board.

Of all of the Jutland wrecks, HMS *Defence* is special. This is because in 2001 she was found to be unsalvaged and upright. These two characteristics made her a perfect site to study, as all of her features were present. The extent to which this was the case is best represented by two images (Fig. 4.10).

Fig. 4.11A shows the left-hand corner of the interior of turret P4. Within it are stacked 7.5-inch rounds, ready for firing. The practice of stacking ammunition

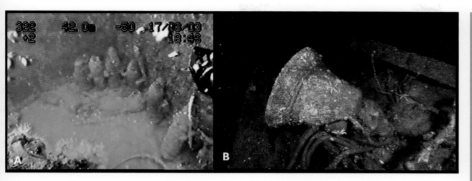

Fig. 4.10 *The extent of intact features on HMS* Defence*: A shows ammunition piled in the corner of turret P4, a dangerous practice. B shows the stern bell of HMS* Defence *as found on the wreck in 2002. (Pictures: A McCartney/Ideal World Productions, B Bradley Sheard)*

in gun houses, ready for use, has long been thought to have been the reason why British ships seemed to immolate so easily when struck near turrets. This practice can be seen here, certainly for projectiles, and it is of significant archaeological note. Interestingly, the turret was supplied with stowage racks for the ammunition at the location where the rounds are seen.[22] This suggests that the ship's designers may not have recognised how dangerous the practice could be, especially if a matching amount of cordite was brought into the turret in the belief it would aid in rapid firing, as has been suggested.[16] Human agency on the Jutland wrecks is not always easy to detect and this is a notable case.

The stern bell of HMS *Defence* was found by a diving expedition who visited the wreck in 2002 (Fig. 4.10). In this case the divers recovered the bell and donated it to the Strandingsmuseum in Thorsminde, Denmark, where it is on public display. At this time there was no protective legislation in force. A more unscrupulous group could have kept it. Who would have known? The broader issues relating to conservation, management and protection will be returned to later, but the point to be made here is *Defence's* huge untapped and unmanaged archaeological potential.

Notes

1 Parkes O. *British Battleships*. London: Seeley Service & Co.; 1970. pp.447–49.

2 Corbett JS. *History of the Great War based on Official Documents: Naval Operations, Vol. I*. London: Longmans, Green and Co.; 1920. p.89.

3 *Ibid.*, pp.291,314.

4 *Ibid.*, pp.341–65.

5 *Ibid.*, pp.404–09.

6 Gordon A. *The Rules of the Game*. London: John Murray; 1996. p.444.

7 Harper JET. *Reproduction of the Record of the Battle of Jutland*. London: HMSO; 1927. p.117.

8 von Hase G. *Kiel and Jutland*. London: Skeffington & Son; 1921. pp.179–80.

9 Liddle PH. *The Sailor's War 1914–18*. Poole: Blandford Press; 1985. pp.113–14.

10 Fawcett HW, Hooper GWW. *The Fighting at Jutland*. Glasgow: Maclure, Macdonald & Co.; 1921. pp.160–61.

11 *Ibid.*, p.159.

12 Wyllie WL, Owen C, Kirkpatrick WD. *More Sea Fights of the Great War*. London: Cassell; 1919. p.131.

13 Amos Papers, Liddle Collection, Leeds University (various dates).

14 Haldane Papers, Liddle Collection, Leeds University (various dates).

15 McCartney I. The armoured cruiser HMS *Defence*: a case study in assessing the Royal Navy shipwrecks of the Battle of Jutland 1916 as an archaeological resource. *International Journal of Nautical Archaeology* 2012; 41(1):56–66.

16 Lambert NA. 'Our bloody ships' or 'our bloody system'? Jutland and the loss of the battle cruisers, 1916. *Journal of Military History* 1998; 62:29–56.

17 Constructor's plans of HMS *Minotaur*. Ship's plans collection, National Maritime Museum (various dates) Controller's Department, Admiralty (undated), London.

18 Brown DK. HMS *Invincible* – the explosion at Jutland and its relevance to HMS *Hood*. *Warship International* 2003; 40(4):339–49.

19 Yates K. *Graf Spee's Raiders*. Annapolis: Naval Institute Press; 1994. p.218.

20 Admiralty. *Battle of Jutland: 30th May to 1st June 1916: Official Dispatches with Appendices*. London: HMSO; 1920. p.270.

21 Steel N, Hart P. *Jutland 1916*. London: Cassell; 2003. p.201.

22 Friedman N. *Naval Weapons of World War One*. Barnsley: Seaforth; 2011. p.76.

Fig. 4.11 *The* Georgios Averof *in Athens shows several similar design features with HMS Defence. (Picture: Patricia McCartney)*

5
BATTLECRUISER HMS *INVINCIBLE*

Sunk by gunfire at 18.27 on 31 May 1916

Fig. 5.1 HMS Invincible, the world's first battlecruiser. Displacement 17,250 tons, length 530 ft, eight 12-inch guns, sixteen 4-inch guns. (Picture: Topical Press Agency / Hulton Archive / Getty Images)

The wreck of HMS Invincible was first examined in 1991. In 2000–03 diving and ROV surveys led to a good understanding of the site's main features. The site was finally accurately mapped in 2015. New evidence seems to suggest that account of the ship sinking in seconds are most probably correct, accounting for the very high loss of life.

HMS *Invincible* (Fig. 5.1) was the world's first battlecruiser. It was by any measure a famous and revolutionary warship and, along with the battleship HMS *Dreadnought,* ushered in a transformation of naval technologies. Turbine propulsion and all big gun armament embodied the technological heart of this revolution.

Unprecedentedly, HMS *Invincible* could cruise endlessly at 25 knots, enabling her rapid deployment anywhere in the world. This was achieved by fitting turbines to each of her four propeller shafts. They were powered by 31 Yarrow boilers, laid out in four boiler rooms, enabling the ship to exceed 26 knots on trial.[1] Compare this with the 42 boilers required on HMS *Queen Mary*.

The ship was fitted with all 12-inch gun main armament, carrying eight guns in four twin turrets, two of which ('P' and 'Q' turrets) were situated slightly in echelon amidships. Unlike the slightly elongated Indefatigable class, the Invincible class could not fire both central turrets in broadside. The *Invincible* was able to easily outgun any enemy cruisers likely to be encountered in the far reaches of the globe, including armoured cruisers, from whose design ethos *Invincible* had been born. In fact, the ship was originally referred to as an 'armoured cruiser'; the term 'battlecruiser' was not officially used until 1911.[2]

Of the three battlecruisers laid down in 1906, HMS *Invincible* was the first to be completed. She was built at the Armstrong shipyard on the Tyne, launched in April 1907 and completed in March 1908. HMS *Invincible* joined the Home Fleet in March 1909 and was present in the Spithead review of that year. From 1910 to 1913 the ship took part in manoeuvres in home waters and in the Mediterranean. In 1914 she underwent a major overhaul in Portsmouth, in part to convert the unsatisfactory electric turret operation to hydraulic.[3] This refit was just being completed when war broke out.

On 28 August 1914 the *Invincible* was present with Beatty's battlecruiser force at the Battle of Heligoland Bight, the first major naval action of the war. Her first 18 rounds fired in anger failed to hit the stricken German light cruiser *Köln*, which was then sunk by the other battlecruisers.[4] North Sea patrolling followed until November 1914 when, along with the *Inflexible*, the *Invincible* formed a special squadron (as flagship) under the command of Admiral Sturdee. This was dispatched to the South Atlantic to find and destroy von Spee's squadron.

The squadron picked up a cruiser escort off Brazil (where it took on board HMS *Defence*'s radio, see page 90) and arrived off the Falkland Islands on 7 December to coal. Fortuitously, von Spee arrived off the islands the following day and so ensued the Battle of the Falklands. Despite brave resistance, the German cruisers *Scharnhorst* and *Gneisenau* and their escorts were no match for the faster and more heavily armed battlecruisers. The whole affair was over in four and a half hours. It was, on paper at least, a vindication of the battlecruiser concept.

In reality, the battlecruisers had come close to running out of ammunition. The *Invincible* had fired 513 rounds (and the *Inflexible* 661) for perhaps as few as 62 hits. Long-range shooting was shown to be poor, mechanical problems many and funnel smoke constantly hindered visibility. The *Invincible* had been hit 22 times, but damage was largely superficial.[5]

The *Invincible* then headed for Gibraltar where repairs were made, including the extension of the fore funnel to ameliorate the smoke problem that had obscured the view from the bridge and foremast in action. By February the ship had returned to Britain and was refitted again in April to May before becoming the flagship of the Third Battlecruiser Squadron under the command of Rear Admiral Sir Horace Hood (Fig. 5.2) on 27 May 1915.[6]

Fig. 5.2 *Rear Admiral Sir Horace Hood, commander of the Third Battlecruiser Squadron was killed when HMS* Invincible *blew up at the Battle of Jutland. The ill-fated battlecruiser HMS* Hood *was named in his honour. (Picture: Print Collector / Getty Images)*

In April 1916 the Third Battlecruiser Squadron was involved in the abortive hunt for the German ships that had bombarded Lowestoft and Yarmouth. During her return passage, the *Invincible* was involved in a collision, her fourth since launching. This necessitated repairs in Rosyth, with work going on day and night until 22 May. The Third Battlecruiser Squadron was then ordered to Scapa for gunnery exercises.[7]

Loss

At Jutland, the *Invincible* was the flagship of the Third Battlecruiser Squadron, under the flag of Rear Admiral Sir Horace Hood, and in normal circumstances would have formed part of the Battlecruiser Fleet. However, nine days before the battle the Third Battlecruiser Squadron had been directed to Scapa Flow for gunnery practice and so found itself steaming eastward across the North Sea as consort to the battle fleet. On receiving signals at around 16.56 that the Battlecruiser Fleet was engaged with German battlecruisers, Hood instinctively went to support them, although he was nearly 50 nautical miles away.

The distance between the Third Battlecruiser Squadron and the Battlecruiser Fleet closed rapidly and within half an hour flashes were seen and gunfire heard. Initially, the Third Battlecruiser Squadron engaged the light cruisers of the Second Scouting Group and fatally damaged SMS *Wiesbaden*. This is sometimes directly credited to the *Invincible*. The Second Scouting Group retired, firing torpedoes which the Third Battlecruiser Squadron was able to avoid. At around 18.16 contact was made with the Battlecruiser Fleet and Hood steered the Third Battlecruiser Squadron to take position at the van of the Battlecruiser Fleet, effectively at the head of the entire British battle fleet, deploying astern of it. As was remarked many years later:

> And so it was a ship designed to hunt down merchant cruisers… now found herself
> as the leading ship of the battle fleet and about to become engaged with vastly superior
> battlecruisers and the powerful battleships heading the van of the German fleet.
> Invincible *was steaming into annihilation.*[8]

The battle situation during this time is depicted in Fig. 5.3. The track of the Third Battlecruiser Squadron is shown in red. The *Invincible*'s movements can be traced to the point of her destruction.

Conditions at this time saw visibility varying from around 2,000 to 16,000 yards as banks of mist rolled over the surface of the sea. Firing began around 18.20 and initially conditions favoured the Third Battlecruiser Squadron, which targeted the First Scouting Group and repeatedly hit SMS *Lützow* and also struck SMS *Derfflinger* and SMS *Seydlitz*. Reminiscent of the Battlecruiser Fleet predicament at the onset of the 'Run to the South', the Germans could see little more than muzzle flashes for the first ten minutes or so. But at around 18.30, a break in the mist revealed the *Invincible* in sharp relief against a background of smoke.[9] Both the *Lützow* and *Derfflinger* ranged in and straddled her. Then,

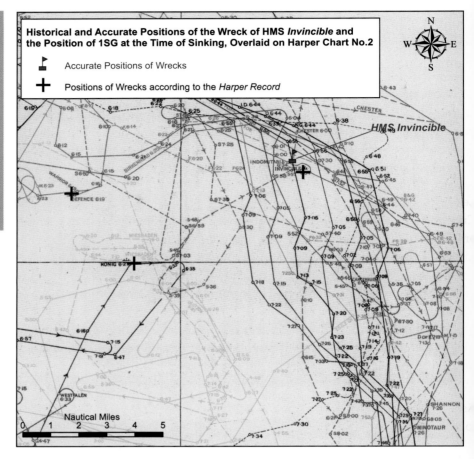

almost inevitably, the *Invincible* blew up, taking all but six of her complement of 1,031 to their deaths.[10] Gunnery ranges had been closing rapidly and at the range of around 9,000 yards or less a catastrophe was only a matter of time.

Eyewitness accounts

The concentration of so many ships around the point where the *Invincible* sank means that, not surprisingly, there is no shortage of first-hand accounts of what happened. However, only a select few that I found have much detail of the actual moment of the explosion that destroyed the ship, with most focusing on a huge plume of smoke and the dreadful sight of the two halves of the ship standing clear of the water afterwards.

From the German side, von Hase on the *Derfflinger* witnessed a third British ship blow up:

[T]he veil of mist in front of us split across like a curtain in a theatre. Clear and sharply silhouetted against the uncovered part of the sky was a powerful battleship with two funnels… and thirty seconds after the first salvo, the second left the guns. I observed two short splashes and two hits… and then for the third time we witnessed the dreadful spectacle that we had already seen in the case of the Queen Mary *and* Defence. *As with the other ships there occurred a rapid succession of explosions, masts collapsed, debris was hurled in the air, a gigantic column of black smoke rose towards the sky and from the parting sections of the ship, coal dust spurted in all directions. Flames enveloped the ship, fresh explosions followed and behind this murky shroud our enemy disappeared from sight.*[11]

Leading Seaman Reginald Bowden on HMS *Yarmouth* (of the Third Light Cruiser Squadron) passing just to the north of the *Invincible* (the dashed range line in Fig. 5.3) reported:

Suddenly a dark smudge seemed to pass along the leading ship's side, the Invincible. *Then she suddenly disappeared into a huge cloud of smoke and flame. It was awful that a ship go in seconds like that, not so much the ship but those living souls with her. A strange thing happened… The upper bridge awning ('Monkey's Island') was blown high above the smoke and flame and looked like a huge parachute with the iron stanchions which supported it dangling below it. As soon as the force of the explosion was over the whole thing plunged into the sea.*[12]

Assistant Clerk Hubert Fischer in the Plotting Room on HMS *Indomitable*, following the *Invincible* and *Inflexible*, recalled his shipmates relating:

[W]e observed 2 dull glows amidships. The appearance was that the armour was withstanding the impact of the shells. But a few moments later a great mushroom of smoke rose to the clouds. When it cleared our flagship was in two halves sticking out of the water in opposite directions and slowly sinking into it. We young Indomitable *officers had particularly poignant feelings since the day before we sailed the junior officers of* Invincible *had come aboard us as a riotous evening was had by all. Now every one of those was 'asleep in the deep'.*[13]

Of the six survivors, Marine Bryan Gasson had the most remarkable of escapes. He was actually inside 'Q' turret when it was struck by a shell but survived, badly burned:

We were engaging the Derfflinger *on which I was ranging & passing information to the Fore Top. Suddenly our starboard midship turret manned by the Royal Marines was struck between the two 12 inch guns and appeared to me to lift off the top of the turret and another from the same salvo followed. The flashes passed down to both midship magazines. The*

explosion broke the ship in half… I owe my survival I think to the fact that I was in a separate compartment at the back of the turret with my head through a hole cut in the top. The rangefinder had only a light armour covering. I think this came off as the ship sank and I floated to the surface.[14]

The most senior survivor, Gunnery Officer Hubert Dannreuther (ironically Richard Wagner's godson), who was stationed in the foremast control top, recorded in his report, of 2 June 1916:

The ship had been hit several times by heavy shell but no appreciable damage had been done when at 1834 a heavy shell struck 'Q' turret and bursting inside blew the roof off. This was observed from the control top. Almost immediately following there was a tremendous explosion amidships indicating 'Q' magazine had blown up. The ship broke in half and sank in 10 or 15 seconds. The survivors on coming to the surface saw the bow and stern of the ship only, both of which were vertical and about 50 feet clear of the water.[15]

Fig. 5.4 *Captain Carslake's sketch of the moment when he saw the* Invincible *blow up at Jutland, as recorded during the inquiry into the loss of HMS Hood in 1941. (Picture: National Archives)*

In 2012, while conducting research before a survey of the wreck of HMS *Hood* (named after Sir Horace Hood, who went down with the *Invincible*), I came across a remarkable testimony, given under oath to the Admiralty inquiry into the loss of the *Hood* to the *Bismarck* in the Denmark Strait in 1941. Despite the passage of years, the account is enlightening about the last moments of the *Invincible*. Questioned as an expert witness, Captain JB Carslake described seeing the *Invincible* blowing up at Jutland:

I was on the bridge of the Inflexible *which was two cables or less astern of the* Invincible. *I was looking at the* Invincible *at the time. She was struck by a salvo which hit her in the neighbourhood of 'Q' turret. There was an appreciable interval after the enemy shell had hit her before the resulting explosion was noticeable. The first thing I remember seeing was the turret roof blown into the air, I would judge some 600 ft. or more, where it opened out into a mushroom of dark brown smoke with pinkish coloured flames. The ship broke clean in half… By the time we were on her quarter the two halves had sunk so that the bows and stern were sticking up some distance apart, with the other ends of the sections on the bottom.[16]*

Asked if he heard any noise Carslake replied:

My immediate reaction after the excitement was that I had heard no noise at all and I remarked upon this at the time to another Officer on the bridge, who said that the noise 'had nearly broken his eardrums'. My deduction was the whole of my attention had been concentrated on sight whereas he had not seen the explosion but heard it first.[16]

Carslake was then asked to make a pencil sketch of what he saw, which to my knowledge is the only one that has endured. It shows how Carslake remembered the strike on 'Q' turret of the *Invincible* and the flames emitted (Fig. 5.4).

Photography

The loss of HMS *Invincible* appears to be the best photographically captured sinking at Jutland. At least four photographs showing the destruction of the ship survive and at least three exist of her ghostly remains before they too sank. The most remarkable of these images are a pair that, according to the naval constructor and historian DK Brown, were taken around an eighth of a second apart (Fig. 5.5 and Fig. 5.6). According to Brown, they appear to show the ship exploding, with Fig. 5.6 depicting the foremast as it began to topple. Brown also noted the movement of the puffs of smoke over the quarterdeck and the 8 ft wide dot in front of the compass platform as evidence of the movement of the ship in the time elapsed between the two images being taken.[17]

The photographs appear to have been taken from the starboard side of the ship and show her entire length. There is a major conflagration engulfing the central part of the ship, with smoke and flame drifting aft. Startlingly, there is also a jet of flame emitting from the area of 'A' turret barbette, including a piece of debris in the air in line with the compass platform. The photograph would have to have been taken from a passing destroyer, but it is similar to the view von Hase would have had from his station on the *Derfflinger*. Such was the rapidity of events that it is perhaps remarkable that this photograph was

Fig. 5.5 The commonly published photograph of HMS Invincible *exploding at Jutland, which has fallen under suspicion in recent years. (Picture: World Ship Society)*

Fig. 5.6 *The other photograph from the Parkes collection (original now lost), which Brown claimed was taken a fraction of a second after the image in Fig. 5.5. (Picture: Originally Imperial War Museum SP956, via David K Brown)*

taken at such an important time in what was happening to the ship, because a few seconds later all was lost in smoke.

If Brown's analysis is correct it suggests that these images may have come from a sequence of moving film, subsequently lost or never in the public domain. This makes sense as it would have been impossible to take two photographs that quickly with a camera of that era. An alternative scenario that has been suggested is that the photograph in Fig. 5.5 is fake.[18] In fact, the earliest representation of the image I have been able to find is in the original version of *The Fighting at Jutland*. In this book there are a number of what are described as photogravures, a process used to produce high-quality plates. In the case of the one depicting the *Queen Mary* blowing up, the caption honestly describes the image as a composite. But, conversely, the same book may have used an image of *Queen Mary* blowing up to depict the *Indefatigable* being destroyed (see page 54). So ultimately there is some doubt over the provenance of these two images. Was Fig. 5.6 a first failed attempt at a photogravure or a poorly developed version of Fig. 5.5?

However, these images depict the destruction of the *Invincible* in an extremely plausible way; especially the venting of flame under 'A' turret and similar flames venting out of the forward boiler intake, details not given by any eyewitness accounts I have found, and certainly Brown detected movement between them and did not consider them fakes. There was a period shortly after the battle when the naval censor did not control news of the event and it is just possible these images slipped out at that time. The truth may never be known now, but there is just enough doubt cast over these images to make me cautious in accepting what they show as incontrovertible.

Fig. 5.7 *The commonly shown photograph of the tragic end to HMS* Invincible. *(Picture: Robert Hunt Library/Windmill Books/ UIG via Getty Images)*

Leaving them aside, there are at least five other photographs of the *Invincible* sunk at Jutland. The most commonly seen (Fig. 5.7) shows the two halves of the *Invincible* on the seabed after she blew up. It seems to have been published for the first time in *The Fighting at Jutland*.

Aside from *The Fighting at Jutland*, there is another collection of photographs, which could have been published as early as 1917. *Photographic Records of the 3CF August 1914–December 1916* is now a rare book. It bears no publishing details, and the photographs it contains end in August 1916. Yet within it are some rarely seen photographs of the battle, among them some of the last images of the *Invincible* (Fig. 5.8). It seems likely that these photographs were taken by midshipman John Croome from the top of 'P' turret of HMS *Indomitable*, the last of the three battlecruisers in the Third Battle Squadron line, astern of the *Inflexible*. In fact, Croome's notes from a public lecture he gave confirms he was serving on the *Indomitable* and took a photograph of the *Invincible* at this time.

[T]here was a terrific flash from the *Invincible*… *and she went up in a column of smoke several hundred feet high decorated at the edges by bits and pieces of what a second before had been a Battle Cruiser… Of this astonishing spectacle I took a photograph which I expect was probably unique and came out so extremely well that it was confiscated from me and presented to the Imperial Service Museum where anybody with six-pence to spare may go and see it masquerading as an official war photograph. I must have got the explosion almost at its height since the column of smoke and debris took certainly two or three seconds to get to its full height, and the photograph shows quite a lot of debris falling back into the water from the bottom of the column of smoke while a number of smaller pieces can be seen coming out towards the top of the plume.*[19]

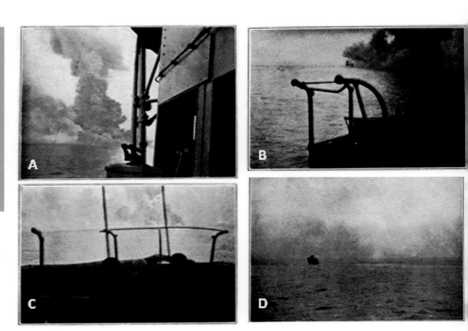

Fig. 5.8 *Four photographs of the final moments of HMS* Invincible, *probably taken by Midshipman J Croome from aboard HMS* Indomitable. *The chronological sequence is probably clockwise from A. (Pictures: Photographic Records of the BCF)*

Croome's description of his photograph certainly fits Fig. 5.8A and, although he doesn't state that he took more, it seems likely that he took the other three in quick succession afterwards. However, the *Photographic Records of the BCF* captions the images as having come from HMS *Inflexible,* the next ship astern of the *Invincible.*[20] Moreover, the single image from the series (A) in the Parkes collection at the Imperial War Museum is also captioned as taken from the *Inflexible.* Most likely, this is an error and the photograph is Croome's, but this is not certain.[21]

To have attempted to establish as much provenance as can be found for the surviving photographs of the losses of all the Jutland wrecks has been important because the presence of these images could have affected the way later accounts by eyewitnesses recalled what happened to the ships. Alongside chatter among the crews, it is likely that many developed a memory of events built out of a collective grouping of personal memories, photographs and conversations. This is why, as much as has been possible, accounts depicting extra personal detail have been sought out.

The photographs, considered in conjunction with the Carslake sketch and the eyewitness testimonies, allow for a testable scenario for the destruction of the *Invincible* to emerge, which can be compared to what can be uncovered from exploring the shipwreck. At least one round from the deadly salvo struck the area around 'P' and 'Q' turrets, as witnessed by the survivor accounts

t detonated the joint magazine below, which contained around 50 tons of propellant. As Brown has suggested, the instant detonation of so much cordite would have created a pressure wave of around 1,000 psi. This would have caused the *Invincible* to burst open. However, as shown below, there is unburned cordite in 'Q' turret, suggesting only a partial detonation of the stock. This was clearly still enough to cause the ship to break in half.

The two halves of the wreck are known to have remained upright for many hours. The cruiser HMS *Galatea* witnessed the stern section finally sink the following day at 14.35. The bow section remained clear of the water, but had sunk by the time a British submarine, tasked with demolishing her, arrived in the area on 3 June.[22]

The wreck

When Harper was ordered to compile his record of the battle, he sent the minesweeper HMS *Oakley* to the North Sea to locate the wreck of the *Invincible*. This was done in order to reconcile Jellicoe's and Beatty's track charts and means that the *Invincible* was the first Jutland wreck to be located. At present it is not known how the identification of the wreck was made, but it is possible that divers visited the site as early as 1919.

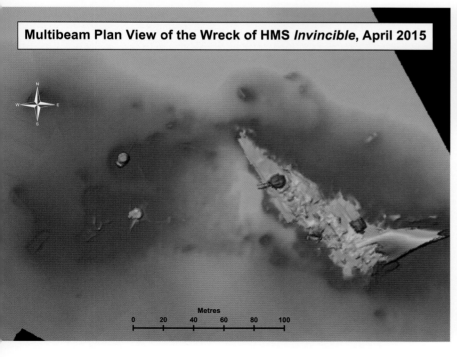

Multibeam Plan View of the Wreck of HMS *Invincible*, April 2015

Metres
0   20   40   60   80   100

Fig. 5.9 *Plan view of the wreck of HMS* Invincible, *as seen on Vina's multibeam system in April 2015. (Picture: McCartney/JD-Contractor)*

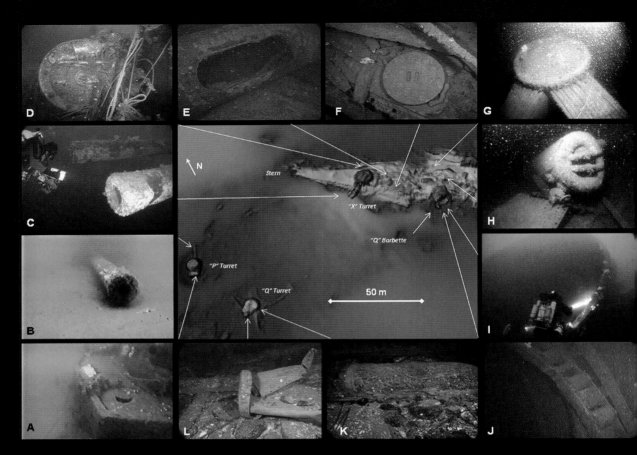

Fig. 5.10 *How HMS* Invincible *looks today, using the multibeam record as a basis for a visual tour of some of the wreck's features. (Pictures: McCartney/JD-Contractor/Ideal World Productions)*

In 1991 the 75th Anniversary Expedition also visited the site and used diver and an ROV to examine what was there. Their description of the wreck wa that she was in two parts, as seen in the photographs of the sinking. The bow was upside down and the stern upright with 'X' turret still in position.[23]

Using the satnav positional data from the 1991 expedition, I located the wrecl of the *Invincible* on 24 July 2000 and have returned to the site on five othe expeditions, culminating in the 2015 survey expedition. During this time much of the wreck has been surveyed, the stern section is understood in detai and the actual circumstances of the sinking have become much better knowr The 2015 multibeam survey finally accurately mapped the entire wreck site.

The first dive in 2000 was carried out on the first large piece of wreckag located by bottom sounder. This, remarkably, turned out to be a 12-inch gun turret, inverted on the seabed with some scattered wreckage around it, but n shipwreck in sight. Later that day the main body of the wreck was located to the east of the single turret. Initially it was proposed that the turret might be 'A' turret, blown out of the ship in the jet of flame in 'A' turret barbette seen in the famous photograph that has now fallen under suspicion (see page 113).

This turret was located again in 2003 for filming purposes and the ROV was then used to explore the seabed around the turret and trace the path back to the main part of the wreck. During this process another turret was located using the ROV's echo sounder. This was also inverted and behind the wreck. The presence of two turrets and an empty armoured sleeve in the debris field between the two halves of the wreck means that they are almost certainly 'P' and 'Q' turrets, which were ejected from the ship when she blew up.

The wreck site of the *Invincible* is not clearly defined by the two sections of the wreck. There is dispersed debris lying in the path of the ship and off to both sides. While the site is not as dispersed as the *Indefatigable* or *Queen Mary*, it cannot be satisfactorily surveyed by diving and ROV alone because it is simply too large and, in places, too confused to safely draw together all the data gathered this way into an accurate map. In 2001 and 2003 side scan images of the main wreck area were taken, confirming the dispersed nature of the entire site, but the surrounding seabed was not scanned. A tentative site plan was drawn in 2003 to show how the wreck was dispersed.[24] It proved broadly correct but has now been superseded by the 2015 multibeam survey (Fig. 5.9).

The multibeam survey significantly added to the data from the 75th Anniversary Expedition and my 2000–03 dives / site surveys. Moreover, it accurately mapped the spatial relationship between the two turrets that were ejected from the ship and the two portions of the wreck. It has now been possible to produce a detailed diagram of key discoveries made on the previous expeditions (Fig. 5.10).

The stern section and part of the debris field of the wreck was surveyed by ROV, diver-operated video or both. The wreck lies at a maximum depth of 54 metres and the visibility on the site in calm conditions can be in excess of 15 metres. Image A shows the counterbalance section at the back of 'P' turret. The entire turret is upside down. Circled is the partially opened escape hatch in its underside. B shows that unlike 'Q' turret, the remains of 'P' turret hold only one of its two 12-inch guns. This makes the turrets easy to differentiate.

Image C shows the muzzles of the two 12-inch guns of 'X' turret pointing to starboard, the direction in which they were firing when the ship sank. D shows the bronze breech of the port-side gun of 'X' turret. This turret is

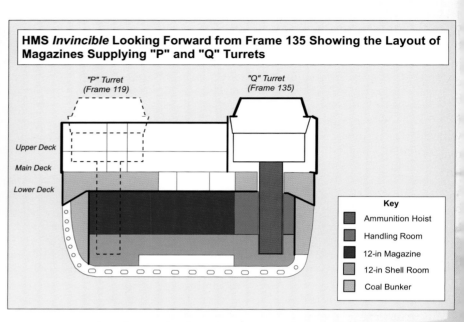

Fig. 5.11 *The layout of the combined magazine feeding both 'P' and 'Q' turrets on HMS Invincible. The cordite store was situated above the shell room in British Dreadnoughts. The explosion of the magazines forced the turrets upwards, with their sleeves effectively functioning as short gun barrels.*

missing its roof and its sides have collapsed inwards. Brown claimed that the roof was blasted off by the explosion amidships passing a pressure wave through the ship and lifting it off.[17] It is equally plausible that it slid off while the stern section was vertical after the ship broke in half. Image E shows a portion of the remains of the mainmast lying across the wreck, just forward of the remains of 'X' turret. The entrance door at its base is shown in the image. Image F shows one of countless smaller items of interest scattered all over the wreck site. In this case it is the cover of a coaling hatch. Image G shows the steam drum of one of *Invincible*'s boilers.

To meet the 25-knot speed requirement of her design the *Invincible* was fitted with 31 Yarrow boilers. The remains of No. 1 to No. 3 boiler rooms forward of the centre turrets and under the two forward funnels are scattered throughout the debris field between the two halves of the wreck.

Image H shows one of two water troughs fitted to the Yarrow boilers seen in the debris field. The manhole hatch with the two locking bars is clearly visible. Image I shows the armoured turret barbette sleeve in the debris field on the starboard side of the wreck. It is most likely that this once held 'Q' turret. The position of this sleeve, roughly where you'd expect to find it, means it fell to the seabed exactly when the ship snapped in half and was not blown out of the wreck earlier in the explosion and sinking process. J shows the roller bearings in the 'Q' turret barbette sleeve, on which the turret would have rotated. K shows that the interior of 'Q' turret contains several unexploded 12-inch rounds. Around these are pieces of coal, which were in a bunker next to the barbette. The thin brown spaghetti-like sticks are unburned pieces of cordite, which strongly indicates that, for some reason, not all the cordite burned in the turret. L shows the ruptured base of a 12-inch 'Clarkson case' cordite container, burst open along its line of rivets, is likely to have been one of the ignition sources causing the magazine detonation, bursting open as the cordite flared out of it. This seems to support Lambert's contention that additional charges of cordite were stored in the turrets of the Grand Fleet's ships at Jutland.[25]

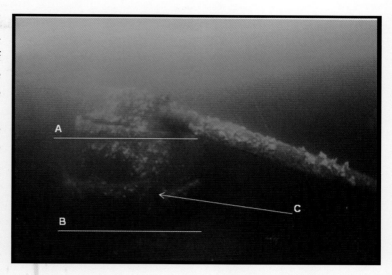

Fig. 5.12 HMS Invincible's 'X' turret in its entirety, showing the slumped guns and surrounding deck. The distance by which the deck has collapsed is highlighted by the distance between lines A and B. Line C points to the collapsing armoured sleeve.

Undoubtedly, my discovery of 'P' and 'Q' turrets in 2001 and 2003 has enabled us to complete the story of how the *Invincible* was destroyed. As the photographic evidence and the testimonies of survivors concur, it is certain that the detonation responsible for sinking the ship occurred in her mid-section, in the area of 'P' and 'Q' turrets. The magazine that fed these turrets was joined and contained at least 50 tons of volatile British cordite (see Fig. 5.11), which, when exposed to flash, simply blew up.[17]

Interestingly, the presence of the 'Q' turret barbette sleeve in the debris field between the two halves of the wreck means that it was on the ship when she snapped in half. The fact that the two turrets are astern of the ship's path means that they had to have been bodily ejected by the force of the explosion, before the ship finally broke. They seem to have been launched out of their sleeves by the force of the blast, which DK Brown calculated to have created as much as 1,000 psi of pressure.[17] The sleeves simply functioned as a short gun barrel.

The remains of the two turrets are different. Although 'P' turret is missing a gun, it is generally in much better condition than 'Q' turret. For instance, it still has part of its armour walls and its counterbalance (Fig. 5.10A), whereas 'Q' turret has only the turret walls surrounding the guns. Interestingly, the missing gun of 'P' turret is the starboard gun (when the turret faces forward)

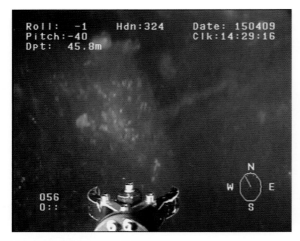

```
Roll:   -1      Hdn:324      Date:  150409
Pitch:-40                    Clk:14:29:16
Dpt:   45.8m




056
0::
```

Fig. 5.13 *The curved armoured plate of 'X' turret sleeve, as seen during the 2015 ROV survey. The curved plate seen displaced in 2001 has now completely fallen out, leaving a void on the right-hand side of the image. (Picture: McCartney/JD-Contractor)*

and this would have been the one nearest to 'Q' turret at the time of the explosion (neither centre turret could be turned across the ship).

We can therefore conclude that, as Dannreuther, Carslake and others reported, it was 'Q' turret that was hit. Initially its roof blew off, then the flash ignited the magazine under the turret, forcing it upwards and over the side, probably taking 'P' turret's missing gun with it (or at least blowing it off). Almost instantaneously, 'P' turret too was blown out of the ship. The *Invincible* staggered on under her own momentum before finally snapping in half and settling on the seabed. Bryan Gasson's survival from inside 'Q' turret was certainly miraculous.

One key advantage arising from the multibeam survey has been the ability to accurately measure distances between various portions of the wreck. In the case of HMS *Defence*, the distance from the remains of S1 turret to the location where you'd expect to see them helped develop a theoretical timeline for the ship's destruction of no less than 12 seconds. The same process can be employed on the wreck of HMS *Invincible*. The distance between 'Q' turret and 'Q' turret sleeve is around 120 metres. It is known from the *Inflexible*'s report that the *Invincible* was travelling at least 20 knots at the time she sank.[26] So, coincidentally, this seems to show that the *Invincible* too sank in no less than 12 seconds. Allowing for some slowing of the ship, the process would have still been very rapid, like for the *Defence*. This seems to support Dannreuther's account of the ship sinking in 10–15 seconds.

The multibeam survey has done much to derive as accurate a record of the wreck as possible without very extensive close-up survey work. Measurements of the two portions of the wreck reveal the bow section to be around 56 metres long and the stern 66 metres long. This means that around 40 metres of the ship broke up during the sinking. Inspections of the ship's plans show that the stern broke off at around frame 145, across No. 4 boiler room and just forward of the main mast. The bow section broke off at around frame 73, across No. 1 boiler room and just abaft the foremast.[27] This is confirmed by the debris field between the two halves being dominated by boilers.

The data from the previous expeditions can now be placed in accurate contexts. This gets us to a point where, alongside HMS *Defence*, the fullest record of any of the Jutland wrecks has now been made. But that is not to say that the book can be closed on this wreck site, as there are still areas worthy of further work, especially attempting to evaluate how rapidly the wreck is degrading.

The stern section of the wreck is dominated by the ghostly remains of 'X' turret, which continues to be the major draw for the few hardy divers who visit the wreck. Yet there is much it can reveal about the state of the shipwreck today. Fig. 5.12 is particularly revealing.

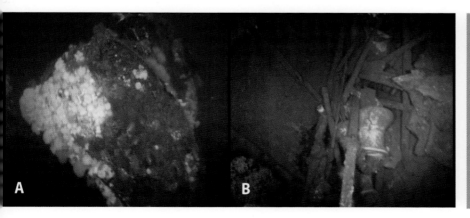

Taken with a fisheye lens on a day of excellent visibility in 2001, the photo shows the entire turret in one shot. What is immediately recognisable is that the guns themselves have slumped downwards at the muzzle end, and actually point toward the seabed. In time they will inevitably become detached.

Fig. 5.12 also reveals the extremely degraded nature of the rest of the stern section. The deck can be seen in the lower portion of the image and is surprisingly low. In fact, it has collapsed down from the level of line A to line B, a distance estimated at around 3 metres. This means the stern section has collapsed on itself and is less than half as high as it would have been when the ship first sank.

'X' turret has so far withstood this process because its strong armoured sleeve has held it together, although it is possible that the sleeve has collapsed down into the shell room below it. But now 'X' turret is also collapsing under the weight of the guns it still supports. Line C points to the break between the curved pieces of armour plate that make up the sleeve, and in 2001 they were parting and beginning to collapse. Despite poor visibility in 2015, the ROV

Fig. 5.14 *Piles of cordite cases now collapsed on each other, as seen in the area underlying 'X' turret in 2003. (Picture: McCartney/Ideal World Productions)*

Fig. 5.15 *The extreme stern of HMS* Invincible, *as seen in 2001 in A. B shows a toilet now collapsed right down to the bottom of the wreck. This area was reported intact a decade earlier, with divers peering into the heads through portholes. That area has now completely gone.*

A

B

was deployed to examine the stern portion of the wreck. The curved plate has now fallen out completely (Fig. 5.13).

The underlying handling room and magazines appeared to have experienced some state of collapse when divers inspected that area from the port side in 2003. In deference to the site being a grave, the area was not entered, so this conclusion is only tentative (see Fig. 5.14) but is supported by the overall condition of the stern section and the jumbled nature of the cordite cases seen in the area.

It has been obvious since 2000 that the wreck is degrading. The 1991 expedition reported that the stern section was in a much better condition than what was seen in 2000–03. Of particular note was the description in the 1991 report that 'it is possible to look into the starboard stern portholes into the seamen's toilets'.[23] However, when I filmed this area in 2001, it had completely changed. The heads have all collapsed into the bottom of the wreck and the hull plating that held the portholes has simply corroded away. This seemingly rapid change in condition in a decade shows that the wreck is most likely in a process of accelerating deterioration (Fig. 5.15).

HMS *Invincible*: in summary

The accurate data now available for this wreck site shows that she sank very rapidly indeed, perhaps as fast as the survivor Dannreuther described. The explosion tore the ship apart in seconds, with a supersonic shock wave travelling throughout the internals of the ship, rapidly killing most of the crew. Gasson's survival from a turret seemingly ejected from the wreck remains one of the most miraculous escapes from a shipwreck I have ever come across.

The haunting remains of 'X' turret represent one of the truly special elements on the entire battlefield and it continues to be an awe-inspiring sight whenever I visit. But it will not survive forever. The armoured sleeve of 'X' turret has now descended deep into the ship's structure, perhaps as far down as the seabed, as the decks around it have collapsed. It too is corroding. Compared with the description of the stern from 1991, the findings from 2001 show a rapid deterioration of the wreck in recent years. In 2015 we observed that even the strong armoured sleeve of 'X' turret was in the process of breaking up. In the next few decades it seems this most emotive and inspiring of shipwrecks will be swallowed up by the seabed, so that by the bicentenary of the battle there will be nothing left.

Notes

1   Burt RA. *British Battleships of World War One*. Barnsley: Seaforth; 2012. pp.49–55.

2   Roberts J. *Battlecruisers*. Annapolis: Naval Institute Press; 1997. p.25.

3   Burt RA. *British Battleships of World War One*. Barnsley: Seaforth; 2012. pp.49–57.

4   Tarrant VE. *Battlecruiser* Invincible. London: Arms and Armour Press; 1986. p.33.

5   *Ibid.*, pp.71–74.

6   *Ibid.*, pp.75–84.

7   *Ibid.*, pp.95–97.

8   *Ibid.*, p.106.

9   Campbell NJM. *Jutland: an Analysis of the Fighting*. London: Conway; 1986. p.159.

10 Harper JET. *Reproduction of the Record of the Battle of Jutland*. London: HMSO; 1927. p.117.

11 von Hase G. *Kiel and Jutland*. London: Skeffington & Son; 1921. pp.183–84.

12 Church Papers Misc 1010. RH Bowden correspondence, Imperial War Museum (various dates), London.

13 Church Papers Misc 1010. H Fisher correspondence, Imperial War Museum (various dates), London.

14 Church Papers Misc 1010. B. W. Gasson correspondence, Imperial War Museum (various dates), London.

15 *Jutland: Reports of Flag and Commanding Officers*. ADM 137/302. National Archives (various dates), London.

16 Loss of HMS *Hood* in action with German Battleship *Bismarck*: Boards of Inquiry. ADM 116/4351, National Archives (various dates), London.

17 Brown DK. HMS *Invincible* – the explosion at Jutland and its relevance to HMS *Hood*. *Warship International* 2003; 40(4):339–49.

18 Marshall PA. The *Invincible*'s explosive photo. *Naval History* 2012; 26(1):44–46.

19 Croome Papers Doc. 5141. Imperial War Museum (various dates), London.

20 Anon. *Photographic Records of the BCF August 1914–December 1916*. Unknown.

21 Surgeon Parkes Collection. SP2469. Imperial War Museum (various dates), London.

22 Tarrant VE. *Battlecruiser* Invincible. London: Arms and Armour Press; 1986. p.113.

23 Moor G. *Battle of Jutland 1916. 75th Anniversary 1991: the Expedition Report*. 1991. Unpublished copy in author's collection.

24 McCartney I. Jutland 1916: The archaeology of a modern naval battle: the wreck of HMS *Invincible*, the world's first battlecruiser. *Skyllis* 2012; 2:168–76.

25 Lambert NA. 'Our bloody ships' or 'our bloody system'? Jutland and the loss of the battle cruisers, 1916. *Journal of Military History* 1998; 62:29–56.

26 Admiralty. *Battle of Jutland: 30th May to 1st June 1916: Official Dispatches with Appendices*. London: HMSO; 1920.

27 Constructor's plans of HMS *Invincible*. Ship's plans collection, National Maritime Museum (various dates) Controller's Department, Admiralty (undated), London.

6
LIGHT CRUISER SMS *WIESBADEN*

Foundered around 01.45 on 1 June 1916

Fig. 6.1 SMS Wiesbaden as seen from the port side. The 5.9-inch gun turrets were arranged with a pair forward and aft (superfiring) and two along each side. Launched in January 1915, she had a displacement of 5,120 tons and length of 477 ft, with eight 5.9-inch guns, two AA guns and four 19.7-inch torpedo tubes. (Picture: Archiv Deutscher Marinebund)

The sinking of SMS Wiesbaden after a titanic struggle for survival in which there was a single survivor still resonates a century later. One of the least understood of the warships sunk at Jutland, the wreck is as mysterious as she is enigmatic.

SMS *Wiesbaden* (Fig. 6.1) was the named ship of her class, which was the first class of light cruisers purposely designed to take the 5.9-inch gun, although earlier classes received retrofits.[1] The eight main guns were fitted in single casemates, two forward, two down each side and a superfiring pair to the stern. Secondary armament consisted of anti-aircraft guns and four torpedo tubes. The ship was commissioned in August 1915 and saw her first major action at the Battle of Jutland, where she formed part of the Second Scouting Group, consisting of her sister ship SMS *Frankfurt* (the lead ship), followed by the *Pillau*, *Elbing* and *Wiesbaden* screening the battlecruisers of the First Scouting Group.

Loss

During the Battlecruiser Action the *Wiesbaden* and Second Scouting Group had been on the eastward, unengaged side of the German line. But at around 17.36 the British light cruiser HMS *Chester* appeared from the north-east and came under fire from all of the Second Scouting Group. These were the gun flashes spotted by the Third Battlecruiser Squadron as her battlecruisers searched to southward for contact with the Battlecruiser Fleet (see page 109). As the *Chester* was outnumbered, she turned away north and rapidly closed the distance with the Third Battlecruiser Squadron. At around 17.55 the Third Battlecruiser Squadron spotted the German light cruisers and opened fire on the Second Scouting Group, which was completely taken by surprise by the appearance of battlecruisers to the east of the Battlecruiser Fleet.[2] During this short engagement, it is thought that the *Wiesbaden* was hit by the 12-inch rounds of the Third Battlecruiser Squadron on at least two occasions. One hit, generally credited to HMS *Invincible*, disabled both *Wiesbaden*'s engines, leading ultimately to her destruction.[3]

Unable to manoeuvre – a nightmare scenario for any warship in battle – the *Wiesbaden* now found herself in a very hot corner as the centrepiece of the unfolding Fleet Action. It seems that over the next hour or so several British ships sighted the *Wiesbaden* and fired at her. Her allure was irresistible to some, including Admiral Sir Robert Arbuthnot on HMS *Defence* who lost his life and two ships of his squadron as a consequence of attempting to sink this remarkable ship (see Chapter 4).

Fig. 6.2 depicts the progress of the battle from 17.55 and shows the Harper position where the *Wiesbaden* was thought lost and her actual position as a wreck, eight nautical miles further north. This discrepancy will be examined later in this chapter. The map clearly shows the central location the disabled ship occupied as the height of the battle raged around her and the British fleet passed by from west to east, with the *Wiesbaden* in the centre of its arc of fire.

Ships of the Battlecruiser Fleet fired as they passed: HMS *Tiger* with her secondary guns from 18.07 to 18.12 and with probably all her guns from 18.19 to 18.24. HMS *Lion* fired a torpedo at her at around 18.15, but missed. Minutes later, under a hail of fire from the German battlecruisers, the destroyer HMS *Onslow* struck the *Wiesbaden* with a torpedo. This was around the same time that Arbuthnot was killed when HMS *Defence* blew up.

Fig. 6.2 *Harper's chart No.2,*
adapted to show the positions
of the wrecks of HMS Defence,
SMS Wiesbaden *and HMS*
Invincible. *The Wiesbaden's*
position is shown from 17.55;
she is said to have been disabled
shortly thereafter.

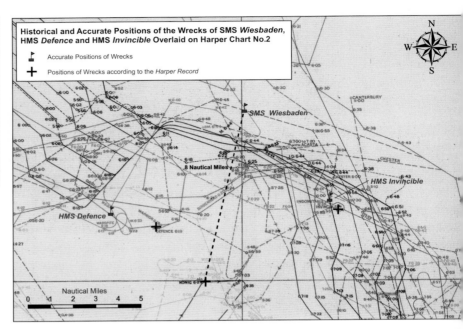

Subsequently the British battle fleet joined the target practice and fired at the *Wiesbaden* as they progressed past. The ship was a target for heavy shell from at least HMS *Agincourt, Revenge, Hercules, Iron Duke, Bellerophon, Marlborough, Superb, Thunderer, Royal Oak, Monarch, Vanguard, Colossus, Collingwood, Conqueror, St Vincent* and *Temeraire*. Secondary guns were fired when the opportunity arose, as it did for at least the light cruisers HMS *Yarmouth, Falmouth, Dublin* and *Southampton*. Leading Seaman Bowden aboard HMS *Yarmouth* who had witnessed *Invincible* destroyed recalled:

> *[Wiesbaden was] stopped and helpless, but still firing one gun. That was soon out*
> *of action. We were firing at point blank range, 1000 yards in our sights. Rapid or*
> *individual firing, and believe me they got a peppering.*[4]

As Campbell has pointed out, it is impossible to know how many times the *Wiesbaden* was struck by shells. But it had to be at least 15 times by heavy rounds, six times by 9.2-inch or 7.5-inch from the First Cruiser Squadron and any number of six-inch and four-inch rounds from the light cruiser and HMS *Onslow*.[5]

The *Wiesbaden* was ablaze from around the time of the torpedo strike and it is practically impossible to imagine the carnage on board. Periodically in the shifting mists, German warships had witnessed their fellow sailors and countrymen going through hell. At 19.00 four torpedo boats of the Third Flotilla attempted to rescue the crew but reluctantly turned back under heavy fire from the British battle fleet. Later the same flotilla made another attempt to reach the *Wiesbaden* and save her surviving crew. This was after the mass torpedo boat attack that finally had managed to push the British battle fleet away from Scheer. However, on this occasion, the *Wiesbaden* could not be located.[6] From this point the ship was on her own, but she clung to life until around 01.45 when she finally succumbed to the sea.

Eyewitness accounts

During the First World War the Admiralty's Naval Intelligence Division compiled files on each German ship from whatever sources it could find. In these files is an Admiralty translation of the book supposedly written by the *Wiesbaden*'s only survivor, Leading Stoker Zenne.[7] He was the only living eyewitness of how the ship met her gruesome end.

The actual author of the book that was published in Germany was Lieutenant-Commander Freiherr Edgar von Spiegel von und zu Peckelsheim who, as commander of *U93*, became a prisoner of war in Britain in 1917. Under interrogation he revealed that he had compiled the book under the direction of the German Admiralty and, while the testimony given by Zenne was accurate, he did not believe the calumnious charges of inhumanity by the Royal Navy that were included in the text. Nevertheless, Naval Intelligence Division produced a translation of selected passages from the book for limited distribution. They serve as a rare account in English of how the *Wiesbaden* finally sank. Zenne's station was between decks at the stoke hold turbo fans. Of how the ship came to be disabled he stated:

> It must have been about 0630 when she was first hit. A tremendous blow was felt, and the light went out. As soon as it had been switched on again from the accumulators, it was found that a shell had penetrated into compartment 6, putting both engines out of action. There was great danger from escaping steam, the hissing sound of which could be plainly heard. All the after part of the ship was already full of it and the heat could be felt, even at the fans. The fan turbines slowed down and finally stopped all together… Once again the order passed down, this time by word of mouth, like a cry of despair through the ship: 'Full speed ahead, both engines', – and the reply came back: 'Engines disabled, struck by heavy shell, engine room had to be abandoned.'[7]

With the ship disabled but not yet entirely helpless, Zenne described the maelstrom that now ensued as the British fleet passed her:

Hit after hit followed, and each time a tremor ran through the ship, but she remained afloat. The gun's crews had suffered heavy casualties, and had been filled up by some of the stokers off duty… the enemy had realised Wiesbaden's helpless plight and their armoured ships were shelling her from all sides… The Commanding Officer and the entire personnel of the bridge had already become casualties… A smell of gas and burning permeated the lower part of the ship, and reports of flooding and damage multiplied.[7]

Zenne goes on to describe the torpedo hit and the subsequent devastation wrought on the *Wiesbaden* up until night fell:

Shortly after 1900 a shock was felt throughout the ship, worse than any that had gone before. A terrific, dull explosion followed, and it felt as though the ship and all on board had been hurled into the air. She had undoubtedly been hit by a torpedo… and immediately afterwards the order was given 'Abandon Ship'… the lifebelts were distributed… Some of the wounded were carried up on deck so at least they might die in the open… The wreckage of the two after funnels was hanging over the side, the still remaining half of the foremost one was full of holes… No.3 starboard gun had disappeared entirely. In the place where it had been was a black gaping hole stretching across the deck to amidships… The lifeboats had been burned in the davits and the motor boat on the boat deck was in flames… Darkness fell, and after a considerable interval firing suddenly ceased.[7]

In the darkness, the surviving crew took stock of their predicament:

[A] devastating fire had been concentrated on her from a number of armoured ships, and from guns of every calibre, during part of the time at very close range; furthermore, a British torpedo had torn open her stern, fires were raging in every direction – yet she remained afloat… The survivors gathered in the light of a fire which had broken out in the ship's office… Sixteen unwounded men remained… The wounded were collected from every part of the ship and laid on the quarterdeck and, as far as possible, attended to.[7]

The only surviving officer now miraculously appeared and ordered an inspection of the ship, to see how long she would float. Three rafts were patched up and lowered into the sea:

[T]he wooden raft was lowered… from the stern of the Wiesbaden… – and not a moment too soon. A dreadful, hollow, gurgling sound was heard from the interior of the ship, and with unexplained suddenness she listed to starboard, right up to the rails. This was after 0100… The three rafts held 22 men in all, some of them wounded… They drifted in an easterly direction until separated by the current.[7]

Zenne was found alone on a raft at 1900 on 2 June, having been in the water and latterly on a small steel raft for nearly 40 hours. He was interned in Norway and later returned to Germany.

Zenne's account, when the embellishments are removed, is informative about the damage this remarkable ship sustained. We hoped that some of it might still manifest itself on the wreck of the *Wiesbaden* when she was surveyed. The torpedo had hit aft, but it was the bow that was noticeably down in the water by 3 metres or more. The starboard No. 3 gun had gone entirely, No. 2 starboard gun was split at the muzzle and the ship had sunk to starboard, the side from which she received much of her punishment. Portions of the masts were still standing at this time.

The wreck

The position of the wreck of SMS *Wiesbaden* was unknown to me until the 2015 survey. JD-Contractor had not previously visited the wreck and, in fact, little was known about what we would find. So it was with great anticipation that the multibeam system was put to use on the wreck. Fig. 6.3 shows the plan view of the wreck, as seen on *Vina* during the survey.

The multibeam survey shows that the wreck lies on an east–west axis. There is no widely scattered debris field; all wreckage is in close proximity to the hull. This was to be expected because the ship sank in one piece without exploding. There is a noticeable piling of wreckage along the north side of the wreck, while the south side is cleaner by comparison. The westerly end of the wreck is much more collapsed than the easterly. The mid-section looks much more solid. It was clear from the survey that the wreck was upside down.

The ROV was deployed to circumvent the wreck site and record its features. The conditions on the seabed were very poor, with less than 1 metre visibility. The risk of entangling the ROV was too great and it had to be recovered. The multibeam was therefore the only evidence that could be gathered on site. From close inspection, it seems to suggest that the bow of the wreck lies to the west. It is known that the ship was down by the bow before sinking, so some of the collapse shown could be related to that.

The wreck was found by the German Navy in 1983 and it seems that some artefacts were recovered at that time, including a torpedo, which is now on display at the Sea War Museum Jutland. Anecdotally, it is also reported that

Fig. 6.3 *Plan view of the multibeam image of the wreck of SMS* Wiesbaden, *as seen on* Vina *in April 2015. (Picture: McCartney/JD-Contractor)*

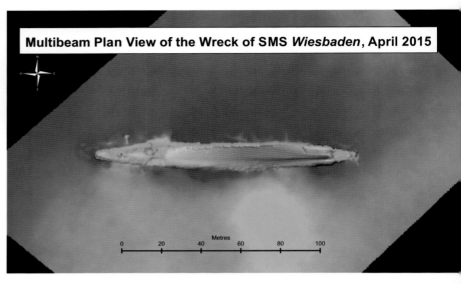

Multibeam Plan View of the Wreck of SMS *Wiesbaden*, April 2015

the propellers were recovered from this wreck. The easterly end of the wreck manifests damage in the area where the propellers would be. Its localised nature tends to support the view that it has been caused by targeted salvage operations. Fig. 6.4 shows the wreck at an angle, depicting the stern area in the foreground. The streamlining of the hull aft of the two propeller shafts on the top of the wreck is clearly visible.

Another notable point to arise during the survey of *Wiesbaden* is her actual position, compared with the one given by Harper. In Fig. 6.2, the distance

Fig. 6.4 *SMS* Wiesbaden, *as seen on* Vina's *multibeam in April 2015. The damage to the stern area is localised and aft of the two propeller shafts. (Picture: McCartney/JD-Contractor)*

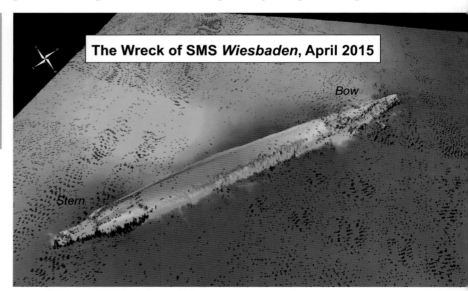

The Wreck of SMS *Wiesbaden*, April 2015

Bow

Stern

between the wreck and the Harper position is shown as eight nautical miles. This is a significant disparity, especially when the more accurate positions for the *Invincible* and *Defence* are taken into consideration. It seems likely that during her time as a disabled ship the *Wiesbaden* drifted northward. Accepting the timings in this chapter to be broadly correct, the ship was unable to manoeuvre for nearly eight hours, giving a northward drift of around 1 knot.

More important than the gentle, predominantly northerly current in the area was the strength and direction of the wind. Also struggling to survive during the night was the British armoured cruiser HMS *Warrior*, slowly losing her fight around 70 nautical miles to the west when the *Wiesbaden* foundered. In her case, the weather is reported as strengthening, with the wind backing from south-south-west to south-west and the sea continuing to rise.[8] The Meteorological Office records for 31 May to 1 June 1916 predicted increased winds from the south-west.[9] Observations on 1 June 1916 confirm that the wind was coming from the south at Force 3 at the station at Blåvands Huk, west Denmark, and the wind was reported as blowing Force 6 from the west at Skagen, north Denmark.[10] The *Wiesbaden*, it seems, was blown by the wind and carried by the tide roughly north-north-east for around eight nautical miles before she foundered. The orientation of the wreck suggests she was probably beam on to the waves at the time she sank.

SMS *Wiesbaden*: in summary

The tragic and yet epic tale of how SMS *Wiesbaden* fought for her life at Jutland is yet another dramatic example of the harsh reality of naval conflict in the First World War. Of the larger wrecks at Jutland, her ghostly upside-down remains will endure long in my memory. It is hoped that further surveys of this wreck will be possible in the future in order to better understand what is present.

On board the *Wiesbaden* as a lookout was the famous marine writer and poet Johann Wilhelm Kinau, better known by his pen name Gorch Fock

Fig. 6.5 Matrose (Seaman) Johann Kinau, otherwise known as the writer and poet Gorch Fock, who lost his life on SMS Wiesbaden at the Battle of Jutland. (Picture: Deutscher Marinebund)

(Fig. 6.5). His body was washed ashore and buried in Sweden. His memory was immortalised in 1933 with the naming of the first of two German Navy training barques in his name. No memorial to the brave crew of this tough ship seems more appropriate. The ship survives in Stralsund, Germany, as a public exhibit (Fig. 6.6).

Fig. 6.6 Gorch Fock I, *named after Johann Kinau, the writer and poet killed on SMS Wiesbaden, as seen in Stralsund in 2012.*

Notes

1   Royal Navy. *German Warships of World War I*. London: Greenhill; 1992. pp.115–16.

2   National Archives (various dates). Groos O. *The Battle of Jutland: Official German Account*. Translated Bagot WT. ADM 186/626. London: Admiralty; 1926. p.91.

3   Campbell NJM. *Jutland: an Analysis of the Fighting*. London: Conway; 1986. p.113.

4   Church Papers Misc 1010. RH Bowden correspondence, Imperial War Museum (various dates), London.

5   Campbell NJM. *Jutland: an Analysis of the Fighting*. London: Conway; 1986. p.395.

6   National Archives (various dates). Groos O. *The Battle of Jutland: Official German Account*. Translated Bagot WT. ADM 186/626. London: Admiralty; 1926. pp.128–45.

7   Jutland: later reports, 1916. ADM 137/1664. National Archives (various dates), London.

8   Admiralty. *Battle of Jutland: 30th May to 1st June 1916: Official Dispatches with Appendices*. London: HMSO; 1920. p.289.

9   Daily Weather Reports 17–31 May 1916. Meteorological Office, Exeter.

10 Daily Weather Reports 1–16 June 1916. Meteorological Office, Exeter.

7
DESTROYER WRECKS OF THE FLEET ACTION

HMS Shark, SMS S35 and SMS V48 sunk by combinations of gunfire and torpedo between around 19.00 and 19.40 on 31 May 1916

Fig. 7.1 *HMS Shark, as seen pre-war. Length 268 ft, displacement 1,072 tons, with three 4-inch guns (one forward and two aft) and two 21-inch torpedo tubes (fore and aft of the after funnel). (Picture: Richard Osborne Collection)*

For the destroyers and torpedo boats in particular, being disabled in 'no man's land' inevitably meant having to endure punishment from whatever enemy units turned their guns at them. This happened to both HMS Shark and SMS 48; Commander Loftus Jones of the Shark received a posthumous Victoria Cross. For S35, the end came quickly: She was blown in half by heavy shell, sinking immediately. The wrecks have been located and surveyed and this chapter investigates their remains and identities.

The previous two chapters covered the intervention of the Third Battlecruiser Squadron and its engagement with the Second Scouting Group at around 17.55 when SMS *Wiesbaden* was disabled. The fighting began while the Third Battlecruiser Squadron was on a northerly track. On the engaged side were four British destroyers, HMS *Shark* leading, *Acasta*, *Ophelia* and *Christopher*. They were all part of the Fourth Destroyer Flotilla and normally would have formed part of the Battlecruiser Fleet screen. They had been detached to screen the Third Battlecruiser Squadron and, as a consequence, now found themselves engaged with the German van in the minutes before the main Fleet Action began.

Astern of the Second Light Cruiser Squadron, the destroyers spotted the First Scouting Group and developed an attack on it. As they closed, the *Shark* fired a torpedo at a 'four-funnelled cruiser'.[1] This was probably SMS *Regensburg*, screening the First Scouting Group (earlier *Nestor's* nemesis) which had altered course with its accompanying destroyers of the Sixth Torpedo Boat Flotilla and Eleventh Half Torpedo Boat Flotilla and possibly others, to thwart the British attack. An unequal fight then broke out. The other destroyers fired torpedoes. Around this time, the *Shark* received a critical hit in the fuel pipe leads and had her main steering gear destroyed, slowing her to a halt.[2]

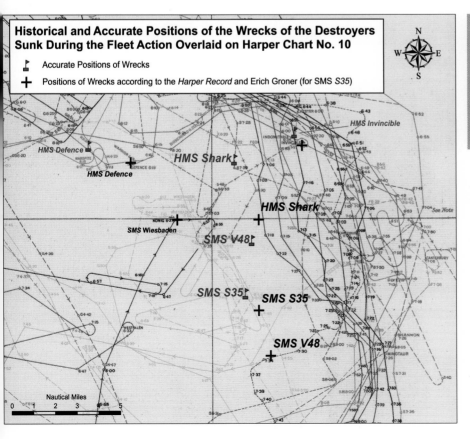

Fig. 7.2 *The historic and accurate wreck positions of HMS Shark, SMS V48 and SMS S35 overlaid on Harper Chart No. 10. These losses occurred while the Fleet Action was raging around them.*

HMS *Acasta* came to the *Shark*'s aid and was hit at least three times while doing so. *Shark*'s captain Commander Loftus William Jones apparently waved the *Acasta* away (as had *Nestor* in the same position), telling her 'not to get sunk for him'.[3] Interestingly, *Acasta*'s captain made no mention of this in his narrative of the battle, simply stating that he received no answer to his offer of help.[4] In any case, the *Acasta* was hardly in a condition to help and could only limp away, unable to steer and just reaching the disengaged side of the British battle fleet before coming to a stop. Temporary repairs got her going and, luckily, during the afternoon of 1 June HMS *Nonsuch* appeared and towed the *Acasta* back to Aberdeen. The *Christopher* and *Ophelia* were also driven off at this time, later joining the screen of the Battlecruiser Fleet, which was now rapidly approaching from the north-west.

Now alone in 'no man's land', the *Shark* was attacked by two German torpedo boats at around 18.15. These are thought to have been *V48* and *S54*, returning from their own foray.[5] *V48* was hit and slowed down, but *S54* struck the *Shark* with a torpedo, which ultimately caused her to sink at around 19.00.[6] The positions of the three wrecks examined in this chapter can be seen in Fig. 7.2.

Now SMS *V48* was in trouble as she was fired on by the passing British ships. Seeing *V48* disabled, *G42* attempted to tow or at least to rescue *V48*'s crew but had to retire or also risk the near certainty of getting sunk.[5] With the tables turned, *V48* now endured hits from the Second Light Cruiser Squadron, the Second Destroyer Flotilla, Fifth Battle Squadron and ultimately the Twelfth Destroyer Flotilla, and finally succumbed to the sea at around 19.35.

Fig. 7.3 *Commander Loftus Jones of HMS* Shark, *who lost his life at the Battle of Jutland. He was posthumously awarded the Victoria Cross for fighting his ship to the last. His body was washed ashore in Sweden where he is buried. (Picture: Crown Copyright)*

Meanwhile, SMS *S35* of the Ninth Torpedo Boat Flotilla, still with portions of *V29*'s crew on board (see Chapter 3), had formed part of the mass attack on the British battle fleet that began at around 19.15 and was made up of the survivors of the Ninth Torpedo Boat Flotilla's earlier action and the Sixth Torpedo Boat Flotilla. Having approached under heavy fire to around 7,700 yards, the ships fired torpedoes and reversed their courses, while making smoke in order to escape safely. It was while heading southwards away from danger that *S35* was hit by heavy shell, breaking in half and sinking immediately with all on board.[7] It is thought that the deadly salvo was fired by Jellicoe's flagship HMS *Iron Duke*.[8] According to her battle report, HMS *Iron Duke* struck an enemy torpedo boat with a main turret salvo and this torpedo boat was then seen to have blown up. The time the salvo was fired was recorded as 19.27.[9]

HMS *Shark*

HMS *Shark* (Fig. 7.1) was of the Acasta, or K, class of British destroyers of 1911–12. Uniquely among the destroyers and torpedo boats lost at Jutland, this class was mainly fitted with four boilers. During the Night Action, three of the *Shark's* sister ships, *Ardent, Fortune* and *Sparrowhawk,* were also sunk.

Loss

The *Shark* had led the attack on the First Scouting Group and had then ended up in a fight with German torpedo boats in which she was outnumbered and had been hit in a vital spot. This made her slow to a stop and she was later torpedoed. There were only six survivors and it is from them that the details of the *Shark's* last moments are known. Only the centre gun was working when the *Shark* had driven off *V48* and *S54*. Those not fighting had been ordered to lie down on deck, which saved lives. Although around 30 crew got on to two Carley floats, only seven survivors were pulled from the sea, with one dying shortly thereafter. Commander Loftus Jones (Fig. 7.3) had lost his left leg and, although wearing a lifebelt, was not thought to have survived for long.

The surviving crew were fortunately rescued after around four hours by the Danish SS *Vidar* and returned to Britain. They were perhaps the last to see the burning *Wiesbaden* in the distance. The torpedo that sank the *Shark* is reported to have struck the ship 'abreast the after funnel'. The *Shark* listed immediately and sank rapidly.[10]

The wreck

During the 2015 multibeam survey, we believe that we located and scanned all three destroyers and torpedo boats sunk during the Fleet Action. The wrecks of both SMS *S35* and *V48* were also examined by ROV and confirmed to be German. By default, the last wreck had to be HMS *Shark*. The multibeam image of her wreck is shown in Fig. 7.4.

The scan showed that the wreck was very broken down and in at least three parts. The central, seemingly most intact part, was measured at around 8.1 metres wide, which is correct for a ship of *Shark's* type. It was impossible

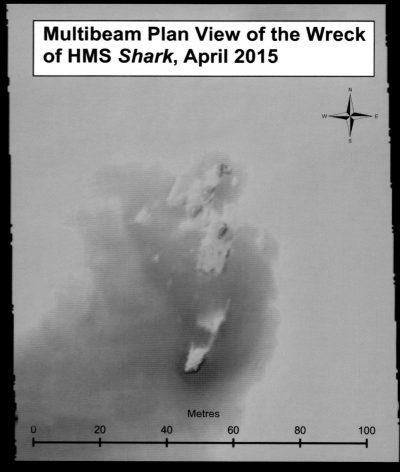

Multibeam Plan View of the Wreck of HMS *Shark*, April 2015

to estimate the overall length of the wreck correctly; this has been common with the smaller Jutland wrecks. It was for cases such as this one that I developed my typology of hull forms and machinery distributions of the smaller ships (see Introduction). By overlaying the correctly scaled schematic of the K class over the plan view of the multibeam scan and aligning it with the orientation of the wreck, a number of features seemed to coincide (Fig. 7.5).

The aftermost boiler of boiler room No. 2 and the engine room seem to match up well. The broken portion of the stern also fits the dimensions of the schematic. It probably broke away on impact with the seabed, as seen in other cases. The three high points on the port side of the wreck are the three forward boilers of the ship, which would confirm the identity of the wreck and show that the ship broke apart at this point.

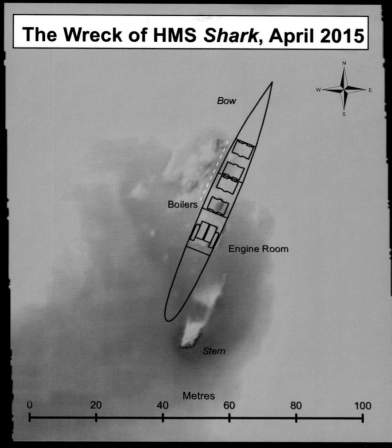

The Wreck of HMS *Shark*, April 2015

Bow

Boilers

Engine Room

Stern

Metres

Fig. 7.5 The hull form and machinery distribution plan for HMS Shark overlaid on the plan view of the multibeam image (Fig. 7.4) revealed that the wreck is probably HMS Shark. (Picture: McCartney/JD-Contractor)

The *Shark* was torpedoed in the region of the after funnel. An inspection of the arrangement of the K class shows that the after funnel actually sat right over the bulkhead between No. 2 boiler room and the engine room.[11] If the ship broke in half roughly where the torpedo hit, the impact would have been a few feet forward of the after funnel and therefore approximately in the right area.

The matches with the hull form, machinery and damage, plus the fact the other two small warship wrecks nearby are confirmed to be German, thereby eliminating them as candidates, suggest that this site is indeed the *Shark*.

As our 2015 study neared completion, Gert Normann Andersen took the ROV back out to the battlefield to check on a few wrecks we had not previously seen by eye. One wreck he looked at was HMS *Shark*. Fig. 7.6 shows some of the features observed on the wreck.

Fig. 7.6 Images of the HMS Shark wreck, as seen by ROV in July 2015. A shows the starboard-side condenser, B the No. 4. boiler, C the water trough of one of the boilers in the northerly debris area and D the starboard-side propeller. (Pictures: McCartney/JD-Contractor)

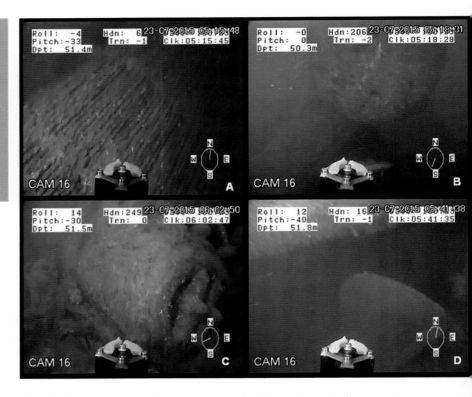

The ROV landed on the wreck site in the region of the engine room and found the starboard-side condenser with its tight pattern of bronze tubes (Fig. 7.6A). Just forward of the engine room it came across a Yarrow boiler with its characteristically straight water tubes (see pages 25-26); this can be clearly seen on the multibeam images. Moving to the north and west the ROV inspected the remains of the forward boilers. They were seen to be more collapsed. In Fig. 7.6C, the water trough of one boiler can be seen, with its distinctive oval shape and locking bars. Finally the stern portion of the wreck was examined and found to be buried to within around a metre of the deck. The tip of the starboard-side propeller could be seen jutting out of the seabed, with the underside of the hull above.

The July 2015 ROV survey confirmed the identification of the wreck as HMS Shark. Up to that point only multibeam had been used to reach this conclusion and it was gratifying to know that it turned out to be correct. Ultimately it was one of the key moments validating the idea that the hull form typology could identify wrecks of this type down to the class level.

SMS V48

SMS *V48* was of the *V25* class of torpedo boats, similar to *V27* and *V29* as described in Chapter 3. *V48* was slightly heavier and longer, but in most details was similar. Fig. 7.7 shows a photograph of SMS *V48* in service.

Loss

The exact circumstances surrounding the loss of SMS *V48* are not documented by the German official historian and nothing is recorded in British Naval Intelligence files. Some sources report that one survivor was picked up from the sea, others three.[12] Of the four destroyers of Twelfth Destroyer Flotilla assigned to sink her, HMS *Obedient, Mindful, Marvel* and *Onslaught,* only the *Obedient* reported a detail of *V48*'s sinking. The ship was apparently flying a Commodore's pennant when she sank, which *V48* would not have been as *S54* was the senior officer's boat of the Sixth Half Torpedo Boat Flotilla.[13]

Fig. 7.7 *The torpedo boat SMS V48, as seen underway. Length 272 ft, displacement 924 tons, with three 3.46-inch (88 mm) guns of 45 calibre, mounted singly fore, central and aft, and six 19.7-inch torpedo tubes (single tube each side at the bow and two double mounts central and aft). (Picture: Archiv Deutscher Marinebund)*

The wreck

The wreck currently thought to be *V48* was first surveyed in April 2015 by multibeam (Fig. 7.8). It is largely in one piece, with one end broken, probably during impact with the seabed. The overall length and width of this wreck made her a good candidate to be one of the smaller warships sunk during the battle.

In order to gather further data about this wreck site, the ROV was deployed. The underwater visibility was extremely poor, but as fate would have it, the ROV came down alongside the wreck, right down on to a torpedo tube, which is more than two-thirds buried in the seabed. Later, detailed examination of the tape revealed that the design of the tube was typically German (Fig. 7.10). Image A shows the tube to have external ribs; typically the German torpedo

Fig. 7.8 *Multibeam plan view of the SMS V48 wreck, as seen on Vina's multibeam system in April 2015. (Picture: McCartney/JD-Contractor)*

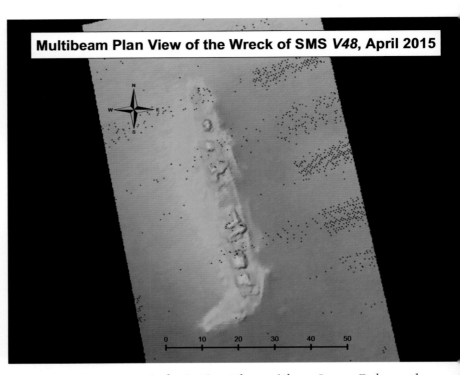

Multibeam Plan View of the Wreck of SMS *V48*, April 2015

Fig. 7.9 *The hull form and machinery distribution plan for SMS V48, overlaid on the plan view of the multibeam image seen in Fig. 7.8. (Picture: McCartney/JD Contractor)*

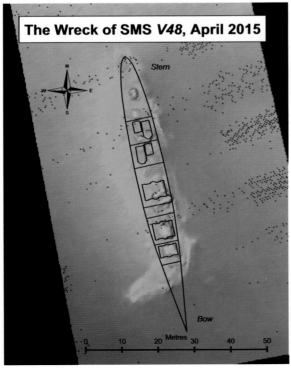

The Wreck of SMS *V48*, April 2015

tube had at least three of these. Image B shows the open end of the tube with a wolf fish living it. The tube i over two-thirds buried in the seabed. The clinching evidence showing this to be German was the triangula window in the fore end of the tube, which covered the top of the warhead of the torpedo. This can be seen very clearly in C and D. No other evidence seen during the rest of the ROV survey conflicted with the view that thi wreck was a German torpedo boat.

With the nationality of the wreck now confirmed, the hull form and machinery schematic was overlaid on the multibeam scan to see how well the two matched up The results are shown in Fig. 7.9. From the description given of the disabling of *V48* given above, it is known that it was returning from an attack and was therefor likely to be heading in a southward direction. Thi appears to be confirmed by Fig. 7.9. If correct, then the *V48* sank by the bow. The dislodging of the boilers in the central boiler room and the damage to the engin

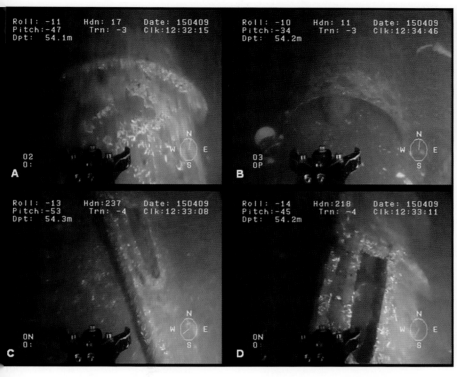

Fig. 7.10 Images of the torpedo tube seen on the wreck of SMS V48, which confirmed the wreck to be of German origin. (Pictures: McCartney/JD-Contractor)

room was probably caused by the shellfire that sank the ship. It is known that the *Shark*'s 4-inch rounds, which disabled *V48*, hit the engine room.[14] Of course, this evidence alone does not confirm that this wreck is *V48*, as it could, in theory, also be *S35*. It is to her case that we now turn.

SMS *S35*

SMS *S35* (Fig. 7.11) was of the V25 class of torpedo boats, similar to *V27* and *V29* (see Chapter 3) and *V48* above. *S35* was slightly longer but in most details similar.

Fig. 7.11 The torpedo boat S35 (background), as seen underway. Length 260 ft, displacement 971 tons, with three 3.46-inch (88 mm) guns of 45 calibre, mounted singly fore, central and aft, and six 19.7-inch torpedo tubes (single tube each side at the bow and two double mounts central and aft). The single tube on either side just aft of the forecastle can be seen in this image. (Picture: Archiv Deutscher Marinebund)

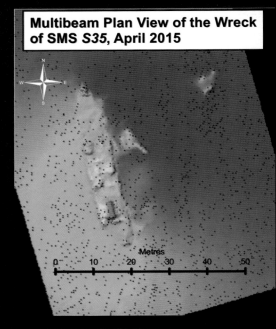

Multibeam Plan View of the Wreck of SMS *S35*, April 2015

Fig. 7.12 Multibeam plan view of the SMS S35 wreck, as seen on Vina's multibeam system in April 2015. (Picture: McCartney/ JD-Contractor)

Loss

One of the most interesting things about the loss of SMS *S35* is that the actual circumstances of her loss appear to have been unknown to the British at the time that the *Harper Record* was compiled, as no estimated position for her wreck is given. In fact, Harper recorded *S35* as 'position uncertain'.[15]

Attempting to place the possible position of the SMS *S35* wreck on the base map used in this study therefore required information from another source. Interestingly, the official German history does not list where they thought the ships had sunk. The charts supplied with both the original publication[16] and the British intelligence translation[17] do not give any geographical information and are little more than pictorial depictions of the text. This is also a feature of the work by other Jutland luminaries such as Corbett[18] and Marder.[19]

The only recorded position for the sinking of *S35* was found in Gröner's history of German major surface vessels and this is the one depicted in Fig. 7.1 at 56°56'N; 06°04'E.[20] Gröner does not cite his source and it must be considered a coincidence that his position matches as closely as it does with the wreck considered to be SMS *S35*.

There were no survivors from this ship. The details of what happened are therefore only those seen from other ships. The German official history states that *S35* was retiring from a torpedo attack when she was 'hit by heavy shell amidships and broke in two and sank'.[7] This is thought to have been caused by fire from HMS *Iron Duke*,[21] which, according to the director gunner, 'blew up an Enemy T.B.D.'[9]

The wreck

The wreck believed to be SMS *S35* was first surveyed in April 2015 by multibeam (Fig. 7.12). The wreck as seen appeared to be too short to be a torpedo boat, but her width was correct for such a vessel. There were substantial pieces of wreckage off to her eastern side.

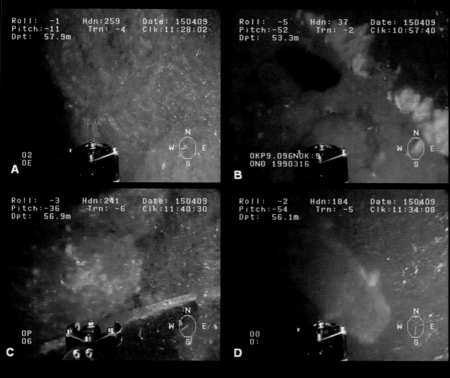

Fig. 7.13 Images of items seen during the ROV survey of the wreck of SMS S35, confirming the wreck to be of German origin. (Pictures: McCartney/JD-Contractor)

In order to confirm that this was one of the smaller warship wrecks, the ROV was deployed to record the wreck. The underwater conditions were very poor, with around one metre of visibility. Nevertheless, by working carefully through the wreck, enough was seen to confirm that she was of German origin. Some of the items seen during the ROV survey are shown in Fig. 7.13.

Image A shows the end of a water tube of one of the wreck's boilers. It can be clearly seen to be of the Schulz-Thornycroft type by the curved water tubes. The central high point of the

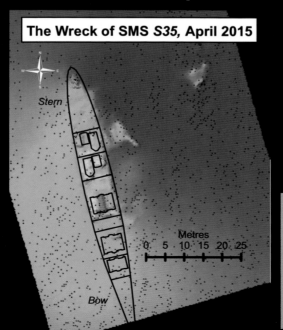

Fig. 7.14 The hull form and machinery distribution plan for SMS S35 overlaid on the plan view of the multibeam image seen in Fig. 7.12. (Picture: McCartney/JD-Contractor)

wreck turned out to be a complete boiler of the same type, which, in complete contrast to those seen on *V27* and *V29*, was largely intact, with portions of the outer skin covering all three water tubes. The intact top of this boiler, at the highest point of the wreck, can be seen in image B. The ROV then left the main portion of the wreck and investigated the wreckage to the east. In this area, a torpedo tube was seen jutting out of the seabed at a 45-degree angle and on its side. C shows the warhead of a torpedo clearly seen in one of the tubes, with the open end of the tube, which would usually cover the warhead, seen behind. D shows the forward end of this tube and the tapered warhead cover which is a feature of the German torpedo tube design.

With the nationality of the wreck no longer in doubt, the hull form and machinery schematic was overlaid on the multibeam scan to see what else could be learned about the wreck (Fig. 7.14). It can be seen that the ship was actually blown in half forward of No. 1 boiler room and that only around two thirds of the wreck is present in one piece. The wreckage seen off to the port side probably represents portions of the forward section. This is most likely the area that was seen blowing up.

The high point of the wreck is seen to clearly be the intact boiler in Fig. 7.13B which is the one in boiler room No. 1. The machinery in the engine room seems to be intact, with both the turbines and the condensers still in place. I would seem that, as with *Shark*'s, the scavengers are yet to loot this site.

Destroyer Wrecks of the Fleet Action: in summary

The German wrecks investigated in this chapter have been satisfactorily differentiated by nationality through the items found on the wrecks of *V48* and *S35*, but in no case is identification 100% certain. *S35* and *V48* have been differentiated primarily on the description that *S35* was seen to be blown in half, and one wreck manifests this type of damage far more than the other. But it is possible that they could be the other way around. Further investigations of both wrecks would reveal the absolute truth.

In the case of HMS *Shark*, the hull form schematic seems to show that three of the forward boilers are together in a line to the port side of the wreck. Since the other two wrecks are German, HMS *Shark* seemed the most likely identity for this wreck and this was confirmed in July 2015 by the ROV survey.

Notes

1   Harper JET. *Reproduction of the Record of the Battle of Jutland*. London: HMSO; 1927. p.30.

2   Campbell NJM. *Jutland: an Analysis of the Fighting*. London: Conway; 1986. p.114.

3   Admiralty. *Narrative of the Battle of Jutland*. London: HMSO; 1924. p.38.

4   Fawcett HW, Hooper GWW. *The Fighting at Jutland*. Glasgow: Maclure, Macdonald & Co.; 1921. p.239.

5   National Archives (various dates). Groos O. *The Battle of Jutland: Official German Account*. Translated Bagot WT. ADM 186/626. London: Admiralty; 1926. p.117.

6   Harper JET. *Reproduction of the Record of the Battle of Jutland*. London: HMSO; 1927. p.31.

7   National Archives (various dates). Groos O. *The Battle of Jutland: Official German Account*. Translated Bagot WT. ADM 186/626. London: Admiralty; 1926. p.136.

8   Campbell NJM. *Jutland: an Analysis of the Fighting*. London: Conway; 1986. p.212.

9   Admiralty. *Battle of Jutland: 30th May to 1st June 1916: Official Dispatches with Appendices*. London: HMSO; 1920. p.54.

10   *Jutland: Reports of Flag and Commanding Officers*. ADM 137/302. National Archives (various dates), London. p.523–25.

11   March EJ. *British Destroyers: a History of Development 1892–1953*. London: Seeley Service & Co.; 1966. plate 16/A.

12   Steel N, Hart P. *Jutland 1916*. London: Cassell; 2003. p.268.

13   *Jutland: Reports of Flag and Commanding Officers*. ADM 137/302. National Archives (various dates), London. p.563.

14   Campbell NJM. *Jutland: an Analysis of the Fighting*. London: Conway; 1986. p.398.

15   Harper JET. *Reproduction of the Record of the Battle of Jutland*. London: HMSO; 1927. p.110.

16   Groos O. *Der Krieg zur See 1914–1918. Nordsee Band 5: Kartenband*. Berlin: Mittler & Sohn; 1925.

17   National Archives (various dates). Groos O. *The Battle of Jutland: Official German Account*. Translated Bagot WT. ADM 186/626. London: Admiralty; 1926.

18   Corbett JS. *History of the Great War based on Official Documents: Naval Operations, Vol. III*. London: Longmans, Green and Co.; 1923.

19   Marder AJ. *From the Dreadnought to Scapa Flow: Volume III*. Oxford: OUP; 1966.

20   Gröner E. *German Warships 1815–1945. Vol. I*. London: Conway; 1990. pp.179–80.

21   Campbell NJM. *Jutland: an Analysis of the Fighting*. London: Conway; 1986. p.246.

Admiral Scheer was not aware that he faced anything more than the Battlecruiser Fleet until minutes before the British battle fleet opened fire on his leading ships. His successful disengagement from a dangerous situation and subsequent evasion of the Grand Fleet during the night preserved the German High Seas Fleet. (Picture: Archiv Deutscher Marinebund)

PART THREE

THE NIGHT ACTION

8
LIGHT CRUISER SMS *FRAUENLOB*

Sunk by torpedo at around 22.45 on 31 May 1916

S. M. S. Frauenlob

Fig. 8.1 SMS Frauenlob, *as seen from the starboard side. The 4.1-inch gun turrets were arranged with a pair forward and aft and three along each side. Launched in March 1902, the ship had a displacement of 2,565 tons and a length of 328 ft, with ten 4.1-inch guns and two 17.7-inch torpedo tubes. (Picture: Archiv Deutscher Marinebund)*

SMS Frauenlob *was sunk at night in a short and vicious engagement. Foundering rapidly after a torpedo strike, the ship fought to the last. There were only eight survivors. The wreck has proven to be one of the most archaeologically important of the German losses, being upright and seemingly unsalvaged.*

Shortly after the loss of HMS *Invincible*, in rapidly closing visibility, Admiral Scheer realised that he had been led into the firing line of the entire Grand Fleet. Outnumbered, the High Seas Fleet performed a 180-degree course change and disappeared into the mists of an early evening in the North Sea. Attempting to pass astern of the British, Scheer blundered into them again, executed another fleet turn and vanished into the dusk. Jellicoe placed the fleet across the Germans' line of retreat and waited to resume action in the morning. But in the darkness Scheer managed to cross Jellicoe's stern and escape. It was during the night that several confused actions took place, one of which claimed SMS *Frauenlob*.

SMS *Frauenlob* (Fig. 8.1) was of the improved Gazelle class of German light cruisers. She was built at AG Weser, Bremen, and commissioned in February 1903. She served in a reconnaissance role with the High Seas Fleet throughout her career. Her first action was in the Battle of Heligoland Bight, where she successfully engaged her enemy counterpart HMS *Arethusa*, hitting her 25 to 35 times before the *Arethusa* was able to slip back into the fog. The *Frauenlob* was only lightly damaged in this engagement.[1]

Loss

By the time of the Battle of Jutland SMS *Frauenlob* bordered on obsolescence. She formed part of the all light cruiser Fourth Scouting Group, which was made up of the lead ship SMS *Stettin*, followed by the *München*, *Frauenlob* and *Stuttgart*. Throughout the battle, the Fourth Scouting Group, under the command of Commodore von Reuter (who in 1919 as Admiral would oversee the scuttling of the High Seas Fleet in Scapa Flow), had been on the wing of the German battle fleet and had not been engaged during daylight.

As night fell, the Fourth Scouting Group took a position on the port wing astern of the battle fleet. At around 21.15 the Fourth Scouting Group

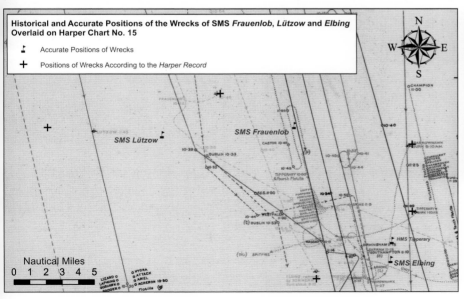

Fig. 8.2 *Map showing the actual location of the wreck of SMS* Frauenlob *overlaid on Harper Chart No.15. The path of the Second Light Cruiser Squadron is shown in dashed red and the Fourth Scouting Group in dashed yellow.*

witnessed a brief exchange between *Hamburg* and *Elbing* (astern and to port) and the British Eleventh Destroyer Flotilla on the port side. While this continued, the battlecruisers *Moltke* and *Seydlitz* came up on the starboard side and cut across in front of the Fourth Scouting Group. This caused the Fourth Scouting Group to briefly go to 'slow'. Having been drawn to the ensuing action, the British Second Light Cruiser Squadron closed on the Fourth Scouting Group from the port quarter astern, on a converging course.[2] When challenged by lamp, the Second Light Cruiser Squadron opened fire at the fearfully short range of 770 yards.

German searchlights focused on the two leading ships of the Second Light Cruiser Squadron, HMS *Southampton* and *Dublin*, and the fire from all of the Fourth Scouting Group was aimed at them. In particular, the *Southampton* was badly mauled, suffering 89 casualties in only a few minutes of fighting.[3] Following behind and having wisely kept their lights off, the *Nottingham* and *Birmingham* poured uninterrupted fire into the Fourth Scouting Group.

This noticeably violent engagement was interrupted at around 22.35 by a loud explosion as a torpedo found its billet in the *Frauenlob*. Down by the stern, she sheered to port. The torpedo had come from HMS *Southampton* and had been fired as soon as the engagement had started. Both lines now disengaged, with both the *Southampton* and *Dublin* on fire. Fig. 8.2 shows the positions of the ships at this time and the location of the SMS *Frauenlob* wreck.

Meanwhile, the *Frauenlob* rapidly foundered. Rolling to port, shells probably tipped out of their racks, adding to the devastation wrought by shellfire and torpedo. The ship was still firing as she sank beneath the waves. In the few minutes after the torpedo hit, few crew managed to escape; 320 went down with the ship.

Eyewitness accounts

There were no British witnesses to the actual sinking of the *Frauenlob*, but the decision to fire a torpedo at the outset of the engagement was recalled by Admiral Sir William Goodenough, the commander of the Second Light Cruiser Squadron, in his autobiography:

> At about 10.30 Arthur Peters (signals officer) said, 'Look, sir, one, two, three, four, five – those must be Germans.' The night was misty and visibility not great. At

such moments things move more quickly than one can write of them. I said, 'Make the Challenge.' A star-shell went up from one of the opposing ships. The Torpedo-Lieutenant said: 'I've got a high-speed torpedo in the tube sir; shall I fire?' Peters said: 'The Donegal's got three tall funnels.' I knew Donegal was away somewhere else and said, 'I can't help who it is – fire.' I had no doubt in my mind that the ships were those of the enemy, but I admit I was reassured when I found pieces of German shell on the deck at daybreak.[4]

The Naval Intelligence Division at the Admiralty in London compiled files on all the German ships of the High Seas Fleet from any scraps of information it could glean. In the *Frauenlob* file is an Admiralty translation of an article in *Norddeutsche Allgemeine Zeitung* of 25 June 1916, compiled from interviews with two of the *Frauenlob*'s nine survivors.[5]

Among them were Fähnrich zur See (Midshipman) Stolzman and Maschinist (Engineer) Max Müller who had been found by a Dutch steamer after drifting in the sea for ten hours. Their unique account of the *Frauenlob*'s last minutes reveals much. Stolzman, as signals officer, was in the upper bridge when at around 22.30 the ship became involved in a firefight at only 800 metres range with what he thought were cruisers. Stolzman switched on the searchlights:

The guns immediately opened fire. This was followed by a furious rain of shells, which nearly all hit the after part of the ship, that it looked as if several enemy ships were concentrating their fire on us. A very few seconds later I heard a shout: 'Fire in the after part of the ship!' and then, only a few seconds later, a terrific crash there, with the characteristic tremor of a ship which has been hit by a torpedo. We had been torpedoed. The light went out. The searchlights which till then had fulfilled their mission well, went out also, and the gun layers continued firing independently. As all my functions of range-finding, searchlight and signal officer had now come to an end, I left the upper bridge. The ship already had a heavy list to port. I hurried to the after bridge, to give any help I could. As I passed the conning tower, I heard orders given to the engine-room quartermaster with a view to turning the ship to starboard. It was all in vain, only the rudder seemed still under control. From now on searchlights did not play on us and the bombardment ceased. Owing to the machinery having been put out of action by the explosion, we were soon left behind. For the first minute the ship merely seemed to sink slightly, but after that it went down rapidly. On reaching the after bridge, I barely had time to fasten on a lifebelt, and glance hastily at the havoc in the after part of the ship, a shapeless mass of wreckage, cowls and corpses, before the water reached the deck of the after bridge and I threw myself onto a raft. A few seconds later we saw the ship sink without any internal explosion.[5]

Müller's account begins in the port-side engine room and states:

> At around 22.40 there was a tremendous explosion in the after part of the ship, which
> could only have been caused by a torpedo. At the same moment both engines stopped,
> probably owing to damage to the propeller shafts, the light went out and there was a
> roar of water pouring in. As I followed the sound, to find out where the hole was, the
> water was already rushing over the floor plates, so that it was no longer possible to
> locate the hole. I went on deck and enquired through the speaking tube to the starboard
> engine room whether the engine room was still intact. The chief engineer replied: 'We
> will try to get rid of the water from the port engine room.' This took some time, and
> meanwhile the action was proceeding on the port side with unabated fury. The ship
> had a heavy list to port. At the same time the water was rushing over the deck and
> flooding the port side. Three cheers rang out on the starboard side. Just then I saw the
> chief engineer coming up from the starboard engine room, probably he was the last to
> leave. I just had time to put on a lifebelt, and was carried away by the sea and washed
> overboard, after becoming entangled several times in the open hammock lockers. After
> swimming about for some time, I reached a raft, and just as I climbed into it with some
> difficulty, I saw the funnels of the Frauenlob disappear. For some time an acetylene
> buoy marked the place where she sank.[5]

These two accounts tell us that the ship lost motive power when she was
struck by the torpedo, because the prop shafts were damaged, although the
rudder was still functioning. The battle rapidly moved on from where the ship
now succumbed to the sea. The *Frauenlob* turned and listed to port, sinking
rapidly. There appears to have been no order to abandon ship.

The wreck

Quite when the *Frauenlob* wreck was discovered is unknown to me. The
Hydrographics Office position was proved false in 2000.[6] I first dived on the
wreck on 29 April 2001 with one diving group and returned on 14 May 2001
with another. The wreck had been discovered some time previously and the
position had come from contacts in Denmark. The site is characteristically
quite dark and muddy. Nevertheless, the wreck proved to be fascinating to
explore and to be a significant untapped archaeological resource.

The wreck was found to be largely upright, although very rotten in places.
The extent to which the ship had actually broken down was readily apparent
by much collapsed superstructure, with portholes seen lying scattered on the
upper points of the wreck (Fig. 8.3A). One particularly interesting feature was
observed running along the starboard side. The hull itself appeared to have

been a composite of iron sheet backed with interleaved layers of timber. At the point of observation I could not be certain whether this was in fact a portion of the ship's armoured protection (which was never more than two inches of plate on the vertical) or a means of filling watertight spaces to create rigidity and prevent crushing.[7] I have seen this practice on German submarines of the period, but this was the first time I saw it used in a warship (Fig. 8.3B).

Another clue to just how collapsed the site had become was the remains of one of *Frauenlob*'s Schulz-Thornycroft type boilers. Only the base remained, with the first few layers of fire bricks in place (Fig. 8.4B). The fire bricks are marked 'KM' (Fig. 8.4A), presumably for *Kaiserliche Marine* ('Imperial Navy'). This is noticeably different from a fire brick found on the wreck of HMS *Black Prince,* which has the manufacturer's name embossed on it. The KM-stamped fire bricks are a common feature on German Navy wrecks of this period, as any diver who has been to Scapa Flow will know.

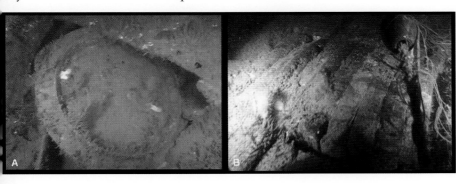

Fig. 8.3 *Items seen on the first dive on SMS* Frauenlob *in April 2001. A shows a porthole from the rotten superstructure. B shows interleaved sheets of timber seen in construction of the ship's side.*

Further evidence pointing to a much degraded wreck came from the turrets; the ones seen during the dives had all toppled on to their sides and had seemingly fallen on the seabed (Fig. 8.5). Nevertheless, it was a surprise to find the wreck upright, as according to the witnesses the ship had leaned

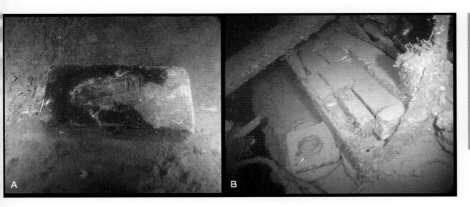

Fig. 8.4 *Boiler features seen on SMS* Frauenlob *in 2001: A shows a fire brick stamped 'KM'. B: Only the base of this Schulz-Thornycroft boiler survives.*

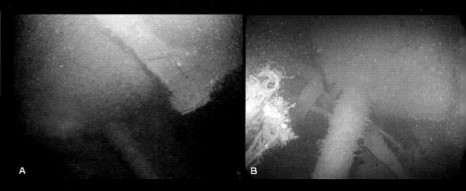

Fig. 8.5 *Two of Frauenlob's 4.1-inch gun turrets seen toppled on their sides.*

A

B

heavily to port when she foundered. Curiously, Müller's account that the funnels were seen to go down suggests that somehow, perhaps, the *Frauenlob* managed to right herself slightly. This may have been due to the efforts to pump out the flooding port engine room, but this is only speculation.

During the dives in May 2001 the focus was on the stern portion of the wreck. This area too was markedly collapsed until the divers reached the stern itself. The stern plate stood higher than the rest of the wreck, again pointing to the collapsed state of the surrounding decks. A deep scour had built up on the starboard side, but on the port side one of *Frauenlob*'s 11ft diameter three-bladed propellers was clearly visible. Fig. 8.6 shows the features seen on the stern of the wreck.

Fig. 8.6 *The stern of the SMS Frauenlob wreck. The stern itself remains intact in a scour, as seen in A. B shows that the stern is the highest portion of this area of the wreck. C shows the port-side propeller to be unburied and intact.*

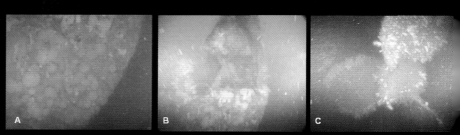

A

B

C

Another noticeable feature in this area was the remains of the mainmast, lying on the seabed on the port side of the wreck. In common with the German light cruiser wrecks in Scapa Flow, a swim along the pole of the mast brought me to the remains of the stern searchlight and its platform (Fig. 8.7).

The dives in 2001 had given a reasonably good appreciation of the extent and condition of the wreck. It did not feature in the 2003 schedule and so consequently it was 2015 before the site was examined again. It was surveyed by *Vina*'s multibeam system and the results proved to be revealing, confirming much of what had been seen previously, but also giving for the first time more

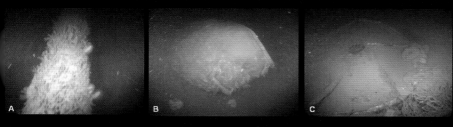

Fig. 8.7 *Features on Frauenlob's mainmast, as seen in 2001. A shows the mast itself, B the now somewhat folded remains of the searchlight housing and C what appears to be the base of the searchlight platform.*

accurate data as to the wreck's orientation and her current state of collapse. A plan view of the multibeam survey can be seen in Fig. 8.8.

The wreck points east, which is consistent with the descriptions that she hauled out of line to port before she sank. This also matches the path of the ship as depicted by Harper (Fig. 8.2). Interestingly, multibeam also shows that the wreck is not upright but has a noticeable lean to port. This is consistent with all the reports of how the ship sank.

An interesting feature on the multibeam image is a noticeable hole, around 25 metres from the stern; this extends right down to the seabed. It is tempting to conclude that this must be the hole made by HMS *Southampton*'s torpedo hit. While this is possible, some form of salvage activity could also be responsible, as could general collapse. Nevertheless, the hole is in about the correct location for the torpedo hit and therefore worthy of note.

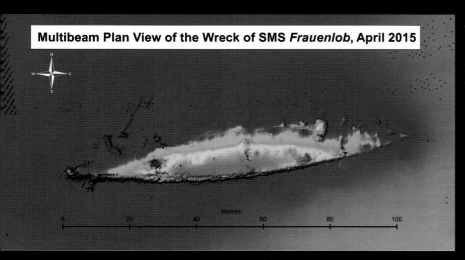

Multibeam Plan View of the Wreck of SMS *Frauenlob*, April 2015

Fig. 8.8 *Plan view of the multibeam survey of SMS Frauenlob, taken from Vina in 2015. The wreck can be seen to be pointing to the east, with the highest portion amidships on the southern side. This demonstrates that the wreck leans slightly to port.*

By reviewing the images and video taken on the dives, we have reconciled some of the observed features with their locations on the wreck compared with the multibeam image. The readily identifiable items that can be safely

Fig. 8.9 *Some of the key features seen on the wreck of SMS* Frauenlob *highlighted on the multibeam image.*

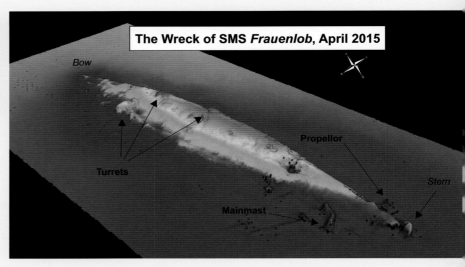

The Wreck of SMS *Frauenlob*, April 2015

placed in their correct locations are shown in Fig. 8.9. Interestingly, the noticeable high point right on the stern shows up well on the multibeam, as do the remains of the mainmast. It is not certain which turrets were filmed in 2001, but they are recognisable on the multibeam and are highlighted as such.

Through diving and geophysics the basics of what is present on this wreck site are now understood. The remains of SMS *Frauenlob* are consistent with the historical reports of her sinking. Her upright state makes her a fascinating dive and a strong candidate for further research in the future.

SMS *Frauenlob*: in summary

The extent to which this wreck is a significant archaeological resource from the Battle of Jutland has been demonstrated in this chapter. In 2001 she proved to be in a very undived condition, which can be deduced by the fact that the divers in April and May 2001 saw the ship's bell in the wreck. In my experience, such a rare item does not endure for long on any wreck that is regularly dived, especially when afforded no protection through legislation and enforcement. The second diving group actually recovered the bell and, in their own time and at their own cost, drove it to the German Naval Memorial at Laboe and donated it to the museum. This gesture was, by all accounts, gratefully received and the bell has been conserved and is now on public display (Fig. 8.10). This unique artefact had been rescued from an uncertain fate (see Chapter 15).

Fig. 8.10 From discovery to display: three images of Frauenlob's bell, as seen A on the wreck, B when recovered and C as a conserved museum exhibit at Laboe.

But, of course, to some the recovery of any items from a naval grave is a very sensitive issue. It is important to remember that the *Frauenlob*, like so many of the Jutland wrecks, sank with a great number of dead. It is easy when diving the wrecks or simply studying them from one's desktop to overlook the terrible and visceral nature of the Battle of Jutland. The fight that led to the sinking of the *Frauenlob* was, because of its close range, noticeably violent.

The wreck had a particular and poignant reminder of the sheer human cost of the battle when I swam over a human skull on the wreck in 2001 (Fig. 8.11). This is the only time I have encountered human remains on a warship wreck and their presence was as much a shock as a reminder of the suffering that accompanies the loss of ships in combat. SMS *Frauenlob*, as much as any of the wrecks of Jutland, is a remarkable monument to what the sailors at Jutland had to endure. The rescue of its bell at least means some tangible remains of SMS *Frauenlob* are accessible to the general public.

Fig. 8.11 A reminder of the human cost of the Battle of Jutland, as seen on the decks of SMS Frauenlob.

Notes

Staff G. *Battle on the Seven Seas*. Barnsley: Pen & Sword Maritime; 2011. pp.8–9.

National Archives (various dates). Groos O. *The Battle of Jutland: Official German Account*. Translated Bagot WT. ADM 186/626. London: Admiralty; 1926. p.173, chart 34.

King-Hall S. *My Naval Life 1906–1929*. London: Faber & Faber; 1952. p.131.

Goodenough W. *A Rough Record*. London: Hutchinson & Co; 1943. p.96.

German surface craft: specifications, movements, details of damage and losses sustained at Jutland. ADM 137/3881. National Archives (various dates), London.

Hydrographics Office. *Record of Wreck No. 32345 SMS* Frauenlob. Taunton: Hydrographics Office; 2000.

Royal Navy. *German Warships of World War I*. London: Greenhill; 1992. p.157.

9
ARMOURED CRUISER
HMS *BLACK PRINCE*

Sunk by gunfire at 00.10 on 1 June 1916

The circumstances surrounding the loss of the Black Prince *and what her wreck
represents today remained one of the most enduring mysteries at Jutland. The site
yielded only clues and no answers until 2015 when the wreck was finally mapped
and an ROV survey began to make sense of her remains. How the ship came to sink
is now understood, alongside her last few terrible minutes.*

HMS *Black Prince* (Fig. 9.1) was a companion cruiser to the pre-Dreadnought
King Edward VII class of battleships. The design ethos of the armoured cruiser
went through a revision when a new director of naval construction, Philip
Watts, was appointed in 1902. A recognition grew that although the design
was primarily for commerce protection, squadrons of armoured cruisers may
eventually form battle lines in a fleet action, requiring heavier guns. This led

to the Duke of Edinburgh class, of which HMS *Black Prince* was the first of two built. Her primary difference over earlier armoured cruisers was a heavier armament of 9.2-inch guns, situated in six single turrets.[1]

The secondary armament of 6-inch guns in five casemates along each side was found to be practically useless in anything but the flattest conditions. In March 1916 at least two had been moved to the upper deck.[2] Other sources claim six to eight guns were in fact moved at this time.[3] Like the later HMS *Defence* (see Chapter 4), HMS *Black Prince* was being rapidly superseded by the battlecruiser.

HMS *Black Prince* was ordered in the 1903 estimates and laid down at the Thames Ironworks and Shipbuilding Company's yard at Blackwall, London, in June. She was launched in January 1904 and completed two years later. The ship was based in home waters until 1912 when she was transferred to the Mediterranean Fleet, where she was stationed when war broke out.

During the hunt for the German battlecruiser *Goeben*, the *Black Prince* was initially based in Malta with Admiral Milne. However, on 10 August 1914, she was ordered, along with HMS *Duke of Edinburgh*, to make for the Red Sea in order to protect a troop convoy from India. On 15 August, the *Black Prince* captured two German steamships, the *Istria* and *Südmark*. These were taken into Suez. After the troop convoy had been escorted up from Aden, the *Black Prince* resumed policing duties at Port Said. On 6 November she was ordered to Gibraltar to form part of a new West Africa Squadron. This was cancelled on 19 November and the *Black Prince* was ordered back to Britain to join the Grand Fleet.[4] Uneventful service followed until she sortied for the Battle of Jutland.

Loss

At Jutland the *Black Prince* was one of the four ships forming Sir Robert Arbuthnot's First Cruiser Squadron. But, along with the *Duke of Edinburgh*, she was to the north of the *Warrior* and the *Defence* when the latter was sunk (see Chapter 4). Her movements from this time remain obscure as she dropped astern of the *Duke of Edinburgh* and was not recorded as seen for certain by either side for the next six hours. The *Black Prince* sent a radio signal at 20.45 warning of a non-existent submarine and gave her position, which was already several nautical miles astern of the British battle line.[5] This opens the possibility that *Black Prince* had been hit just before or during the Fleet Action and had, temporarily at least, lost speed.

Whatever did occur aboard this ill-fated ship will never be known for certain. But what is known is that at around midnight she tragically seems to have mistaken a line of German battleships for British ones and attempted to take station, probably astern. Spotted by searchlight, her end came quickly. Under a hail of fire from German battleships, including SMS *Nassau*, *Thüringen* and *Ostfriesland*, the *Black Prince* was soon alight from stem to stern, after which she blew up, killing all 857 men on board.[6] As terrible as the losses are of so many ships at Jutland, there is something uniquely horrific about the loss of the *Black Prince*. Fig. 9.2 depicts the battle situation at this time.

Eyewitness accounts

The single British eyewitness account originally attributed to the loss of *Black Prince* comes from Lieutenant Bush on the disabled destroyer HMS *Spitfire*:

> I looked up and saw… what appeared to be a battlecruiser on fire steering straight for our stern… she missed by a few feet but so close was she to us that that it seemed that we were actually lying under her guns, which were trained out on her starboard beam… the very crackling of the flames could be heard and felt. She was a mass of fire from foremast to mainmast on deck and between decks. Flames were issuing out of her from every corner.[7]

As Gordon has noted about this account, the mistaking of the *Black Prince* for a battlecruiser could have been caused because her two central funnels had gone and the outer ones, spaced like a battlecruiser, would have given this impression.[8] But the problem with this account is one of timing. The *Spitfire* was actually disabled by colliding with SMS *Nassau* at around 23.11, an hour before *Black Prince* was sunk. During this time the German battle line had travelled around 10 nautical miles southwards. Whatever the *Spitfire* saw was not likely to have been the *Black Prince*. We are left then with German accounts only.

In the darkness, the German eyewitness descriptions of this event are very similar, depicting a blazing ship and an explosion. An example from among the German witnesses is that of Cadet Heinz Bonatz on SMS *Nassau*:

> Due to the *Spitfire* ramming we were excluded from the line and forced to reduce speed… Then, however, we suddenly sighted a cruiser with four funnels (HMS *Black Prince*). It immediately came under fire from three other ships. Within a few minutes the cruiser was a glowing wreck and sank after a mighty explosion, a horrible but imposing sight.[9]

Naturally in the weeks following the battle the British wanted to find out what had happened to the *Black Prince*. The Naval Intelligence Division compiled

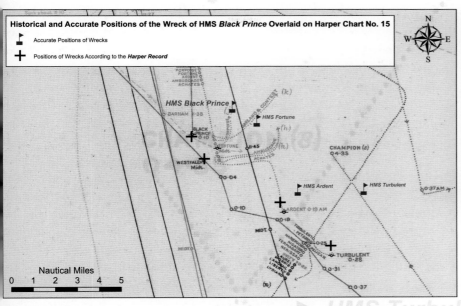

Fig. 9.2 *The loss of HMS* Black Prince*. The Harper and modern positions for the wreck of the* Black Prince *are shown overlaid on Harper Chart No.15. HMS* Black Prince *can be seen approaching the German battle line from the north, mistakenly assuming it was British (the vertical green line).*

any data it could amass from German sources, including newspapers. The following account appeared in the *Tägliche Rundschau* of 28 June 1916. It was entitled 'SMS *Thüringen* in the Battle of the Skagerrak' and allegedly written by an officer who gave an account of the ship's role in the battle and her participation in the destruction of the *Black Prince*. A mysterious ship was seen approaching the ship's line:

> We made some absolutely secret recognition signals, known only to German ships. The enemy, for such she must have been, returned no answer. Searchlights and guns were laid over her. 'Switch on the searchlights!' The beams of light fell at once on their objective. Almost at the same instant came the word: 'British! Salvo – fire!' Our broadsides roared out and fell with a mighty crash into the stern of the enemy, who was seen to be an old, four-funnelled cruiser. An immense column of fire blazed up, and a devastating fire was now opened up on the whole of the enemy ship, raking her from stem to stern, before the enemy could come to her senses. We were only 700 or 800 metres away from her. She failed to put up any effective defence, so quickly was she overwhelmed… Another lofty flame blazed up, and then the vessel sank almost in silence.[10]

In fact, nearly every account of the loss of the *Black Prince* came from the German battle line. And it was these, along with logs, gunnery ranges and so on, that Captain Otto Groos used when he compiled the official German history of the battle and this account appears to be the most reliable we have. He suggested that the *Black Prince* had been damaged earlier in the battle, accounting for her straggling as day turned to night, but did not elaborate.

The Groos account does give a number of important details. First it states that at midnight the *Thüringen* first saw the *Black Prince* on her port bow and, when challenged, the *Black Prince* turned sharply to starboard. The *Thüringen* opened fire immediately at an opening range of 1,100 metres, raking the ship from stern to bow. The *Nassau* fired at 00.07, the *Ostfriesland* at 00.10 and finally the *Friedrich der Grosse* at 00.15, by which time the *Black Prince* was already a flaming wreck, sinking shortly thereafter. This seems to suggest that the *Black Prince* did not survive much beyond 00.15.[11]

Campbell's masterly study of the fighting at Jutland gives a little more detail from German sources. In accordance with the *Tägliche Rundschau* account on the previous page, he says the *Thüringen* initially hit the *Black Prince* near the after turret, which appeared to blow overboard, and set the ship alight. Only 46 seconds had passed after the *Friedrich der Grosse* opened fire when the *Black Prince* exploded fore and aft and sank.[12] This consistent scenario of events needed to be tested against the archaeology of the wreck site. The challenge with the murky wreck of the *Black Prince* was to work out how the entire wreck sat on the ocean bottom.

The wreck

The *Black Prince* wreck has long been the most mysterious of the large British losses. Although her position has been known for as long as I have been looking at the wrecks, the circumstances of the sinking and the generally poor visibility on this murky wreck site have combined to make it a challenge to work out exactly what happened to the ship and how the wreck is dispersed and oriented today. This all changed in 2015 when the multibeam and ROV survey finally revealed many of the *Black Prince*'s secrets.

With positional data from Denmark, I first visited the site of the *Black Prince* on 22 July 2000 and returned to dive it the following year. The site of the wreck received little attention from diving groups because they were generally drawn towards the bigger, more famous battlecruiser wrecks with their generally better underwater visibility.

Because of the large size of the wreck and the murky conditions, the exact area of the dive in 2000 is still not confirmed, but is thought to have been in the region of the engine spaces between the mainmast and amidships. The impression from diving and reviewing the video tape afterwards was that the wreck was probably upside down. In the poor visibility the few items that

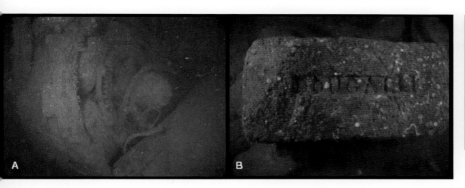

Fig. 9.3 *Images from the first dive on the* Black Prince *in 2000: A shows electrical machinery and B is a fire brick from the well-known Scottish brick manufacturer Dougall & Sons.*

could be identified were recorded, including a Scottish-made fire brick (Fig. 9.3B), but nothing was seen to confirm that this was really the *Black Prince*, although there seemed to be no other plausible alternative.

In 2001, we dived on the western end of the wreck. On this occasion, the unmistakable remains of a 9.2-inch single gun turret, as fitted to HMS *Black Prince*, was seen and photographed (Fig. 9.4). The turret was heavily damaged, it had no roof and the gun was not present. Similarities between this turret and ones seen on the *Defence* and the *Invincible* were obvious. All the propellant in the turret and perhaps most of the underlying magazine must have burned out, driving off the turret roof and gun. There was now no doubt that this was the wreck of the *Black Prince* and her end had most likely been caused by a magazine fire and explosion. The turret lay virtually upright, while the main portion of the wreck around it was seen to be lying almost on its side. This gave the impression that perhaps not all of the wreck was actually upside down. The problem was that it had not been possible to know with any certainty whether the turret was 'A' or 'X' or, in fact, any of the four similar side turrets. The site was not part of the filming schedule for 2003 and further investigations really needed geophysics to unravel what was actually present.

So it was in 2015 that the *Black Prince* was the first name on the list of ships to be investigated using *Vina*'s multibeam system. The results were a total revelation (Fig. 9.5). For the first time the wreck could be viewed in her entirety. She was seen to be oriented on roughly a

Fig. 9.4 *The single 9.2-inch gun turret discovered during the dive on the* Black Prince *in 2001. At the time it could not be ascertained which turret it might turn out to be.*

Fig. 9.5 *The multibeam plan view, as seen on* Vina *in April 2015. The wreck site was observed to be very compact with little dispersed debris. (Picture: McCartney/JD-Contractor)*

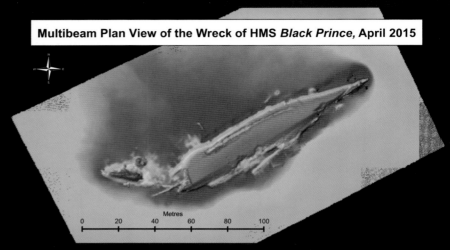

Multibeam Plan View of the Wreck of HMS *Black Prince*, April 2015

Metres
0   20   40   60   80   100

240°/60° line. It was possible to make out the damaged area dived in 2001 on the westward end of the wreck and to see the turret very clearly. Interestingly and in contrast with the remains of several of the other larger warship losses at Jutland, there was hardly any debris field visible around the wreck site, suggesting the ship had sunk rapidly, which would explain why no wreckage lies in an obvious path on the seabed.

Knowing this, the next task was to work out in which direction the wreck pointed. This would tell us much about the circumstances of her destruction. With this objective in mind, the ROV was deployed initially to examine the westerly portion of the wreck. Underwater visibility was poor, as seems to be the case each time the site is visited. Nevertheless, over two hours, much of the area around the entire wreck was inspected.

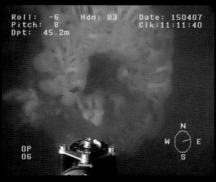

The westerly portion of the wreck turned out to be the stern. This was confirmed when the 'A' bracket, which would have held the starboard-side propeller, was seen still in place on the hull (Fig. 9.6). The propeller had gone, but the bracket was unmistakable. As was thought in 2001, this smaller portion of the wreck lies over on its port side, but very broken in places. The rest of the wreck was obviously upside down.

Fig. 9.6 *The aft side of the bracket that held the Black Prince's starboard-side propeller as seen during the ROV survey in 2015. (Picture: McCartney/JD-Contractor)*

This section was examined in more detail and it emerged that 'X' turret was dislodged from the after portion of the wreck. The gun port pointed to the north-west. At least one of what appeared to be a large calibre shell hole was

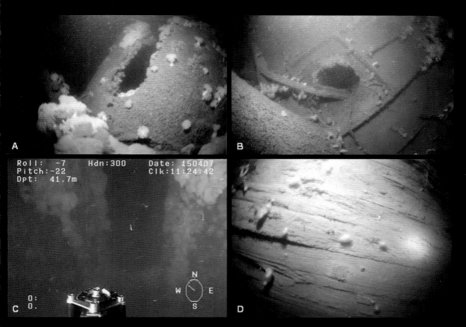

Fig. 9.7 Images showing the remains of 'X' turret: A shows that the turret is roofless and B that the gun has gone. In C, the turret points north-west. The after deck in places was observed to have its planking in good condition after 99 years of immersion in the sea. (Picture: C McCartney/JD-Contractor)

observed in the side of the turret. The ROV was able to look into the top of the turret and out through the port (Fig. 9.7C). The interior of the turret did not appear to hold any unburned propellant containers or projectiles (Fig. 9.7B). The conclusion remained the same as in 2001 that only a magazine detonation could have caused such extensive damage.

The ROV then passed along the northern side of the wreck. Among the items seen were the remains of what appears to be one of *Black Prince*'s 6-inch casemate guns upside down, having apparently fallen out of the wreck. The gun was present pointing roughly north-west. The underside of the gun breech was clearly visible inboard of the casemate (Fig. 9.8).

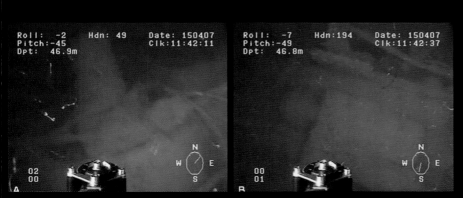

Fig. 9.8 The remains of what is most likely a 6-inch casemate gun turret upside down on the seabed are shown in A, with B showing the gun breech also upside down with its underside facing upwards. (Pictures: McCartney/JD-Contractor)

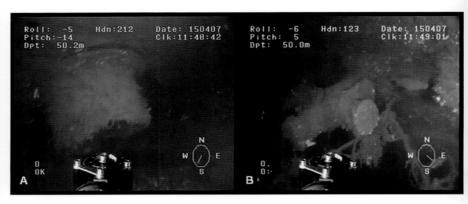

Fig. 9.9 *The remains of a vent are visible in A and B shows a mooring point on the underside of the port side foredeck of HMS* Black Prince. *These images give a good indication of the angle at which the main portion of the wreck lies. (Pictures: McCartney/JD-Contractor).*

The ROV continued to head towards the bow and we noticed that there was clearance of a metre or so under the wreck in this area. Peering into this space revealed a number of features still clinging to the upturned deck. These included the remains of vents and the cross-type mooring points for the ship's tenders (Fig. 9.9).

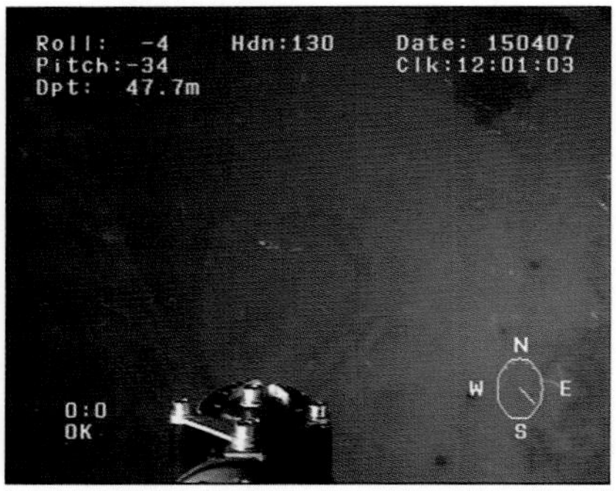

Moving up towards the bow, the raised forecastle deck was observed to be very rotten and collapsed. This portion of the wreck was clearly identifiable by the rotted steel plates containing portholes with their distinctive semi-circular drip

Fig. 9.10 *A porthole of the type seen in the forecastle of HMS* Black Prince. *This area of the wreck is very rotten and in a state of collapse. (Picture: McCartney/JD-Contractor)*

shields on them (Fig. 9.10). The ROV then passed up to and around the bow and began its return run along the southerly side of the wreck.

Much of the south side of the wreck was found to be sealed flat to the seabed. However, in line with 'A' turret next to the wreck, we found a complete, unburned cordite container for a 9.2-inch gun (Fig. 9.11). It must have fallen there when the ship rolled over. Its unburned condition might indicate that the conflagration that destroyed the ship did not extend so far forward. The fact that the bows are not blown off, as seen on HMS *Defence*, for instance, would tend to also support the view that the explosive damage to the ship was limited to the stern.

Fig. 9.11 *An intact, unburned 9.2-inch cordite container on the seabed in the vicinity of 'A' turret. Its condition might indicate that the explosion that sank HMS* Black Prince *did not extend to 'A' magazine. (Picture: McCartney/JD-Contractor)*

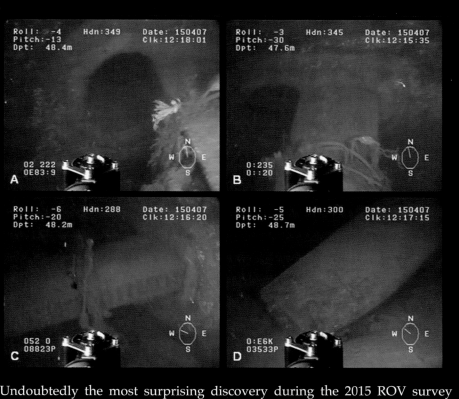

Fig. 9.12 The opened external torpedo door on the port side of HMS Black Prince. The tube is visible in A and B and the fin can be seen in B, C and D. The fact that this tube was readied for use, and may have fired, somewhat belies the German view that the Black Prince *did not respond to the devastating fire she received. (Pictures: McCartney/JD-Contractor).*

Undoubtedly the most surprising discovery during the 2015 ROV survey was that the port-side underwater torpedo tube was open (Fig. 9.12). This design seems to have featured a fin that extended outboard when the external torpedo door was open to the sea. The fin and the open torpedo tube were clearly visible at the level of the seabed. The ROV examined the tube and no torpedo was seen to be present, although it may simply have been too far back to be visible. Nevertheless, there is the real possibility that *Black Prince* fired a torpedo. The German accounts generally agree that the *Black Prince* did little to fight back, with only a couple of 'overs' reported by the *Ostfriesland*.[12] That the torpedo crews were ready at least is no longer in dispute.

Coincidentally, the *Nassau* observed as she opened fire that the *Black Prince* turned in such a way as to be making for a torpedo shot.[12] It is not clear how the *Nassau* reached that conclusion, because it seems more likely that the *Black Prince* would have been doing all she could to withdraw once under the combined fire of battleships. The torpedo crews were most likely ready to fire at targets of opportunity. It would have been the *Black Prince*'s port side that was facing the *Nassau* and it is entirely possible that the torpedo, if fired, was aimed at that ship. Interestingly, the *Nassau* turned sharply to starboard

Fig. 9.13 *A view of the wreck of HMS* Black Prince *seen looking west to east from stern to bow, showing some of the features recorded during the 2015 ROV survey. (Pictures: McCartney/JD-Contractor)*

The Wreck of HMS *Black Prince*, April 2015

Bow

Foremast

6 inch Casemate Gun

Port Side Submerged Torpedo Tube

"X" Turret

Starboard Side Propeller Bracket

Stern

to avoid the *Black Prince,* so, depending on timing, she may have dodged the torpedo, although this is entirely speculative.

Fig. 9.14 *The layout of magazines in the stern of HMS* Black Prince, *showing the likely sources of detonation that sank the ship.*

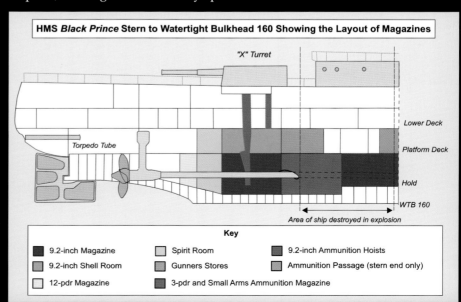

HMS *Black Prince* Stern to Watertight Bulkhead 160 Showing the Layout of Magazines

"X" Turret

Torpedo Tube

Lower Deck

Platform Deck

Hold

WTB 160

Area of ship destroyed in explosion

Key

■ 9.2-inch Magazine	□ Spirit Room	■ 9.2-inch Ammunition Hoists
■ 9.2-inch Shell Room	■ Gunners Stores	■ Ammunition Passage (stern end only)
□ 12-pdr Magazine	■ 3-pdr and Small Arms Ammunition Magazine	

With a broad plan of the wreck now established (Fig. 9.13), this could be checked against the builder's plans of the ship.[13] The key area of interest was the break in the wreck, which was measured on the multibeam plan to be 114 metres from the bow, 8 metres long and 9.5 metres wide. This equated to an area on the ship beginning 2 metres abaft of watertight bulkhead 160 and continuing to 2 metres before watertight bulkhead 179. With the experience of looking at the wreck of HMS *Defence* and the other British ships that blew up, it came as little surprise to discover this area coincided with the presence of the forward one of the two stern 9.2-inch magazines. The aftermost one was under 'X' turret and was linked to the inboard one by an ammunition store for the secondary armament (Fig. 9.14).

An explosion of this 9.2-inch magazine may well have blown the keel out of the ship. The multibeam image shows that the damage extends all the way down to the seabed. A possible scenario would be that 'X' turret was hit and flash travelled into the ship. The pressure build-up could not all be vented out through 'X' turret and consequently the ship burst open in the way four others had already done at Jutland. The shock wave would have instantly killed all inside the hull of the ship. The initiating flash could have also come through the ammunition passage on the platform deck, igniting the foremost of the 9.2-inch magazines (see Fig. 9.14). Further inspection of the visible portions of the side turrets may show damage commensurate with this scenario.

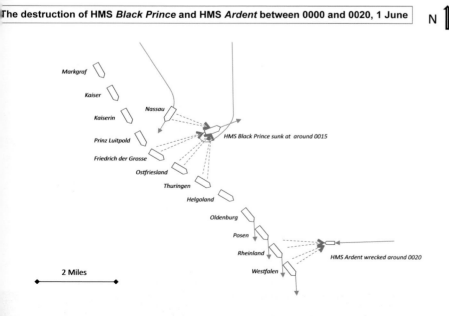

The destruction of HMS *Black Prince* and HMS *Ardent* between 0000 and 0020, 1 June

N

Markgraf

Kaiser

Nassau

Kaiserin

Prinz Luitpold

HMS Black Prince sunk at around 0015

Friedrich der Grosse

Ostfriesland

Thuringen

Helgoland

Oldenburg

Posen

Rheinland

HMS Ardent wrecked around 0020

Westfalen

2 Miles

Fig. 9.15 *Schematic (not to scale) showing a scenario for the loss of the* Black Prince *based on the evidence now known. The location where HMS* Ardent *was disabled shortly thereafter is also shown.*

It is tempting when looking at the multibeam images to think that the stern portion would plug nicely into the square hole in the forward portion, making the wreck complete. In fact, when measured, the result comes up 10 metres short of the full ship's length. So at least 10 metres of the hull were completely blown away when the magazine detonated, as marked on Fig. 9.14. One further observation: Above the further forward of the two 9.2-inch magazines in Fig. 9.14 is a dynamo room. This may well be the original location of the item in Fig. 9.3A, although this is not certain.

The features described have been highlighted in Fig. 9.13, which shows the wreck as seen on the multibeam system looking from stern to bow. The main portion of the wreck can be seen to be tilted slightly to the south side. This noticeable lean, coupled with the fact that the remains for the foremast were seen on the seabed on the north side, tends to indicate that the larger portion of the ship rolled over to port as it sank.

Now that we know the bows point to the east, this indicates that Black Prince managed to turn around 180 degrees and get stern-on to her tormentors before she sank. Taking into consideration all of the evidence from the accounts of her destruction and the archaeology present on the seabed, Fig. 9.15 attempts to draw a scenario for her last quarter of an hour. The Black Prince was sighted port to port by the Thüringen and immediately turned to starboard and managed to turn around 180 degrees before she sank.

During this time, it was the port side of the ship that faced the maelstrom of fire directed at her and ultimately this is probably why she rolled to port when she finally sank. Such a turn is also consistent with the fact that the ship was described as being raked from stern to bow. The fact that 'X' turret exploded should therefore come as little surprise. The detonation of a magazine in the stern looks to be the most likely reason that a portion of the wreck is blown off and is consistent with the heavily damaged remains of 'X' turret. At this point in time, the rest of the ship was quickly overwhelmed by the sea and by the continued firing of four battleships. If the Black Prince fired a torpedo, the Thüringen or the Nassau would have made splendid targets.

One final element that needs considering from the evidence seen in 2015 is the possibility that the wreck has undergone commercial salvage in the past. The fact that the starboard-side propeller was absent and the port side one was not seen point to salvage activity. While it is possible the port-side propeller lies on the seabed somewhere, there is other evidence of salvage on the site. The multibeam image of the ship shows a long strip of missing armoured belt on the north side of the wreck. This could have been lifted out of the wreck at some time in the past. Further survey work would probably confirm whether this is the case.

HMS *Black Prince*: in summary

The wreck of HMS *Black Prince* slowly yielded her secrets during the early phases of diving, but as each feature was recorded it posed more questions. Ultimately it was the multibeam survey conducted aboard *Vina* in 2015 that opened the door to an accurate understanding of how the wreck is oriented and what this can tell us about how she sank. A final scenario of events has been depicted in this chapter. The multibeam and ROV survey also revealed the distinct possibility that this wreck has been subject to commercial salvage in the past.

It is far from certain that the last word has been written about this still enigmatic wreck site. Further survey work could yield more valuable information about what is present, since the 2015 ROV survey did not capture all of the wreck's key features, primarily because of poor visibility. The pair of deck drains seen in Fig. 9.16 serve to illustrate this point. While one is now mapped, the location of the other remains unknown.

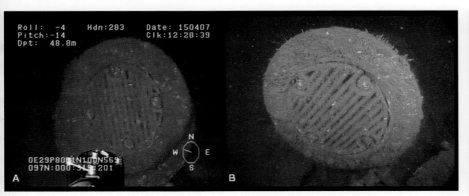

Fig. 9.16 Two deck drains seen on the wreck of the Black Prince: A was recorded in 2015 near the break at the aft end of the main portion of the wreck, while B was recorded in 2000 and its location remains unknown. Both are seen from the top, with the removable strainer plate clearly visible. More of the wreck's external features await recording in the future. (Pictures: McCartney/JD-Contractor)

Another element of the importance lies in the small details the wrecks can yield. When studied carefully, there are myriad pieces of evidence that help enhance the way the Battle of Jutland is seen through modern eyes. Back in 2000 I recorded a watertight door on the *Black Prince*. Reviewing the tape of the dive some months later, its importance suddenly jumped out of the screen. In the aftermath of the battle, the captain of the light cruiser HMS *Chester* wrote:

[W]atertight doors should be properly closed. If a door is closed by [only] one or two clips and a shell explodes in its vicinity it will be blown away bodily and will act as a very large splinter, being hurled the length of the compartment and killing everyone in its way.[14]

Such a door can clearly be seen in Fig. 9.17. It has been shut by only two of its six clips. This is a fine example of how human agency can be clearly detected in a 20th century nautical archaeology context. Moreover, the complacency that was seemingly endemic in the Grand Fleet leading up to Jutland, caused by what Gordon has termed 'the long calm lee of Trafalgar', is nowhere better illustrated than in that one image. Ironically, it comes from the least understood of the British shipwrecks and, if anything, tells us how much more the wrecks can yield with further research.

Fig 9.17 *A watertight door on the wreck of the* Black Prince, *echoing the words of HMS* Chester's *captain after the Battle of Jutland.*

Notes

Parkes O. *British Battleships*. London: Seeley Service & Co.; 1970. pp.441–43.

Friedman N. *British Cruisers of the Victorian Era*. Barnsley: Seaforth; 2012. p.262.

Brown DK. *Warrior to Dreadnought*. London: Chatham; 1997. pp.161–62.

Corbett JS. *History of the Great War based on Official Documents: Naval Operations, Vol. I*. London: Longmans, Green and Co.; 1920. pp.33, 84, 88, 364, 406–07.

Campbell NJM. *Jutland: an Analysis of the Fighting*. London: Conway; 1986. p.122.

Harper JET. *Reproduction of the Record of the Battle of Jutland*. London: HMSO; 1927. p.117.

Fawcett HW, Hooper GWW. *The Fighting at Jutland*. Glasgow: Maclure, Macdonald & Co.; 1921. pp.342–43.

Gordon A. *The Rules of the Game*. London: John Murray; 1996. p.483.

Church Papers Misc 1010. H Bonatz correspondence, Imperial War Museum (various dates), London.

0 Battle of Jutland: press and survivors' reports, press cuttings, extracts from letters etc. Vol I. ADM 137/4808. National Archives (various dates), London.

1 National Archives (various dates). Groos O. *The Battle of Jutland: Official German Account*. Translated Bagot WT. ADM 186/626. London: Admiralty; 1926. pp.183–84.

2 Campbell NJM. *Jutland: an Analysis of the Fighting*. London: Conway; 1986. p.290.

3 Constructor's plans of HMS *Black Prince*. Ship's plans collection, National Maritime Museum (various dates), Controller's Department, Admiralty (undated), London.

4 Gordon A. *The Rules of the Game*. London: John Murray; 1996. p.505.

10
BATTLECRUISER SMS *LÜTZOW*

Scuttled at 01.45 on 1 June 1916

In contrast to the losses of the large British ships at Jutland, the sinking of SMS Lützow *did not happen in battle but on her way back to Germany during the night phase. As a consequence, much is known of the damage the ship sustained. Although upside down and partially salvaged, the wreck remains one of the most fascinating in the Jutland battlefield, with the mark of battle and salvage clearly visible within her remains.*

SMS *Lützow* (Fig. 10.1) and her sister ship SMS *Derfflinger* were the most modern of the battlecruisers in the High Seas Fleet at Jutland. They were the first to be fitted with all the turrets mounted on the centre line. These ships are instantly recognisable by their flush decks, giving them a noticeably low freeboard (Fig. 10.3). Their subdivisions were excellent, as can be attested to by the punishment both ships received during the battle. The class was fitted with 12-inch guns, an advance over the 11-inch guns of previous designs, and for the most part they are regarded as the finest German warships of the First World War.

SMS *Lützow* was laid down on 15 May 1912 at the Ferdinand Schichau Shipyard, Danzig (now Gdansk in Poland), launched in November 1913 and commissioned on 8 August 1915. On 25 October, the last day of trials, it was discovered that a foreign object had caused significant damage to one of her turbines. The repairs took until March 1916 to complete.[1]

Subsequent operations before Jutland saw the *Lützow* missed by a torpedo on 29 March, possibly fired by the British submarine HMS *E24*. More significantly, she took part in the bombarding of Yarmouth and Lowestoft on 24–25 April. On turning away from Lowestoft the German battlecruisers encountered Commodore Tyrwhitt's Harwich Force of light cruisers and destroyers. An uneven fight briefly ensued, in which Tyrwhitt's flagship HMS *Conquest* was hit five times and badly damaged before withdrawing. In this engagement the *Lützow* had fired thirty-three 12-inch rounds, also claiming a hit on the destroyer HMS *Laertes*.[2]

LOSS

Admiral von Hipper had transferred his flag from the *Seydlitz* to the *Lützow* only eight days before the Battle of Jutland. The role of the First Scouting Group during the Battlecruiser Action and the Fleet Action up to the time of the loss of HMS *Invincible* has been described previously. During this period the *Lützow* had been struck ten times by heavy shell, initially from the Battlecruiser Fleet, then the Fifth Battle Squadron and finally a flurry of a further eight hits from the Third Battlecruiser Squadron were received before the *Invincible* was blown up. Immediately thereafter, the *Lützow* hauled out of line, down by the bow.[3] Hipper disembarked on a destroyer at this time so he could take command of the nearest serviceable ship in the First Scouting Group.[4] During this period another six hits were registered by the British battle fleet. As she attempted to limp back to Germany, flooding continued to advance through the ship from forward.

Heavily down by the bow, the ship ultimately became unstable and was abandoned and scuttled at 01.47 on 1 June. Fig. 10.2 shows the Harper and actual positions where this occurred relative to the movements and wrecks of other ships in the area, as drawn by Harper. Of note is the fact that Harper's written position for the wreck in the *Harper Record* does not match where it is plotted on Harper Chart 15. This discrepancy is hard to explain other than being a plotting error.

In Wilhelmshaven Naval Cemetery, a memorial to the fallen of *Lützow's* complement lists 128 killed. The crew is thought to have numbered around 1,305 at the time of the battle. The surviving crew were given ten weeks' leave

Fig. 10.2 *The position of the SMS* Lützow *wreck as now known, plotted on Harper Chart No. 15, showing the relative movements of other ships in the area. Of note is the difference of where Harper plotted the wreck on the chart and the position given in the* Harper Record, *separated by the black dashed line.*

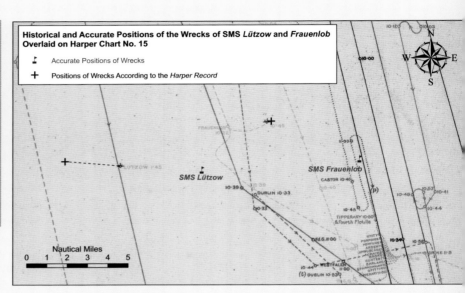

and were later transferred en masse to become part of the crew of the brand-new SMS *Baden*.

Probably because of the somewhat chaotic nature of their recovery and return, some survivors seem to have thought the number of casualties among their crewmates to have been much higher. An alleged survivor account by P Krug, published in Holland in 1917, stated that as many as 597 died and only 1,003 survived. This account appears highly propagandistic and is dubious on many points.[5] However, Charles Jubilee, petty officer on HMS *Nestor* and a prisoner of war after Jutland, related on his return to Britain in 1918 how he had met a *Lützow* survivor on 2 June 1916 while being held prisoner in the naval barracks in Wilhelmshaven. This man also stated that around 500 had died. This must have been nothing more than a guess or a rumour among the survivors shortly after the battle, because official statistics recently checked by the Archiv Deutscher Marinebund suggest that 128 is correct.[5]

Eyewitness accounts

With the circumstances of the sinking being such that most of the crew survived, there were plenty of witnesses. A number of sources detail how the *Lützow* was damaged throughout the battle and how she was scuttled ultimately, so, unlike with the five large British losses where the ships took most of their crews to the bottom, a great deal of information is known about how and why the ship came to be scuttled – although not all sources agree on all points.

Reports were collated in the weeks after the battle. A report on SMS *Lützow*'s performance at Jutland was filed on 8 June 1916 by her commander, Kapitän zur See (Captain) Harder.[6] Subsequently, a hit diagram was compiled. This shows that it was thought the ship had been hit by heavy shell on no less than 31 occasions.[7] However, an analysis of these hits by John Campbell suggests that the actual total of heavy shell hits was 24.[8] While some caused only superficial damage to the fighting capability of the ship, eight hits working in combination ultimately proved extremely damaging, forcing the *Lützow* to be scuttled in the early hours of 1 June.

The first rounds to strike the *Lützow* were received at around 16.00 from HMS *Lion* and formed part of this dangerous cluster of hits. Two 13.5-inch rounds penetrated the foredeck between the capstans and 'A' turret. The hits effectively made one large hole. Later, when the ship's draught had increased, this allowed water to pour into the ship above the armoured deck. Of the hit nearer 'A' turret, Hermann Jung, the officer commanding 'A' turret, later recalled:

> The turret was lifted by the vibration and rocked from one side to the other several times because of the ferocity of the blow… The fallen lie lifelessly on the deck. After some time they recovered and could again man their battle stations. They later stated that with the opening of the breech suddenly they had lost consciousness. The explosion on the forecastle developed poisonous gases which penetrated the gun barrel and when the breech was opened in the turret the gases laid three men low.[9]

At 17.13 during the 'Run to the North' a 15-inch round from HMS *Barham* of the Fifth Battle Squadron hit *Lützow*'s lower portion of the armour belt below the waterline just abaft of 'B' turret. The round seems to have broken up on impact, but its force was enough to distort the belt and permit water ingression into the wing compartments at that point. Initially this was of little consequence, but it later contributed to the build-up of water in the forepart of the ship.

Up to this point, seven other hits had been registered on the *Lützow*, causing mainly localised damage. But between 18.26 and 18.34 when the *Lützow* was engaged against the Third Battlecruiser Squadron, five hits out of eight caused very serious damage. Captain Harder stated that the hits received by the Third Battlecruiser Squadron at this time immediately caused heavy flooding.[6] First, a pair of 12-inch rounds from either HMS *Invincible* or *Inflexible* hit the *Lützow* forward, in line with the broadside torpedo room and below the waterline. It is thought both hits penetrated, causing the room to flood. These two hits seemingly then initiated a sequence of events that proved catastrophic. Second, a 12-inch round, again from either HMS *Invincible* or *Inflexible*, crashed through the foredeck in front of the two hits received at 16.00. The result was similar as it created a further hole through which water would later fatally enter the ship. Third, around 18.34 a further pair of 12-inch rounds from either HMS *Invincible* or *Inflexible* struck the bow below the waterline in line with the forward torpedo room, causing it to flood. This added to the volume of water accumulating in the fore part of the ship. As *Lützow*'s gunnery officer, Lieutenant-Commander G Paschen, later recounted:

> *Seemingly at this moment we had already received a fatal wound from them [Third Battlecruiser Squadron], as it later transpired. Every ship has a weak point and our Achilles heel was the broadside torpedo room, situated before A turret. Here unfortunately, out of considerations for space, the torpedo bulkhead had been omitted; this incomparable protection against underwater hits, that distinguished the German ships so advantageously against all from abroad. And so two enemy shells successfully penetrated here beneath the armoured belt and their explosive result was so thorough, that the entire forecastle before turret A practically immediately filled. It gave the ship a powerful jerk, and our artillery direction position did not miss out as I was thrown powerfully with my head against the armoured wall.*[10]

The absence of the torpedo bulkhead (a secondary wall on the inside of the outer hull to protect the ship from flooding in the event of an underwater hit) meant that the damage from the first pair of hits allowed the entire space to fill instantly with 354 tons of water. Damaged bulkheads, voice pipes and an ill-suited bulkhead door quickly allowed around another 1,000 tons of water to fill the ship forward of this room. The third pair of hits on the bow torpedo room then contributed to the flooding by letting in another 500. So including

Fig. 10.3 *SMS* Lützow *from the port side, also during trials. This picture gives a good impression of the extremely low freeboard of these ships. (Picture: Archiv Deutscher Marinebund)*

the water already inside the forward portion of the ship from the hit at 18.13, at least 2,000 tons were present by 18.34.[11] This effectively finished the *Lützow* as a fighting ship. As 'A' turret commander Jung related:

> *The entire forecastle is shot through like a sieve and is already full of water. With the opening of a door from the working chamber to the turret substructure, water mixed with oil penetrates. Outside there stand two stokers. They are the last survivors of the Leak Countermeasures Personnel in the forecastle. They escaped into the turret. The leaking door was further closed and sealed with the shirts of the working chamber crew. However, despite this water continues to penetrate.[9]*

While the damage parties and the crew of 'A' turret fought to stem the ingress of water, the *Lützow* hauled out of line so that the First Scouting Group's commander, Admiral von Hipper, could disembark to a destroyer and later board the battlecruiser SMS *Moltke*. A further six hits were registered on the *Lützow* up to around 19.40 when she began to limp away from the fight. During the battle the main batteries had fired around 380 rounds.[12]

Over the next five hours the forecastle slipped deeper into the water, until it was entirely submerged. At around 21.00, speed had to be reduced from 11 knots to 5 knots because of the pressure on the bulkhead, which now effectively operated as the ship's bow. Around this time it is thought that the holes in the foredeck were beginning to allow more water into the ship. The flooding could not be halted, owing in part to the failure of the forward pumping group. The ship was one of the first fitted with a grouped drainage system, fore, mid and aft. Paschen observed that the midship group alone could not prevent the ingress of the sea.[10]

By 01.00 on 1 June it was estimated that the ship was holding more than 8,000 tons of water.[3] At this time an attempt was made to drive the ship in reverse, but the sea conditions and the fact the ship could not be steered made it impossible. After towing proved fruitless, the ship had to be abandoned and sunk. This took place at 01.47, by which time Jung noticed that the barrels of 'A' turret's guns were underwater.[9] By this time the *Lützow* was in a parlous position, some 45 nautical miles astern of the German battle fleet.[13] Harper Chart No. 15 used along with the actual position of the wreck corroborates this distance to be correct. Criticisms that the *Lützow* ultimately sank because she was being driven too hard seem unfair in the light of just how isolated she had become.[14]

After all the survivors had been brought on board four escorting destroyers, two torpedoes were fired at the stricken ship. One passed under the elevated stern and the other hit amidships. The *Lützow* rolled over to starboard and sank bow first.[10] Tragically, six men in the forward dynamo room in the flooded bows could not be reached and went down with the ship. The room

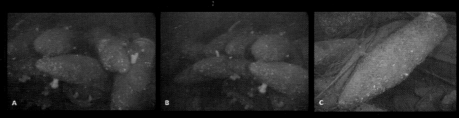

had been entirely cut off by water on all sides.[15] *Lützow*'s survivors were later transferred to the light cruiser *Regensburg*, but not before further casualties had been sustained in a scrape with British destroyers.[16]

The wreck

According to the UK Hydrographic Office the location of the wreck of SMS *Lützow* has been known about since at least 1960.[17] From 1 to 13 September 1960 salvage operations were carried out on the wreck. This was not the only time salvage has occurred. The wreck has been dived since at least 1990,

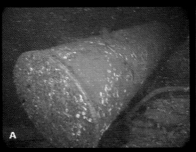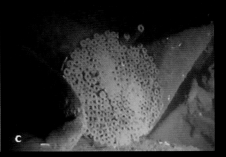

when Gert Normann Andersen and JD-Contractor filmed her for the 75th anniversary commemorations.

Fig. 10.6 *12-inch cartridges as seen on the wreck of SMS Lützow. Both full and empty ones are present on the wreck. The German Navy reused them and it is thought that at Jutland they were returned to the magazines after use.*

I first dived the site on 17 July 2000 and have returned on three further occasions, culminating in the 2015 multibeam survey of the wreck. On the first dives on the wreck I observed that she had been extensively salvaged. The dives were focused on the forward end and initially it was a challenge to work out whether it was upright or upside down. Ultimately I concluded it was upside down as some recognisable features, such as the 5.9-inch guns, were clearly in that orientation. Fig. 10.4 shows how the secondary armament looks on the wreck today.

Owing to the salvage works on the wreck site, much of the interior can now be seen. In places it is dominated by assemblages of ammunition and propellant for the main and secondary armament. This can be seen extensively where the hull has been cut down or has collapsed in the regions of the magazines. The types visible are shown in Fig. 10.5, Fig. 10.6 and Fig. 10.7. Fig. 10.5 shows an assemblage of 12-inch rounds as seen on an area of the wreck thought to be in the region of a shell room below 'A' or 'B' turrets. All rounds seen in this area appear to be of the high explosive type.

The German 12-inch gunnery system used a two-part charge. The fore charge, loaded after the round, was in a thin metal case that disintegrated when fired out of the gun. The second charge was held in a reusable brass cartridge, which was either returned to the magazine or ejected out of the back of the turret. At Jutland it is thought that the cartridges were routinely returned to the magazines after being used.[18] Fig. 10.6 shows these cartridges on the wreck. The cartridges seen in images A and C were full of cordite. The cordite is of a tubular type, differing from the stick type seen on British wrecks. In C the cordite is clearly visible, with the thin metal cover long since rotted away. The cartridge seen in B is empty, suggesting that reuse was probably being practised on *Lützow*.

Fig. 10.7 Shells and cartridges in the region alongside the foremast. A and B show 5.9-inch shells and cartridges. C shows what is believed to be a carrier for ammunition as commonly seen on German naval wrecks from the First World War.

Images A and B in Fig. 10.7 show 5.9-inch shells and cartridges as seen in region alongside the foremast. The guns appear to have been supplied with a separate round and propellant cartridge. The cordite is of a similar type to that in the 12-inch cartridges. C shows an item very commonly seen on German warship wrecks of this period from torpedo boat upwards. It is normally seen in an ammunition context and has been thought to be a carrier for propellant charges.

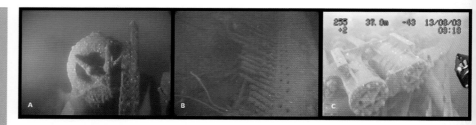

Fig. 10.8 Items of machinery seen on the wreck of SMS Lützow. A and B show the water troughs as seen in the boilers. C is possibly part of the ship's pumping arrangements. (Picture: C McCartney/Ideal World Productions)

Aside from the gunnery systems on the ship, a plethora of other items can be seen wherever you look. In at least two parts of the wreck, boilers and other associated machinery can be seen. Fig. 10.8A and B show the water troughs on the *Lützow*'s boilers. The typically round profile of the water trough is consistent with it being of the Schulz-Thornycroft design. The item in Fig. 10.8C was observed by the ROV in 2003 and is possibly a pump. If so, it would be notable because of the *Lützow*'s novel pumping arrangements, mentioned above.

During the dives carried out in 2000–03, a great deal of the wreck was observed and recorded. The challenge was to establish exactly where each dive took place on the wreck. The site is 197 metres long and much of it is extremely broken down, making this difficult. Nevertheless in 2015 the site was recorded using *Vina*'s multibeam system. For the first time the wreck could be seen in her entirety.

Fig. 10.10 shows a plan view of the multibeam results. This proved to be remarkably detailed, allowing for an unprecedented understanding of how the

remains of the ship are extant today. The wreck points to the south, as would be expected because she was heading broadly in that direction at the time Captain Harder took the decision to abandon ship. The image also confirms that the entire structure is upside down. The fact that there appears to be more wreckage to the western side seems to confirm that the ship rolled to starboard while she was sinking. Two larger pieces seen in line with where the masts were could turn out to be portions of both. Interestingly, although the ship was 210 metres long, the wreck is around 10 metres shorter than this. This may be due to some crumpling of the forward portion of the wreck as it hit the seabed.

Closer examination of the multibeam images reveals details that are almost certainly the result of the salvage work on the ship. By consulting the builder's plans in conjunction with the multibeam, it has been possible to see the areas of damage to the upturned hull in a new light. The salvage operations were clearly focused on extracting the valuable non-ferrous metal and the locations of areas in the ship that contained items of interest closely match the areas of damage. The fact that the ship was upside down made her an attractive target for salvage because the valuable machinery (having been in lower decks) was near the top of the wreck, which could be fairly easily cut open.[19]

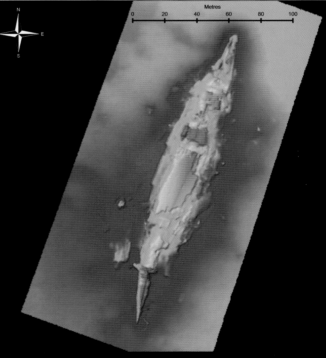

Multibeam Plan View of the Wreck of SMS *Lützow*, April 2015

Metres
0 20 40 60 80 100

Fig. 10.10 *Plan view of the wreck of SMS Lützow, as depicted on Vina's multibeam system in April 2015.*

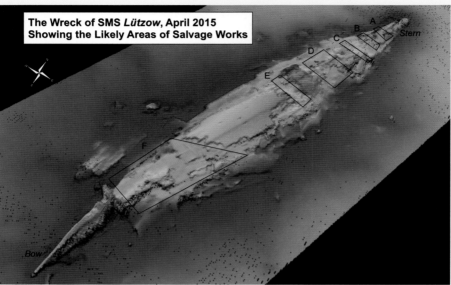

The Wreck of SMS *Lützow*, April 2015
Showing the Likely Areas of Salvage Works

Fig. 10.11 The wreck of SMS Lützow *showing the areas where it is thought commercial salvage has taken place in the past.*

Fig. 10.11 identifies six areas on the wreck that have probably been subjected to salvage works. Starting at the stern, area A is situated in the region of frames 20–25 and, like area B (frames 40–45), this is where *Lützow*'s propellers would have been. The damage appears to be the result of the use of explosives to cut them off the shafts and probably a grab to recover them. Area C coincides with the area around frames 55–60. This portion of the ship contained the ship's steering engine, which is probably why this area has been rather neatly cut open. Area D is much larger, covering a region around frames 75–100. This area of the ship contained the condensers; seemingly a major prize on any ship salvage project, as evidenced by the sheer numbers of them now missing from the Jutland wrecks. The fresh water plant and low pressure turbines were also nearby. Area E is situated in the region of frames 115–130. This area of the ship housed the forward end of the high pressure turbines.

The very large area F falls roughly in the region of frames 195–250. The after end of this area covers a portion of boiler room V and all of boiler room VI. This area is aft of the portion of the ship that flooded during the battle. But it is also most likely in the area in which the *Lützow* received her *coup de grâce* by torpedo. This probably explains some of the damage seen in this area, but it is too extensive for one torpedo to have been the only cause. So some form of salvage seems likely to have taken place in this area, too.

SMS *Lützow*: in summary

The long fight to save the *Lützow* from sinking means that the circumstances of her loss were well documented, although little, if any, of the damage described is visible on the wreck today. Perhaps some of the damage in the fore part of this ship relates to the torpedo that finally sank her.

Nevertheless, the wreck still holds some notable archaeological features, perhaps none more so than the ammunition stores seen in various portions of the ship. The very fact that some of the 12-inch cartridges have been found to be empty seems to show that reuse was planned and that they were not just dumped on the decks after firing, as some paintings of the battle seem to show. As von Hipper's flagship at the First World War's greatest naval battle, this is a historic wreck that should yield new information about the Imperial German Navy in the years to come.

Notes

1   Staff G. *German Battlecruisers of World War One*. Barnsley: Seaforth; 2014. pp.265–67.

2   *Ibid.*, pp.269–70.

3   *Ibid.*, pp.277–80.

4   Philbin TR. *Admiral von Hipper: the Inconvenient Hero*. Amsterdam: BR Grüner; 1982. p.134.

5   German surface craft: specifications, movements, details of damage and losses sustained at Jutland. ADM 137/3881. National Archives (various dates), London.

6   Harder V. *Report concerning the Battle on 31 May 1916*. Translation by Gary Staff, in the author's collection.

7   Hit diagrams: SMS *Lützow*. Bundesarchiv-Militärarchiv (various dates), Freiburg.

8   Campbell NJM. *Jutland: an Analysis of the Fighting*. London: Conway; 1986. pp.351–57.

9   Jung AK. *Skagerrak with the Battlekreuzer* Lützow *at the Head*. Undated. Translation by Gary Staff, in the author's collection.

10 Paschen G. SMS *Lützow* in the Skagerrak Battle. *Marine-Rundschau* May 1926. Translation by Gary Staff, in the author's collection.

11 Campbell NJM. *Jutland: an Analysis of the Fighting*. London: Conway; 1986. p.183.

12 National Archives (various dates). Groos O. *The Battle of Jutland: Official German Account*. Translated Bagot WT. ADM 186/626. London: Admiralty; 1926. p.270.

13 Campbell NJM. *Jutland: an Analysis of the Fighting*. London: Conway; 1986. p.294.

14 Preston A. *Battleships of World War I*. New York: Galahad Books; 1972.

15 Harder V. Letter to E von Mantey. 1930. Translation by Gary Staff, in the author's collection.

16 Anon. *Medical Report of SMS Lützow*. Undated. Translation by Gary Staff, in the author's collection.

17 Hydrographics Department of the Admiralty. *Record of Wreck No. 32344 SMS* Lützow. Taunton: Hydrographics Office; 2000.

18 Friedman N. *Naval Weapons of World War One*. Barnsley: Seaforth; 2011. p.127.

19 Staff G. *German Battlecruisers of World War One*. Barnsley: Seaforth; 2014. pp.258–62.

11
LIGHT CRUISER SMS *ELBING*

Scuttled at around 02.00 on 1 June 1916

SMS Elbing *scored the first hit of the Battle of Jutland but was later in a collision with the battleship SMS* Posen, *which led to her sinking. Upright on the seabed, she remains a valuable archaeological resource and a time capsule from which much could be learned about the Imperial German Navy.*

SMS *Elbing* (Fig. 11.1) and her sister ship SMS *Pillau* were under construction for the Russian Navy at Ferdinand Schichau shipyard in Danzig (modern-day Gdansk) but were requisitioned on 5 August 1914. Modifications for service in the German Navy followed, including upgrading the main guns from 5.1-inch to 5.9-inch. The *Elbing* was launched in November 1914 and commissioned on 4 September 1915.

After being commissioned, the *Elbing* was assigned to the Second Scouting Group of the High Seas Fleet. Before Jutland she had taken part in the Lowestoft Raid of 24–25 April 1916. During the approach to Lowestoft, Commodore Reginald Tyrwhitt's Harwich Force of three light cruisers and

18 destroyers was sighted and the *Elbing*, *Rostock* and four other German light cruisers engaged Tyrwhitt at long range. The fight was brought to an end by the arrival from Lowestoft of the German battlecruisers, causing Tyrwhitt to withdraw when his flagship, HMS *Conquest*, was damaged along with the destroyer HMS *Laertes*.[1]

Loss

At Jutland the *Elbing* was still part of the Second Scouting Group consisting of the *Frankfurt*, *Pillau*, *Elbing* and the ill-fated *Wiesbaden* which also sank (see Chapter 6). The Second Scouting Group worked alongside the battlecruisers of the First Scouting Group in a scouting role. It was while inspecting the Danish steamer *NJ Fjord* that the *Elbing* was the first German ship sighted at Jutland and came under fire from the British light cruisers HMS *Galatea* and *Phaeton* of the First Light Cruiser Squadron. She returned fire at 02.32 and is said to have scored the first hit of battle when a 5.9-inch round hit the *Galatea* without bursting.[2]

During the battlecruiser engagement that followed, the Second Scouting Group was on the unengaged side of the First Scouting Group, but during the 'Run to the North' at 17.36 the light cruiser HMS *Chester* appeared from the north-east and the Second Scouting Group engaged and pursued. Twenty minutes later, the battlecruisers of the Third Battlecruiser Squadron appeared and in the short engagement that followed the *Wiesbaden* was fatally disabled. Both the *Elbing* and *Frankfurt* fired a torpedo without result and the Second Scouting Group retired to the south.

At around 19.15 the *Elbing*'s port-side engine was put out of action by a leaking condenser; this reduced her speed to 20 knots for nearly four hours.[3] This six-knot reduction in speed meant that she was unable to keep up with the Second Scouting Group, which by 21.15 was heading for the van of the German line in support of the First Scouting Group. It was at that time that von Hipper had managed to board SMS *Moltke* and taken command of the First Scouting Group again after leaving the *Lützow* earlier (see Chapter 10). He took the only two ships of the First Scouting Group which at that time could make 20 knots, the *Moltke* and the *Seydlitz*, to the van of the German line.[4] This left the *Elbing* to find her way into an improvised three-ship line between SMS *Rostock* and *Hamburg*. Shortly ahead of them was the line of four light cruisers of the Fourth Scouting Group: SMS *Stettin*, *München*, *Frauenlob* and *Stuttgart*.

Fig. 11.2 *Harper's Chart No.15 adapted to show the historic and accurate position of the SMS Elbing wreck. Like with several other wrecks during the Night Action, Harper estimated the sinking position to be west of where the wreck has been found.*

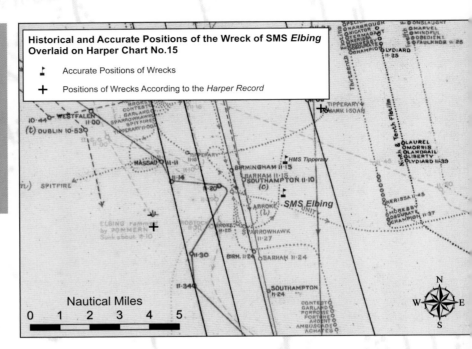

Historical and Accurate Positions of the Wreck of SMS *Elbing* Overlaid on Harper Chart No.15

⚓ Accurate Positions of Wrecks

✛ Positions of Wrecks According to the *Harper Record*

Nautical Miles

0 1 2 3 4 5

At around 22.10 *Hamburg* and *Elbing* engaged the light cruiser HMS *Castor* leading the Eleventh Destroyer Flotilla which had appeared on their port side. On being hit, the *Castor* turned away, firing torpedoes, one of which passed under the *Elbing* from aft to forward without detonating, despite her attempts to avoid it.[5] The line now slowed to allow the *Moltke* and *Seydlitz* to pass ahead. This had the effect of allowing the Second Light Cruiser Squadron to close from astern, leading to the engagement that saw *Frauenlob* sunk (see Chapter 8). During this close action, the *Elbing* had four men killed and her wireless transmitter disabled.[6]

Around 23.00 the German line passed to the rear of the British line and ran into the aft destroyer screen. The resulting action saw the loss of HMS *Tipperary* and a collision of HMS *Spitfire* and the battleship SMS *Nassau*. The German light cruisers were in a parlous position between the British torpedo attack to the east and the German battle line to the west. Evasive action had to be taken to avoid the torpedoes and the light cruisers turned to starboard into the German line. The *Rostock* squeezed through, but the battleship *Posen* discerned the *Elbing*'s manoeuvre too late to do anything more than turn away to soften the blow of the inevitable collision. Holed below the waterline the *Elbing* had both engine rooms fill with water and the ship slowed as the German line passed into the distance.[7]

By 01.00 it was clear nothing could be done to get the ship moving again. SMS *53* came alongside, took off 477 of the *Elbing*'s crew and made for the Danish coast. A small party consisting of the captain, two officers, an explosives party and the crew of the ship's cutter remained on board in the hope that the ship could be saved. A sail was rigged, but it was hopeless and when more British ships were seen around 02.00, the last of the crew disembarked into the cutter. The German official historian suggests that the *Elbing* then came under fire from a cruiser or destroyer.[8] But it seems more likely that scuttling charges caused her to sink. The crew of the destroyer HMS *Sparrowhawk*, lying disabled nearby, saw the *Elbing* founder.[9]

Eyewitness accounts

In fact, the crew of the *Sparrowhawk* were the only British witnesses to see the *Elbing* go under. Sub-lieutenant Percy Wood's account was written from notes when he returned to Britain. With only the stern gun functioning, the *Sparrowhawk* was in no condition to fight and was to sink in a few hours (see Chapter 14). When a German cruiser was sighted:

> A large shape, which we knew was a big ship, then moved up out of the mist. We just prayed it was one of our own. Every man on board was straining their eyes to make her out… Our feelings when we saw that she was one of the latest class of German light cruisers, may perhaps be imagined. Fellows went about sort of whispering that this must be the end of all things, and asked each other what it was like to be dead etc… the Captain ordered us not to be the first to open fire… So we waited; just waited for the flashes of those guns and – thought. I had some spotting glasses and… I thought she started to heel over to one side slightly. Then everyone else noticed it, until there was actually no mistaking it. She settled down forward, very slowly, and then quietly stood on her head, and – sank. We had seemed to be absolutely done, there had seemed to be no hope whatever, then this happened; you can imagine what we felt like.[10]

It seems from this account that the *Elbing* sank bow first and that her stern was probably sticking out of the water when the bows were already buried in the seabed. The sea depth where the *Elbing* sank is just 44 metres and the *Elbing* was 134 metres in length.

The wreck

Quite when SMS *Elbing* was identified as a wreck is not known. In 2000 the position listed in the Hydrographic Office database derived from the

75th Anniversary expedition was checked and found to be false. In fact, the wreck is 5.6 nautical miles away.[11] The actual wreck site was surveyed by JD Contractor with ROV in 2014 and then again with multibeam when I was present in 2015 and the results have proved to be of significant interest.

The ROV survey in 2014 was focused on the fore end of the wreck, identified by the discovery of the *Elbing*'s anchor chains, spread out on the seabed, with what appeared to be the possible remains of the anchor windlass nearby (Fig. 11.3). The wreck in this area seemed to be very broken down and scattered.

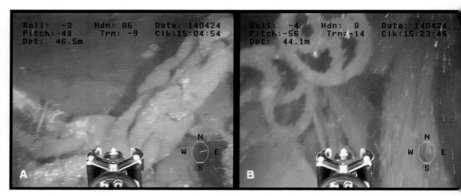

Fig. 11.3 *The fore end of the SMS* Elbing *wreck: A shows an anchor chain and B the possible controls for the anchor windlass. (Pictures: McCartney/ JD-Contractor)*

However, as the ROV moved further aft, it revealed that the main portion of wreck site was upright and, like SMS *Frauenlob* when she was first dived in 2001, seemed largely undisturbed. The ROV passed over a number of portable artefacts (Fig. 11.4), such as bottles and plates.

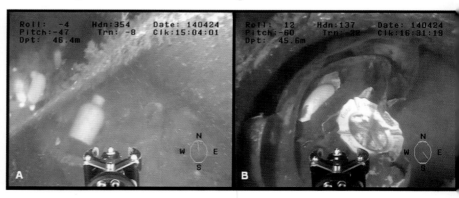

Fig. 11.4 *Portable artefacts as seen during the survey of SMS* Elbing *in 2014: A is an example of a stoneware bottle, common on shipwrecks of this period. B shows a china ashtray, which has been conserved and is on public display at the Sea War Museum Jutland. (Pictures: McCartney/JD-Contractor)*

As the ROV edged its way along the side of the wreck, the unmistakable remains of the armoured conning tower came into view. This cylindrical feature is common on German light cruisers of the First World War and its type is well known to me from similar ones seen on the light cruiser wrecks in Scapa Flow. Here the tower had fallen out of the wreck and was lying with

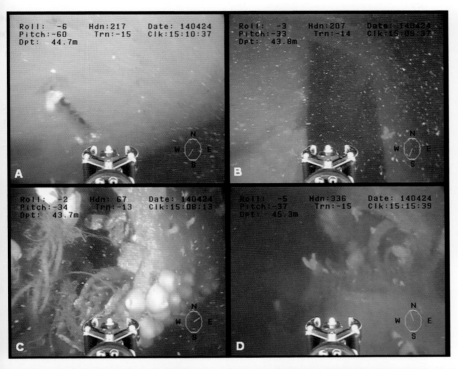

Fig. 11.5 *The armoured conning tower as seen on the wreck of SMS* Elbing. *A shows the side of the tower with one of its slit windows visible in the centre. B shows the access door to the rear of the tower. C shows the termination of the armoured stalk of the tower. D shows the range finder snapped off its base and hanging upside down. (Pictures: McCartney/JD-Contractor)*

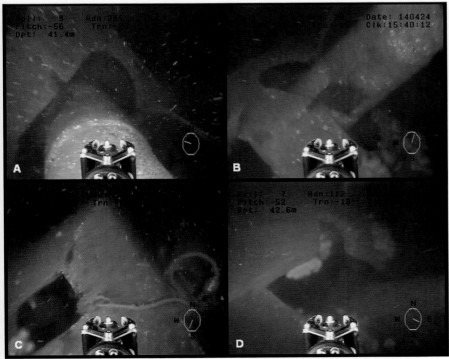

Fig. 11.6 *A pair of 5.9-inch gun turrets, as seen on SMS* Elbing *during the 2014 ROV inspection. A and B depict the first turret seen, with its distinctive German splinter shield design. In C, the muzzle of the gun of the second turret can be seen on the roof of the first (on the right side of the shot, with some stray rope in front of it). D shows the second turret; here, the splinter shield has been bent out of shape. (Pictures: McCartney/JD-Contractor)*

its top pointing down to the seabed where the range finder was still present, although it had partially split away from its mounting. The access door at the rear of the tower was now at the top and its armoured stalk, which led down to the armoured deck, was now the highest point of the feature (Fig. 11.5).

As the ROV continued to examine the wreck, it moved over an unexpected feature. At first it detected a 5.9-inch gun turret, as expected on this wreck. But surprisingly there was another turret very close to it. The second turret was also of the 5.9-inch type and the muzzle of its gun was resting on the roof of the first turret. This second turret was more damaged, with its splinter shield distorted. It was concluded that they must be the pair of turrets situated on the foredeck (Fig. 11.1). On closer inspection, neither turret was still fitted to the ship, both were detached and lying off to the side of the wreck (Fig. 11.6).

A further discovery that helped confirm the identity of this wreck was one of the distinctive 'carrying handles' seen on German naval wrecks of this period (Fig. 11.7). It is identical to the type seen on the *Lützow* and elsewhere at Jutland. Its exact purpose remains unknown, but it is invariably seen in an ammunition context.

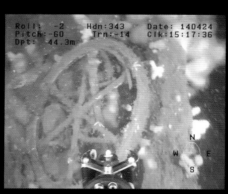

Fig. 11.7 *The distinctive 'carrier' seen only on German naval wrecks of the First World War. (Picture: McCartney/JD-Contractor)*

The ROV survey established that the wreck was upright, although the bow area seemed damaged. Interestingly, in places the superstructure of the ship seemed to have collapsed inwardly into the hull, covering much of the machinery inside, although not all of the wreck was inspected. On the highest point of the wreck, the ROV passed over an open circular feature, either a porthole or a bulkhead cutting. Looking down into it revealed a pile of fire bricks for the boilers (Fig. 11.8).

The ROV survey had revealed a great deal about the orientation and condition of the wreck of SMS *Elbing*. But in common with the larger wrecks of Jutland, her sheer size made it a challenge to fit all of the evidence into an accurate, comprehensive picture of what was present. This was compounded by the generally poor underwater visibility on the site. So we anticipated that the 2015 multibeam survey would add much to what was known of the wreck site and it did not disappoint.

Fig. 11.9 shows the wreck lying east to west and largely in one piece. Her orientation means that she was beam-on to the weather at the time that she sank, as would be expected of a ship that had been disabled and could not move under her own power. The same is seen with SMS *Wiesbaden*. The local weather report from Blåvands Huk recorded the wind to have been around Force 3 from the south.[12]

As described above, the ship is known to have sunk by the bow and 'stood on her head'. This suggests that the bow of the ship was on the seabed when the stern was still showing. The multibeam seems to confirm this, because the westerly end of the wreck is broken down and bent around slightly to the north. It therefore must be the area where the anchor chains were seen spread on the seabed in 2014.

Closer inspection of the multibeam data reveals that the high points seen along both sides of the wreck coincide with the locations where the ship's gun turrets would be found. A couple of questions remained: Where on the wreck were the two turrets seen together? And where is the armoured conning tower? Although not confirmed, their locations are most likely as shown on Fig. 11.10.

It seems possible that the forward turrets and the armoured conning tower became dislodged when the bows of the ship struck the seabed as the ship sank. A pair of features can be clearly seen on Fig. 11.10. These are probably

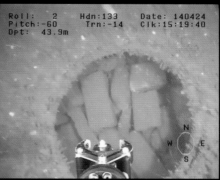

Fig. 11.8 Looking down a circular hole from the top of the wreck revealed a pile of fire bricks within. It appeared that the superstructure had in places collapsed over the internal machinery spaces of the ship. (Picture: McCartney/JD-Contractor)

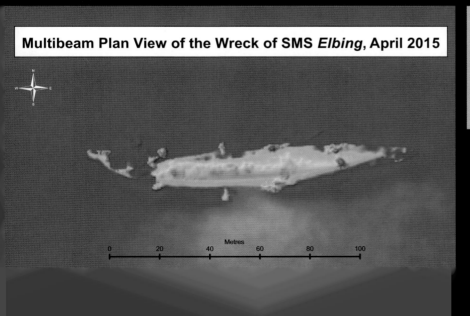

Multibeam Plan View of the Wreck of SMS *Elbing*, April 2015

Metres
0   20   40   60   80   100

Fig. 11.9 Plan view of the SMS Elbing wreck, as seen on Vina's multibeam system in April 2015. (Picture: McCartney/JD-Contractor)

Fig. 11.10 SMS Elbing, *as seen in April 2015, with the suggested locations of the pair of turrets and the armoured conning tower seen in 2014. (Picture: McCartney/JD-Contractor)*

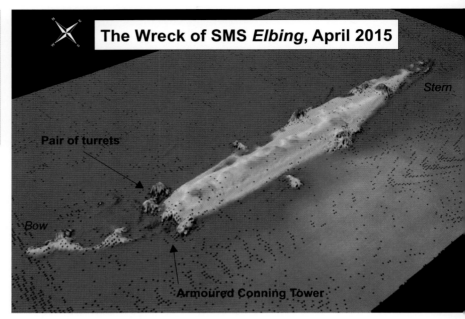

Fig. 11.10 SMS Elbing, *as seen in April 2015, with the suggested locations of the pair of turrets and the armoured conning tower seen in 2014. (Picture: McCartney/JD-Contractor)*

the two forward turrets. The conning tower is probably one of the pair of distinctive features seen to the south of the turrets. This is slightly speculative, but seems to fit with the evidence.

SMS *Elbing*: in summary

The wreck of SMS *Elbing* has proved to be one of the surprise finds among the German wrecks. Similar to the *Frauenlob*, she is upright and in such a condition as to be easily recognisable as a German light cruiser. As the ROV survey has shown, she is in fine condition for a ship immersed in the sea for nearly 100 years. Being upright may well have helped to protect her from commercial salvage in the past, as the armoured deck would pose a challenge to drill through in the hunt for the non-ferrous metal within the ship. A great deal more could be learned about this wreck with careful study and, unlike those where the ships are upside down and have been salvaged, this site currently retains a high degree of archaeological potential.

Notes

1 Tarrant VE. *Battlecruiser* Invincible. London: Arms and Armour Press; 1986. pp.47–48.

2 Harper JET. *Reproduction of the Record of the Battle of Jutland*. London: HMSO; 1927. p.18.

3 Campbell NJM. *Jutland: an Analysis of the Fighting*. London: Conway; 1986. p.201.

4 National Archives (various dates). Groos O. *The Battle of Jutland: Official German Account*. Translated Bagot WT. ADM 186/626. London: Admiralty; 1926. pp.167–68.

5 *Ibid.*, p.172.

6 *Ibid.*, p.173.

7 *Ibid.*, p.179.

8 *Ibid.*, p.208.

9 Campbell NJM. *Jutland: an Analysis of the Fighting*. London: Conway; 1986. p.295.

10 Fawcett HW, Hooper GWW. *The Fighting at Jutland*. Glasgow: Maclure, Macdonald & Co.; 1921. p.354.

11 Hydrographics Department of the Admiralty. *Record of Wreck No. 32334*. Taunton: Hydrographics Office; 2000.

12 Daily Weather Reports 1–16 June 1916. Meteorological Office, Exeter.

12
PRE-DREADNOUGHT BATTLESHIP SMS *POMMERN*

Torpedoed at around 02.10 on 1 June 1916

Fig. 12.1 SMS Pommern, as seen from the starboard side. The 11-inch guns were arranged in two turrets, fore and aft. Launched in March 1905, the ship had a displacement of 13,191 tons and a length of 413 ft, with four 11-inch guns, fourteen 6.7-inch guns and six 17.7-inch torpedo tubes. Note the bow ornament (Bugzier in German). (Picture: Archiv Deutscher Marinebund)

SMS Pommern *was an obsolete ship in 1916. Ultimately this obsolescence was to prove her undoing at the Battle of Jutland. Much dispersed and in an area of poor underwater visibility, what remained of the wreck was unknown until 2015 when the entire site was mapped for the first time using multibeam.*

SMS *Pommern* (Fig. 12.1) was one of the Deutschland class of pre-Dreadnought battleships. She was laid down in 1904 and commissioned in August 1907. She was powered by three triple-expansion engines, fed by 12 boilers; this gave her a top speed of around 18 knots. Armed with four 11-inch guns and fourteen 6.7-inch guns, she was also fitted with six 17.7-inch torpedo tubes. The entire class was obsolescent owing to the construction in secret of HMS *Dreadnought*

The *Pommern*'s armament, speed and armoured protection would continue to decrease in military value in the years running up to Jutland, as both navies continued to build newer Dreadnought types.

After being commissioned, the *Pommern* was assigned to the Second Battle Squadron of the High Seas Fleet, where she remained throughout her life. Routine cruises and training followed where the ship partook in all manoeuvres carried out by the Second Battle Squadron, aside from periods of refit. In 1909 and 1912 the ship was for periods icebound in the Baltic. When war broke out, the Second Battle Squadron was involved in battleship support, over the horizon, during the German raids on Scarborough in 1914 and Yarmouth in 1916.[1]

Loss

By 1916 SMS *Pommern*'s obsolescence lay primarily in her speed. She had been the fastest pre-Dreadnought battleship in the world when launched, but turbine propulsion had changed everything. Along with the other five pre-Dreadnoughts sailing with the High Seas Fleet at Jutland, she was the slowest in either battle fleet with her top speed of 18 knots. She was therefore potentially a liability if high speed became a necessity as the slowest British battleship could make 21 knots, a three-knot advantage in a chase. Also of concern was a perceived vulnerability to more modern battleships; this had earned the Deutschland class the unfortunate moniker of the 'five-minute ships'.

In fact, Scheer had been undecided about taking them on the sortie that led to the Battle of Jutland. Scheer himself had previous connections to the six ships that made up the Second Battle Squadron. In his autobiography he states that the decision to have the squadron accompany the fleet was out of consideration for the morale of the crews and owing to the persistence of the Second Battle Squadron commander Admiral Mauve.[2]

To the rear of the German battle fleet at Jutland, the Second Battle Squadron did not fire during the main Fleet Action. At around 20.33 HMS *Indomitable* scored a hit on the *Pommern* as the Second Battle Squadron suddenly presented itself as a target when the battered First Scouting Group turned away behind it. Firing lasted no more than five or six minutes before visibility closed in. There is some debate as to whether the Second Battle Squadron returned fire at this time as the individual ships' reports differ from the German official history.[3]

The *Pommern's* destruction was only delayed. At around 01.50 the flotilla leader HMS *Faulknor* of the British Twelfth Destroyer Flotilla, accompanied by the *Obedient*, *Marvel* and *Onslaught*, launched an attack on a line of German battleships (Fig. 12.2). Torpedoes were fired at around 02.06. At 02.10 one or more torpedoes found their billet and a heavy explosion marked the sinking of SMS *Pommern*.[4] The ship was seen to blow up and break in two, taking all of her 839 crew to the bottom. The first torpedo fired by the *Onslaught* is usually credited with the fatal hit.[5] As the attack withdrew the four destroyers came under fire and the *Onslaught's* captain, Lieutenant-Commander Onslow, was killed. This marked the end of the last major destroyer engagement in the battle.

Eyewitness accounts

The event was recorded by witnesses in both fleets and they add some detail to what occurred. From the Second Battle Squadron, the report from SMS *Hessen* depicts a succession of explosions after the torpedo strike, with columns of smoke of different colours, followed by dark red flames starting from starboard and overwhelming the entire ship. SMS *Schlesien* observed that there were two columns of smoke visible before the ship broke in two. The sheer power of the final explosion is perhaps best documented by the *Deutschland's* report that fragments fell all around the ship, including one very large splash, perhaps a turret roof or similar. Around three or four minutes after the torpedo hit, the *Hannover* observed the upturned hull of SMS *Pommern*, seeing the rudder and propellers.[6] It is quite likely that the fore part was already resting on the seabed at this time. The sea depth at the location of the wreck is only around 33 metres.

Clearly drawn from these reports, the German official history noted that the *Pommern* must have been hit by either one or two torpedoes. An immediate series of detonations occurred in succession, each causing a column of smoke. Flames were seen rising initially from the starboard side, rising as high as the mastheads and ultimately causing the ship to break in half.[7]

The *Pommern's* port side faced the attacking destroyers and she must therefore have been hit on that side. Logically, the initiator of the events that sank the ship must have started on the port side. To explain how the starboard side was seen as the initial point where the flames were emitting from the ship, Campbell suggests that the ammunition spaces on the far side of the ship must have been unaffected by water flooding in through the torpedo hole, allowing them to burn.[8] This is possible, but the rapidity with which ammunition fires can spread

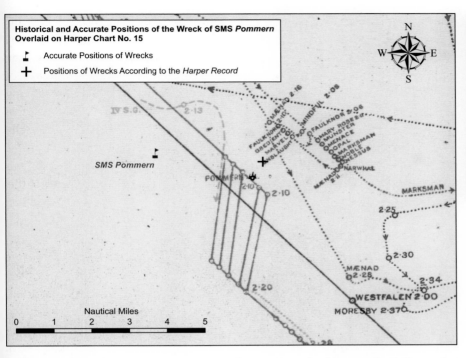

Historical and Accurate Positions of the Wreck of SMS *Pommern* Overlaid on Harper Chart No. 15

⚓ Accurate Positions of Wrecks

✛ Positions of Wrecks According to the *Harper Record*

SMS Pommern

Nautical Miles
0 1 2 3 4 5

Fig. 12.2 *Map showing the actual location of the SMS Pommern wreck overlaid on Harper Chart No. 15. The path of the Second Battle Squadron is shown in pea green and the dark green dotted lines show the movement of the Twelfth Destroyer Flotilla.*

through a ship should be considered. The reader who has reached this point will be familiar with just how rapidly these explosions occurred on the British ships that blew up earlier in the battle. It takes little more than a few seconds.

From the British side, the rapidity of the events was remarked on aboard HMS *Obedient*. The torpedo strike resembled a dull red ball of fire, then:

> *Quicker than one can imagine it spread fore and aft, until reaching the foremast and mainmast it flared upwards, up the masts in big red tongues of flame, uniting between the mastheads in a big black cloud of smoke and sparks. Then one saw the ends of the ship come up as though her back was broken, before the mist shut her out from view.*[9]

The telegraphist Ernest Amos aboard HMS *Faulknor*, who had previously seen HMS *Defence* blow up, recalled:

> *Evidently more than one torpedo struck her to cause that great battleship to blow up in that fashion. It was a similar explosion to that of the* Defence *though with more flame.*[10]

The key difference was that the *Pommern* was destroyed by torpedo, not gunfire. However, the German pre-Dreadnought ships were known to be vulnerable to underwater damage. They were not fitted with torpedo

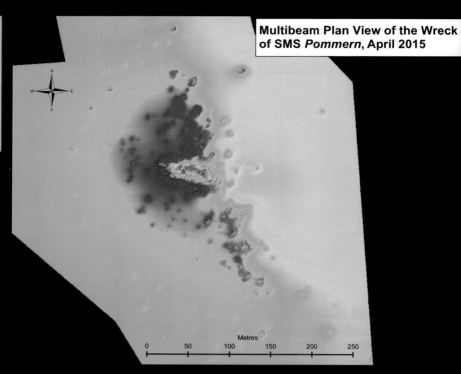

Fig. 12.3 Plan view of SMS Pommern, *as seen on* Vina's *multibeam system in April 2015. (Picture: McCartney/JD-Contractor)*

bulkheads. Measures had been taken to close down any magazines on the outboard portions of these ships. The void created was filled with timber. But by Jutland, this remedial measure was known to be ineffective because in 1915 the armoured cruiser *Prinz Adalbert* had exploded spectacularly when hit by a single torpedo from the British submarine *E8*.[11]

The wreck

Quite when the wreck of SMS *Pommern* was first discovered is not clear. The Hydrographic Office record of 2000 derived from the 1991 75th Anniversary Expedition plots 8.2 nautical miles from the actual wreck.[12] However, it is known that the wreck was subject to extensive salvage in 1957, when her armour and non-ferrous components were recovered.[13] This was three years before the *Lützow* suffered the same fate.

Anecdotally the wreck site was known to be very broken up and situated in an area of poor underwater visibility. In 2001 I did not attempt to dive the site when others had a go one early evening. They reported a mass of steel plates on the bottom in very little visibility, so not much was learned.

However, in 2015 the multibeam survey offered an opportunity to see what the entire wreck site looked like. Like so many others investigated with this technology that year, the wreck threw up some unforeseen surprises. Fig. 12.3 shows the plan view of the site as captured by *Vina*'s multibeam system.

The wreck site was found to be very dispersed. Visually it resembled the shattered remains seen on the multibeam survey of HMS *Indefatigable* (see page 42-43). Very substantial pieces of wreckage had been thrown out to more than 250 metres from the wreck. The dispersal pattern had almost no bias in any direction and the most likely explanation for this is that many pieces of the ship travelled through the air before crashing into the sea.

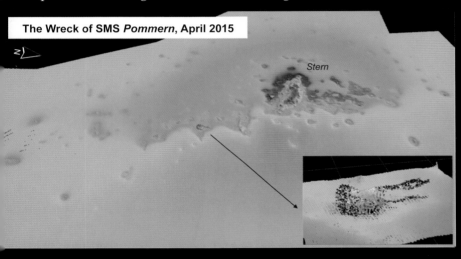

The Wreck of SMS *Pommern*, April 2015

Stern

Fig. 12.4 *Multibeam illustrative view of SMS* Pommern, *showing the location and close-up image of the upside-down remains of what was probably 'A' turret. (Picture: McCartney/ JD-Contractor)*

It is important to recognise that the 1957 salvage operations on this site will have significantly changed the wreck's characteristics, but their targeted work on the wreck to remove components from the engine rooms and the armoured belt would not have caused the dispersal of wreckage seen today. SMS *Lützow* suffered the same fate in 1960 and the multibeam scan of her wreck site reveals very little impact on the seabed outside the immediate surroundings of the wreck (see page 187-88). What the multibeam survey has revealed therefore appears to be, for the most part, caused by the circumstances in which the ship sank.

The large portion of the wreck is oriented at around 280/100 degrees. This is slightly out of line with the track of the Second Battle Squadron seen on Fig. 12.2, suggesting that the ship may have turned slightly to port as she sank. This, of course, assumes that the main piece of wreckage is the stern, which seems most likely because it was seen upside down by the passing ships

Fig. 12.5 *The surviving bow ornament of SMS* Pommern, *which had been stowed ashore before the ship sailed for the last time. This* Bugzier *now forms one of the central exhibits in the German Naval Memorial at Laboe. (Picture: Archiv Deutscher Marinebund)*

This piece of wreckage is 80 metres long at its maximum extent. The ship was around 127 metres long. This means that around 50 metres of the ship's fore part was largely destroyed when the ship sank. It seems that the stern portion of the ship travelled forward under its own momentum, perhaps coming to rest on whatever remained of the forward portion. This would explain why the wreck seen today does not extend further east.

One obvious piece of wreckage was seen to the south; on the multibeam this seemed to resemble a gun turret. Zooming into the raw multibeam data to the pixel level, JD-Contractor's surveyor Sven Heinrichs was able to show that the wreckage does indeed strongly resemble a gun turret, with the 'guns' appearing to be clear of the seabed (Fig. 12.4) and a noticeable acoustic shadow underneath them. A pair of guns means that it must be one of the *Pommern*'s 11-inch turrets.

This was confirmed in July 2015 when JD-Contractor was able to survey the site using ROV, which showed that the 'turret' had been flung out of the ship by the force of a magazine detonation underneath what would have been 'A' barbette. There is nothing unexpected about this phenomenon; similar ones have occurred in other cases at Jutland and elsewhere.

SMS *Pommern*: in summary

Examinations into the loss and the wreck of SMS *Pommern* have revealed that the ship herself proved more of a liability than an asset at Jutland. Her speed and poor protection gave her little chance of achieving much in a fight with the British battle line, let alone her accompanying destroyers. This message was not lost on Scheer who later wrote: 'The fighting value of the ships had decreased with age, and to take them into battle could have meant nothing but the useless sacrifice of human life, as the loss of *Pommern* had already proved.'[14] As a consequence the Second Battle Squadron was disbanded with crews spread across the fleet and used to populate the expanding U-boat arm.

In an area known for poor underwater visibility, the *Pommern* wreck remained unexplored until the site was surveyed in April 2015 with multibeam. The results were a surprise because they showed that the violent explosion that sank the ship was still manifested by the large field of debris surrounding the wreck. It appears that ammunition in the region of 'A' turret exploded, destroying the ship. The remains of 'A' turret have been pinpointed on the seabed, more than 100 metres from the wreck. The turret crashing back into the sea could have caused the large splash reported by SMS *Deutschland* shortly after the *Pommern* was torpedoed.

SMS *Pommern* was the only battleship sunk at Jutland. The loss of her entire crew represented around 40 per cent of all the German sailors who died in the battle. The ship's *Bugzier* or bow ornament (Fig. 12.1 and Fig. 12.5) was safely stowed ashore when the *Pommern* sailed for Jutland. Displayed in the Laboe Naval Memorial, it now serves as a very fitting memorial to the 839 men tragically lost in SMS *Pommern*.

Notes

1   Staff G. *German Battleships 1914–18*. Vol. I. Oxford: Osprey; 2010. pp.11–12.

2   Scheer R. *Germany's High Sea Fleet in the World War*. London: Cassell; 1920. p.133.

3   Campbell NJM. *Jutland: an Analysis of the Fighting*. London: Conway; 1986. p.255.

4   Harper JET. *Reproduction of the Record of the Battle of Jutland*. London: HMSO; 1927. p.95.

5   Campbell NJM. *Jutland: an Analysis of the Fighting*. London: Conway; 1986. p.300.

6   *Ibid.*, p.305.

7   National Archives (various dates). Groos O. *The Battle of Jutland: Official German Account*. Translated Bagot WT. ADM 186/626. London: Admiralty; 1926. p.200.

8   Campbell NJM. *Jutland: an Analysis of the Fighting*. London: Conway; 1986. p.305.

9   Fawcett HW, Hooper GWW. *The Fighting at Jutland*. Glasgow: Maclure, Macdonald & Co.; 1921. p.388.

10 Amos Papers, Liddle Collection, Leeds University (various dates).

11 Campbell NJM. *Jutland: an Analysis of the Fighting*. London: Conway; 1986. pp.378–79.

12 Hydrographics Department of the Admiralty. *Record of Wreck No. 31507 SMS* Pommern. Taunton: Hydrographics Office; 2000.

13 Gröner E. *German Warships 1815–1945. Vol. I*. London: Conway; 1990. p.22.

14 Scheer R. *Germany's High Sea Fleet in the World War*. London: Cassell; 1920. p.195.

13
LIGHT CRUISER SMS *ROSTOCK*

Scuttled at 04.25 on 1 June 1916

The torpedo boat flagship SMS Rostock played a key role in the Battle of Jutland and was present in several engagements. She was struck by an enemy torpedo and later had to be scuttled. The wreck was found to be in two distinct pieces. Her gun turrets have been rescued for display at the Sea War Museum Jutland.

Fig. 13.1 *SMS Rostock, as seen from the port side. She had twelve 4.1-inch guns on single mounts, a pair side by side forward and aft and four down each side, and two 19.7-inch submerged torpedo tubes. Launched in November 1912, she had a displacement of 4,900 tons and a length of 446 ft. (Picture: Archiv Deutscher Marinebund)*

SMS *Rostock* (Fig. 13.1) was the second and last of the 1910 Karlsruhe class of light cruiser. The ships were in many ways very similar to the Magdeburg class of 1908–09. These ships were the first light cruisers to be fitted with vertical side armour. They were considered to be good sea boats. The *Rostock* was built in Howaldtswerke, Kiel. Launched in November 1912 and commissioned on 5 February 1914, she served as the flagship of torpedo boat flotillas.

Before Jutland, the *Rostock* saw action at the Battle of Dogger Bank on 24 January 1915. With a half flotilla of torpedo boats in tow, the *Rostock* formed the port screen of the German force of three battlecruisers and the armoured cruiser *Blücher*. They ran into five British battlecruisers led by

Admiral Beatty in HMS *Lion*. In the ensuing engagement, the *Blücher* was sunk and the rest of the German force, aided by poor British signalling, were able to escape.[1]

The *Rostock* also took part in the Lowestoft Raid of 24–25 April 1916. During the approach to Lowestoft, Tyrwhitt's Harwich Force was sighted and the *Rostock* and five other German light cruisers engaged Tyrwhitt at long range. The fight was brought to an abrupt conclusion by the arriving German battlecruisers, causing Tyrwhitt to withdraw when his flagship, HMS *Conquest,* was badly damaged and the destroyer HMS *Laertes* was hit.[2]

Loss

At the Battle of Jutland, the *Rostock* was the Broad Pendant leader commanded by Commodore A Michelsen of all four torpedo boat flotillas attached to the German battle fleet. In this role the ship played an important part in the battle, coordinating the torpedo boat attacks that were so useful in allowing the battle fleet to break away from the enemy during the Fleet Action.

From the outset of the battle until around 18.30, the *Rostock* had been in position on the forward starboard quarter of the German battle fleet, leading the Third Torpedo Boat Flotilla and the First Half Torpedo Boat Flotilla. She then played a part in laying the smoke screen at the head of the battle line to aid in its withdraw. At 18.50 the First Half Torpedo Boat Flotilla was dispatched to assist the heavily damaged *Lützow* and the Third Torpedo Boat Flotilla made an attempt to reach the stricken *Wiesbaden*, without success, and returned to the *Rostock*. At 19.23, the Third Torpedo Boat Flotilla was ordered to fire torpedoes at the British battle line and attacked accordingly. At 22.00 Michelsen deployed his remaining flotillas to night patrolling.[3]

SMS *Rostock* now took a position behind SMS *Elbing* in a line of seven light cruisers headed by SMS *Stettin*. The ship was one of the light cruisers engaged by the Second Light Cruiser Squadron in the short but fierce fight that saw the *Frauenlob* torpedoed. During this action the *Rostock* had been firing at HMS *Southampton*. At 23.00 the German light cruisers were stationed on the port side of the battle fleet when it crossed behind the British fleet and ran into the British rearward destroyer screen. This led to the fight with the British Fourth Destroyer Flotilla that ultimately saw SMS *Elbing* collide with the *Posen* as the light cruisers attempted to pass through the German line to avoid the torpedo attack.

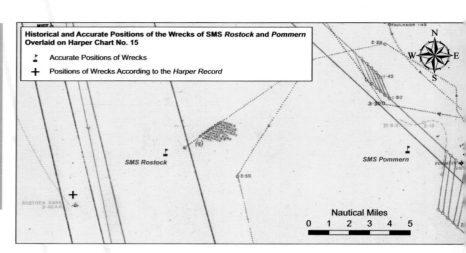

Fig. 13.2 *The position where Harper recorded SMS* Rostock *as sinking and her actual position shown in relation to the wreck of SMS* Pommern, *overlaid on Harper Chart No.15. The* Rostock *was scuttled further north than the Germans presumed.*

The *Rostock* made it through to the unengaged side of the German line without collision and made her way to the port beam of the line. As the engagement continued, a challenge was answered by the *Rostock* turning on her searchlights and opening fire. The battleships SMS *Westfalen* and *Rheinland* joined in. The target was the *Rostock*'s enemy counterpart, the destroyer leader HMS *Broke*. The *Rostock* then turned to starboard to pass between the two battleships to prevent obscuring their fields of fire. While manoeuvring, she was hit by a torpedo, fatally damaging the ship. She had also been hit at least twice by rounds, probably from HMS *Broke*.[4]

The torpedo had been running on the surface and struck the port side of the ship. The lights went out and the steering engine failed. The turbines started giving trouble and, although the pumps kept the water ingression stable at around 930 tons, the ship had a five-degree list and could barely limp away from the fight.[5] The turbines had to be stopped because of salt in the boiler feed water. Although they were restarted, the ship was taken in tow by the torpedo boat SMS *S54*. With the tow, a speed of 10 knots was possible and a track was plotted to take the *Rostock* on a wide arc around Horns Reef, away from danger. At 02.25 the torpedo boats *V71* and *V73* arrived to form a screen.[6]

According to the official German history, all seemed to go well until 03.55 when two light cruisers were seen to the south-west; these soon moved off. Then a report from the airship *L11* informed the *Rostock* of the impending arrival of an enemy squadron. Michelsen ordered the torpedo boats alongside and the crew disembarked under a smoke screen. Scuttling charges were fired and the sinking was accelerated by torpedoes fired by *V71* and *V73*, who then moved off before the British squadron arrived on the scene.[7]

t seems that only one light cruiser was present, HMS *Dublin*. Both the *S54* and *Rostock* flashed 'UA', the first two letters of the British challenge and made smoke. This ruse appears to have kept HMS *Dublin* at bay long enough to scuttle the *Rostock*.[8] Interestingly, the position reported by *V71* for the sinking of the *Rostock* in grid square 080a plots around 24 nautical miles further south than the Harper position, shown in Fig. 13.2.[9] It suggests an overestimate of the progress made while the *Rostock* was under tow.

The wreck

don't know when the wreck of SMS *Rostock* was found. But in 2000 there was no Hydrographic Office record for this wreck to check. The first data available is an ROV survey conducted by JD-Contractor in August 2012. The survey culminated in the recovery of some of the guns from the wreck, which have been conserved and are now on display in the newly opened Sea War Museum Jutland in Thyborøn, Denmark.

n the area that the ROV inspected the wreck was found to be upright and, like both SMS *Elbing* and *Frauenlob,* in a condition that suggested that any post-sinking salvage activity had been minimal in its overall impact on the wreck. Being upright meant that a fascinating array of items lay distributed across the decks. The ROV tapes reveal items such as china plates that have survived intact on the wreck. At one point a small pile of plates was seen, still stacked together. Almost predictably, the ubiquitous 'carrying handles' were also present in numbers on the wreck, as seen on several other German wrecks at Jutland (see Fig. 13.3).

Fig. 13.3 *Small items seen on the deck of SMS* Rostock *in August 2012: A shows china plates and B the item thought to be an ammunition carrier, commonly seen on the German wrecks of the First World War. (Pictures: McCartney/JD-Contractor)*

One gun turret was seen to have toppled backwards into the wreck, leaving its gun pointing vertically upwards. As the ROV passed along the side of the hull, it became evident that the wreck had been collapsing in on itself (Fig. 12.4) Also seen was one of the *Rostock*'s main mooring points, also now sunk into the wreck. The impression given was that the decks were being compressed on to one another as the ship slowly succumbed to the marine environment.

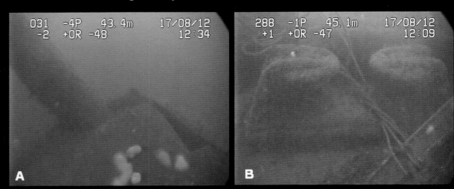

Fig. 13.4 *The wreck of SMS Rostock is slowly collapsing in on itself. A shows one of the gun turrets before recovery. It had tilted back into the wreck, leaving the gun pointing upwards. B shows one of the Rostock's mooring bollards, also now sunk into the structure of the wreck. (Pictures: McCartney/ JD-Contractor)*

Anecdotally, the wreck was known to be in two sections. In April 2015 this was confirmed when it was the *Rostock*'s turn to be examined using *Vina*'s new multibeam system. The wreck was revealed to be in two parts, lying around 55 metres apart (Fig. 13.5). She is oriented north-west to south-east, with the bow to the south. The southerly portion of the wreck is upside down. The northerly portion is upright and was clearly the area of the ROV examination in 2012.

The *Rostock* reportedly sank by the bow once she had been torpedoed.[10] The multibeam suggests that the ship most likely broke in half while still on the surface. Interestingly, the original torpedo hit in action is said to have struck the *Rostock* further aft than the break now seen on the multibeam, in the region between the second and third boiler rooms.[4] The break in the wreck is in line with the bridge. Measurements of both halves of the wreck reveal that around 15 metres of the ship must have been largely destroyed by a combination of the three torpedoes fired by *V71* and *V73* and scuttling charges. There is little wreckage now visible between the two halves of the wreck. The sea depth is only 45 metres so it is possible that the stern portion went vertical, giving the impression that the whole ship sank by the bow.

SMS *Rostock*: in summary

The wreck of SMS *Rostock* was found to be in two halves, with the larger stern portion upright. Like the upright remains of both SMS *Elbing* and SMS *Frauenlob*, this wreck has been among the most fascinating to explore. Their

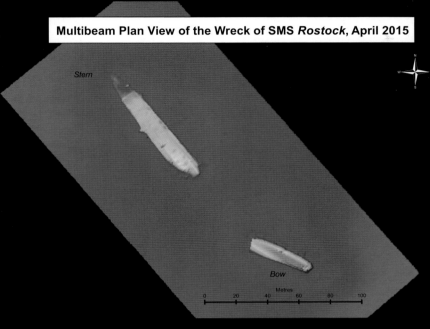

Multibeam Plan View of the Wreck of SMS *Rostock*, April 2015

Stern

Bow

Metres
0   20   40   60   80   100

Fig. 13.5 *Plan view of the SMS* Rostock *wreck, as seen on Vina's multibeam in April 2015. The bow section lies to the south and is upside down. The northerly section is upright. (Picture: McCartney/JD-Contractor)*

upright nature has helped to protect them from the type of commercial salvage seen in the wrecks of at least SMS *Pommern* and SMS *Lützow*. This is probably because the armoured decks have proved to be too uneconomical to cut through to access the engine compartments. This is fortuitous as the wrecks have endured largely intact for a century. However, it is obvious on the wreck of the *Rostock* that she has collapsed downwards on to herself, with spaces between the decks becoming increasingly compressed. It is only a matter of time before they collapse completely and finally surrender to the sea.

What should be done with all the Jutland wrecks to preserve their memory in some way for the future? One solution lies in the selective recovery of items for public display in museums and for educational purposes. This type of rescue and conservation is expensive and not without its critics. Only a tiny minority of the public could ever have the opportunity to dive down to the wrecks. So how can people envisage the Battle of Jutland today, unless they have something tangible from the battlefield to examine? The *Rostock*'s guns (Fig. 13.6) provide such an opportunity and have, by default, also been conserved for the future, hopefully to endure long after the wreck of SMS *Rostock* has succumbed to the waters of the North Sea.

Notes

1   Tarrant VE. *Jutland: the German Perspective*. London: Arms and Armour Press; 1995. pp.33–39.

2   *Ibid.*, pp.47–8.

3   National Archives (various dates). Groos O. *The Battle of Jutland: Official German Account*. Translated Bago WT. ADM 186/626. London: Admiralty; 1926. pp.164–66.

4   Campbell NJM. *Jutland: an Analysis of the Fighting*. London: Conway; 1986. p.287.

5   National Archives (various dates). Groos O. *The Battle of Jutland: Official German Account*. Translated Bago WT. ADM 186/626. London: Admiralty; 1926. p.181.

6   *Ibid.*, p.208.

7   *Ibid.*, p.210.

8   Tarrant VE. *Jutland: the German Perspective*. London: Arms and Armour Press; 1995. p.227.

9   National Archives (various dates). Groos O. *The Battle of Jutland: Official German Account*. Translated Bago WT. ADM 186/626. London: Admiralty; 1926. p.297.

10   Campbell NJM. *Jutland: an Analysis of the Fighting*. London: Conway; 1986. pp.316–17.

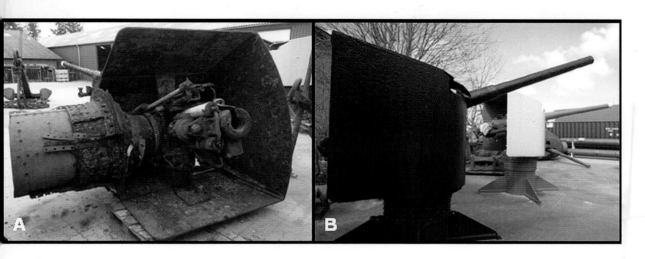

Fig. 13.6 *Some of the Rostock's guns in the process of being conserved. They are now on public display at the Sea War Museum Jutland.*

14
DESTROYER WRECKS OF THE NIGHT ACTION

HMS Tipperary, *HMS* Fortune, *HMS* Ardent *and HMS* Turbulent *sunk by gunfire between 23.00 on 31 May and 02.30 on 1 June 1916*

Fig. 14.1 *The powerful HMS Tipperary. Length 331 ft, displacement 1,610 tons, with six 4-inch guns, three forward and three aft, and four 21-inch torpedo tubes mounted amidships. (Picture: Imperial War Museum SP45)*

The Night Action saw a number of instances where the destroyers screening the stern of the Grand Fleet engaged the van of the High Seas Fleet as it passed behind. These short, vicious engagements claimed five British destroyers, all sunk by gunfire from the First Battle Squadron at short ranges as they attempted to deliver torpedo attacks. The four destroyers listed above have been located and identified. HMS Sparrowhawk was damaged at the same time and sank in the morning of 1 June, but her wreck is yet to be located. Similarly the wreck of SMS V4, sunk around the same time as SMS Pommern, remains elusive.

At around 23.00 on 31 May the Fourth Destroyer Flotilla was made up of one column, led by the large flotilla leader HMS *Tipperary*, followed by the *Spitfire*, *Sparrowhawk*, *Garland*, *Contest*, *Broke* (also a flotilla leader), *Achates*, *Ambuscade*, *Ardent*, *Fortune*, *Porpoise* and *Unity*. It was screening the British Second Battle Squadron and was in a position on the starboard wing of the battle fleet as it progressed southwards. As the German fleet crossed astern of the British fleet, the Fourth Destroyer Flotilla found itself in the way. The position at this time is depicted in Fig. 14.2; the movements of the Fourth Destroyer Flotilla are shown by the orange dotted line, the German First Battle Squadron by the solid green line.

HMS *Tipperary* (Fig. 14.1) probably sighted the German First Battle Squadron led by SMS *Westfalen* some minutes before the engagement began. As the two lines converged and ranges fell to around 1,000 yards, the *Tipperary* made her recognition signal and received heavy, accurate fire from the *Westfalen* in response. Caught in the glare of searchlights, HMS *Tipperary* caught fire and was soon 'burning like a torch'.[1]

The rest of the Fourth Destroyer Flotilla turned away, except HMS *Spitfire,* which, while attempting to draw fire away from the *Tipperary*, passed through the German line, colliding with the battleship SMS *Nassau* before limping home with 20 ft of the battleship's plating lying on her foredeck.

The burning *Tipperary* illuminated the German line and dispelled any doubt that her ships might have been British. Some of the other destroyers then also fired torpedoes at the German line and HMS *Garland* and HMS *Ambuscade* attempted to rescue the *Tipperary*, but were driven off. The column reformed behind HMS *Broke* and returned to its southerly track. Only HMS *Unity* failed to do so, having passed too far to the east. It was only a matter of time before they collided with the German line again. The German line had turned away from the approaching torpedoes, but soon afterwards reverted to its original course.

While this action was taking place, both SMS *Rostock* and SMS *Elbing* were on the engaged side of the German line and attempted to pass through it. The *Rostock* was successful, but the *Elbing* collided with the battleship *Posen* and was disabled. Her wreck lies close to that of HMS *Tipperary* (Fig. 14.2). SMS *Rostock* then took position ahead of the First Battle Squadron.

Only minutes had passed since the first attack when HMS *Broke*, like HMS *Tipperary* before her, made the recognition signal to the vague outlines of a line of battleships ahead and similarly received a reply in the form of searchlights

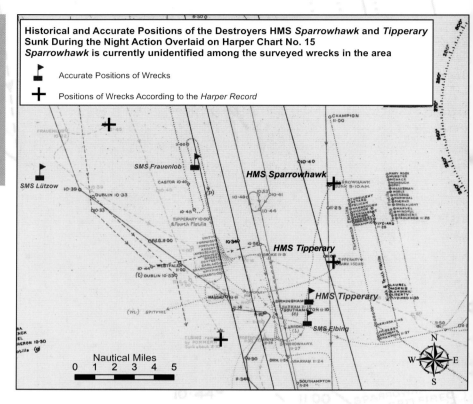

Historical and Accurate Positions of the Destroyers HMS *Sparrowhawk* and *Tipperary* Sunk During the Night Action Overlaid on Harper Chart No. 15
Sparrowhawk is currently unidentified among the surveyed wrecks in the area

▸ Accurate Positions of Wrecks

✝ Positions of Wrecks According to the *Harper Record*

and a hail of gunfire. In this instance, it was the *Rostock*, now ahead of the First Battle Squadron that fired first, followed by the *Westfalen* and the *Rheinland*.[2] At this time the *Rostock* was torpedoed, probably by HMS *Ambuscade* or HMS *Contest,* as she attempted to turn away. HMS *Broke* also hit her with at least two 4-inch rounds.[3]

Under deadly fire, HMS *Broke* turned away but was hit in the bridge, jamming the helm to starboard. Her circular turn was arrested only when she collided with the ship astern, HMS *Sparrowhawk*, which was struck forward of the bridge as HMS *Broke*'s bows sank deep into her, arresting the speed of both vessels. While locked together, the destroyers in the line following behind attempted to get clear, but HMS *Contest* was unable to do so and ploughed into the *Sparrowhawk*'s stern, slicing it off. Only then was HMS *Broke* able to get clear and limp to the north, with heavy damage forward. By then the deadly searchlights had been switched off and the Germans had moved on.

HMS *Sparrowhawk* was now helpless and, according to the German official history, drifted to the north-west.[2] This differs from the track shown by Harper

(Fig. 14.2). HMS *Sparrowhawk*'s rudders had been jammed by the collision with HMS *Contest* and she could only slowly steam hopelessly in circles.[4] The ship stayed afloat, uneasily illuminated by the burning *Tipperary,* until the *Tipperary*'s flames petered out as she sank at around 02.00.

As the first morning light began to illuminate the sea, a German light cruiser (SMS *Elbing* – see Chapter 11) could be seen from the *Sparrowhawk*; this then settled and sank by the bows. At about 06.00 a raft of survivors from HMS *Tipperary* was taken on board the *Sparrowhawk*. Around this time the *Sparrowhawk*'s bows, smashed in the collision with HMS *Broke*, finally dropped off.[5] Shortly thereafter help came in the form of HMS *Marksman*, which, after attempting to tow her, finally sank the *Sparrowhawk*, only a few miles from where she had been disabled initially.[6]

In the minutes after the collision between HMS *Broke* and HMS *Sparrowhawk*, the *Achates* took command of the Fourth Destroyer Flotilla and the column of destroyers reformed, passing east for about three nautical miles and then south, inevitably to meet the German battleships of the First Battle Squadron again. During this time HMS *Contest* straggled because of her damaged stem and fell behind.

Contact with the enemy reoccured around midnight as HMS *Achates* led a torpedo attack on the German line. The deadly searchlights and fire fell

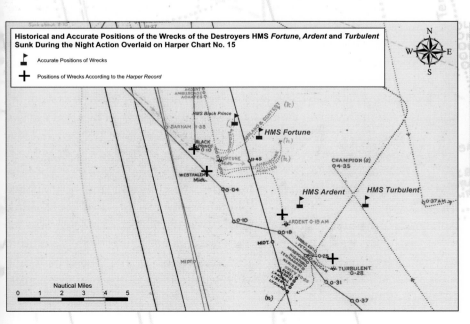

Historical and Accurate Positions of the Wrecks of the Destroyers HMS *Fortune*, *Ardent* and *Turbulent* Sunk During the Night Action Overlaid on Harper Chart No. 15

Accurate Positions of Wrecks

Positions of Wrecks According to the *Harper Record*

Fig. 14.3 *The historic and accurate positions of the wrecks of HMS* Ardent, *HMS* Fortune *and HMS* Turbulent *and surrounding wrecks. The data is overlaid on Harper Chart No. 15.*

most heavily on the fourth and fifth ships of the line, HMS *Fortune* and HMS *Porpoise*. The *Fortune* was disabled and rapidly succumbed to the maelstrom aimed at her, gamely fighting to the last in 'a most gallant manner'.[7] Screened by steam and smoke from the *Fortune*, HMS *Porpoise* limped away.

HMS *Achates* and HMS *Ambuscade* turned away under the impression they were being pursued by a German cruiser, which Harper states may have been from the Fourth Scouting Group.[8] However, the German official historian states that HMS *Achates* and HMS *Ambuscade* in fact saw the ill-fated HMS *Black Prince*,[7] which now too blundered into the German battle line with fatal consequences (see Chapter 9). The position of HMS *Black Prince* and the next three destroyers sunk nearby is depicted in Fig. 14.3.

HMS *Ardent* had become separated at this time and, after searching to the east, turned south and followed smoke, which it thought came from HMS *Ambuscade*. Alone, but now following a predictable pattern that had already claimed HMS *Tipperary*, HMS *Fortune* and HMS *Black Prince*, the *Ardent* discovered to her cost that the smoke was from SMS *Westfalen*, which opened fire at 900 yards at around 00.20. The *Ardent* immediately responded with a torpedo but had been hit several times and was disabled and set on fire. The German searchlights were turned off and the *Ardent*, still ablaze, waited helplessly for bombardment from the next passing German squadron. With no intact rafts, around 40 crew fell into the sea; only three of them were saved some five hours later.[8] Fig. 9.15 shows the *Ardent*'s approach to the German line alongside that of HMS *Black Prince*.

The path of the German fleet was taking it to the south-east and inevitably into the path of the British destroyer flotillas to the east of the Fourth Destroyer Flotilla. The next flotilla to fall in with the First Battle Squadron was a mix of the Ninth and Tenth Destroyer Flotillas and some stragglers. Led by HMS *Lydiard*, *Liberty*, *Landrail* and *Laurel*, the stragglers followed behind. They were: HMS *Unity*, *Nerissa*, *Termagant*, *Nicator*, *Narborough*, *Pelican*, *Petard* and *Turbulent*.

HMS *Lydiard*, under Commander Malcolm Goldsmith, appeared not to notice the additions to the end of the column, which now extended to 12 ships. Goldsmith turned the line to take position on the starboard side of what he presumed to be a line of British battleships, namely Fifth Battle Squadron. Not realising his line was so long, the calculated turn swept the end of his line right under the bows not of Fifth Battle Squadron but of the waiting German First Battle Squadron.[9]

At some time around 00.30 the last four ships of this line encountered the van of the First Battle Squadron approaching from the north-west. HMS *Pelican* and HMS *Narborough* gave the recognition signal and yet again the German searchlights fell on the enemy ships, accompanied by heavy fire. This time it was HMS *Petard* and HMS *Turbulent* that were the focus of attention. The *Petard*, with no torpedoes left, managed to escape, but the *Turbulent* was not so lucky.

According to the German official historian, the *Turbulent* swung away to port for fear of being rammed. Now conveniently on a parallel course to SMS *Westfalen*, she then had twenty-nine 6-inch and sixteen 3.5-inch rounds fired at her at close range. The after gun was seen swept overboard, shortly before an explosion marked the *Turbulent*'s destruction.[10] Inexplicably, Goldsmith did not turn his long line to attack, nor did he make a report to Jellicoe. This marked the point at which the Germans had successfully forced their way through the stern of the British fleet, although the Twelfth Destroyer Flotilla was later to sink SMS *Pommern*, as related in Chapter 12.

Finally at around 02.15, five minutes after SMS *Pommern* had blown up, a group of torpedo boats (SMS *V2*, *V4* and *V6*) on the starboard side of the German line and heading to the van, just passed in line with SMS *Westfalen* when the *V4* exploded. The forward part of the ship, up to a point aft of the bridge, was blown off. In an increasing sea state, the *V2* rescued the survivors (17 had been killed) and then the *V6* sank the stern portion with a torpedo.[11] The wreck of *V4* has not been positively identified as yet and will be the focus of further work in the future.

HMS *Tipperary*

The flotilla leader HMS *Tipperary* (Fig. 14.1) was one of four large and powerful destroyers being built for Chile that were taken over by the Admiralty in 1914. They had amenities unprecedented on British destroyers at the time, including electric radiators, bathrooms for seamen, electric hoists for each gun, range finders fore and aft and a crow's nest from where gunnery was co-ordinated. They were also heavily armed with three 4-inch guns mounted on the foredeck and a further three similarly mounted aft. The *Tipperary* was also armed with four 21-inch torpedo tubes in a pair of double mounts.

HMS *Tipperary* was hit and disabled in the first of the actions described above. The ship burned furiously for around two hours before sinking. The senior surviving officer, Acting Sub-lieutenant Powlett, stated in his action report:

Around 1150 a ship on our starboard beam fired one gun... immediately afterwards the ship fired a salvo which hit us forward. I opened fire with the after guns. A shell then struck us in a steam pipe and I could see nothing but steam... The firing appeared to last around three minutes during which time we were continually hit forward. When the steam died away I found that the ship was stationary and badly on fire forward. The enemy was not to be seen; nearly everybody amidships was either killed or wounded; the boxes of cartridges on the fore guns were exploding one after the other... At around 1.45 the First Lieutenant gave the order 'Everybody Aft'. The ship soon afterwards heeled over to starboard and the bows went under... The ship sank in about one minute, the stern going right up into the air.[12]

It is clear that the forward portion of the ship effectively burned to the waterline before she foundered by the bows, listing to starboard. Stoker First Class George Parkyn was rescued alone from the sea by HMS *Dublin* after around five hours. His report also stated that he saw the *Tipperary* sink by the bows.[13]

Surgeon Probationer Gilbert Blurton RNVR of HMS *Tipperary* stated that shortly after midnight the ship had been hit forward. With the ship immobilised and latterly on fire, the survivors finally took to a raft at around 02.12 (when Blurton's watch stopped working). Blurton was later picked up by SMS *Elbing*'s whaler and later transferred to a Dutch trawler.[14] The *Tipperary*'s survivors had a number of encounters with German vessels during the night. The burning ship had been approached at around 01.00 by a German torpedo boat which clearly did not consider her to be a threat any more and moved off without firing, once the *Tipperary* had revealed her identity.[12]

Later, the *Tipperary*'s survivors on the only functioning Carley raft informed their rescuers aboard HMS *Marksman* that: 'in the morning a German lifeboat had passed them full of men and that they had hailed them and asked to be taken on board, but they had been told to go to hell'.[15] This tale may well be an embellishment, especially in the light of the fact that the lifeboat must have come from SMS *Elbing* and rescued Blurton from the sea. It is more probable that there was simply no room to accommodate a raftload of survivors in the small boat.

According to Harper, 185 crew were killed, two were wounded and eight ended up prisoners of war.[16] The survivors picked up by the British included Parkyn (the only one by HMS *Dublin*). According to Powlett, 22 were picked up by HMS *Sparrowhawk* and they, at least, were still alive when the *Marksman* returned to Scapa Flow on 3 June.[12]

The wreck

The wreck now considered to be HMS *Tipperary* was scanned by multibeam during the 2015 expedition and the results can be seen in Fig. 14.4. Initially they did not look too promising as only some of the ship's machinery was all that seemed to have survived. The length of the wreck was difficult to estimate because it seemed much of it had either buried itself or corroded away.

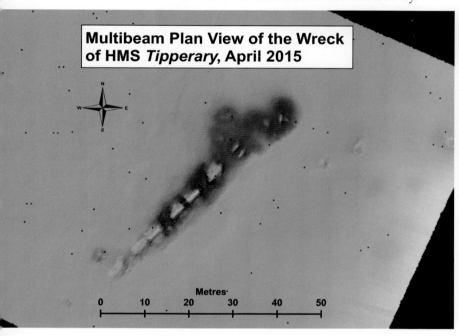

Multibeam Plan View of the Wreck of HMS *Tipperary*, April 2015

Fig. 14.4 Plan view of the HMS Tipperary wreck, as seen on Vina's multibeam system in April 2015. (Picture: McCartney/JD-Contractor)

The wreck looked correct for a destroyer, being longer and slimmer than most, but with so little seemingly remaining could it be positively identified? There were five British destroyers sunk in the Night Action and, in theory at least, this wreck could have been any one of them. The site had been surveyed by ROV in 2014 and the tape was re-examined for evidence (Fig. 14.5). The seabed was of soft mud and it was obvious that much of the wreck was buried.

The ROV started the survey in the south-west area of the wreck. The dominating features were the steam drums at the top of the three-drum boilers seen on warship wrecks of this period. Fig. 14.5A shows the locking arms for the manhole cover in the steam drum. The steam drums are situated directly on the seabed and the ROV had to search carefully to find a couple of places where the water tubes could be seen projecting from the underneath of them. B and C show the water tubes as seen. The actual water troughs are buried under several feet of mud.

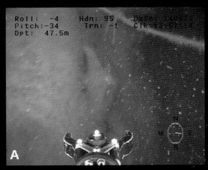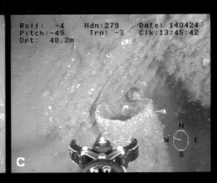

Fig. 14.5 Images of the remains of HMS Tipperary's boilers, now the only recognisable features of this once powerful destroyer. (Picture: McCartney/ JD-Contractor)

So the ROV tape revealed that the highest points of the wreck were the tops of the steam drums of the ship's boilers. Looking again at the multibeam images of the wreck, there seemed to be between four and six boilers present. HMS *Tipperary* was unique among all of the destroyers and torpedo boats sunk at Jutland because she was equipped with six White-Forster boilers. One feature of this boiler type is the slightly curved nature of the water tubes, but, with so little of them now showing, this was difficult to discern on the ROV tape.

The hull form and machinery distribution typology described on page 24 was consulted again in this case. The correctly scaled outline of the hull and machinery of HMS *Tipperary* was overlaid on her multibeam image and proved to be an exact match (Fig. 14.6).

The steam drums of all six boilers remain, with the forward one being the most buried. This is consistent with accounts that the ship sank bow first. Little remains forward of this boiler, with whatever remained of the bow when the ship sank probably buried in the mud. In the area of the engine room, the ROV tape revealed the remains of what appeared to be part of a ship's turbine. The rest of the engine room cannot be seen, being either buried or no longer present. The schematic lined up well with the wreck's surviving features and, alongside the evidence from the ROV tape, has allowed us to satisfactorily conclude that this is the wreck of HMS *Tipperary* because of her unique number of boilers.

The proximity of the HMS *Tipperary* wreck to the SMS *Elbing* wreck is noteworthy (see Fig. 14.2). It seems that the Carley raft with HMS *Tipperary's* survivors on board drifted initially in a south-easterly direction. This would have placed them near the track presumably taken by the *Elbing's* whaler as she headed for land.

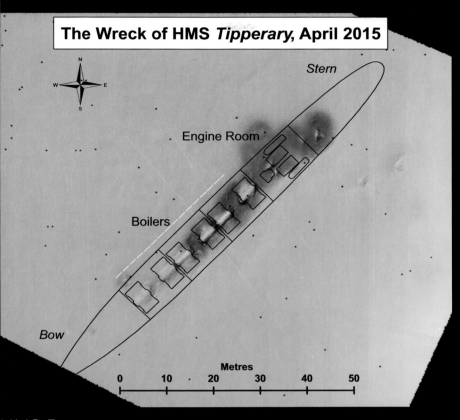

The Wreck of HMS *Tipperary*, April 2015

Stern

N
W E
S

Engine Room

Boilers

Bow

Metres
0   10   20   30   40   50

Fig. 14.6 The hull form and machinery distribution plan for HMS Tipperary, overlaid on the plan view of the multibeam image seen in Fig. 14.4. This clearly identified the wreck as HMS Tipperary. It also shows the crater from where the engines have seemingly been salvaged. (Picture: McCartney/ JD-Contractor)

HMS *Fortune*

HMS *Fortune* (Fig. 14.7) was of the Acasta, or K, class of British destroyers of 1911–12. Uniquely among the destroyers and torpedo boats lost at Jutland, most of this class was fitted with four boilers. During the Night Action, two of her sister ships, HMS *Ardent* and HMS *Sparrowhawk*, were also sunk. However, both the *Fortune* and the *Ardent* were not typical 'Ks'; they were considered 'specials'.[17] In the case of HMS *Fortune*, she was the only one of her class built by Fairfield in Govan. She was unique in appearance for a 'K', having a clipper bow, a gun between No. 2 and No. 3 funnels, a searchlight platform between the torpedo tubes mounted aft of the funnels and all of her funnels of equal height.[18] She was, in fact, built as a 'try-out' for the three-funnel version of the future 'L' class.

HMS *Fortune* was sunk when the Fourth Destroyer Flotilla stumbled into the First Battle Squadron at around midnight. Within a few minutes the *Fortune* succumbed to a deluge of shells. Leading Seaman Thomas Clifford, who was at the torpedo tubes, later recalled:

Fig. 14.7 HMS Fortune had a length of 265 ft and displacement of 981 tons, with three 4-inch guns (one forward, one between funnels No. 2 and No. 3 and one aft) and two 21-inch torpedo tubes aft of the after funnel either side of the searchlight. Note the clipper bow. The rest of the 'K's had a straight stem. (Picture: Richard Osborne Collection)

I was sitting on the tube. It was pitch dark and quiet, when a dark shape appeared in front of me about 200 yards away. I knew it was the enemy but must wait for orders to fire. Then she made her recognitions light and when I got no order to fire I looked at the bridge and it was blown away… We were that close I could see searchlights crew on the big ship. I… helped to get any survivors into Carley float… At last only Sub Lt Patterson and I were left on quarterdeck, he thinking of 33 golden sovereigns he had down cabin, when another foremost bulkhead collapsed and the stern rose to a sharper angle, so I suggested we dive over the side.[19]

Lieutenant-Commander Otto Busch, searchlight control officer on the battleship SMS *Oldenburg*, four ships back from the leader SMS *Westfalen*, saw a more violent end to HMS *Fortune*. He stated that 'clear in the glare of our searchlights I could see a petty officer and two seamen loading and firing her after gun until she disappeared'.[20] HMS *Ardent*'s captain also recalled seeing the *Fortune* sinking while still firing her guns.[21] In either case, though, it seems that the ship sank from forward. This was potentially a useful clue when it came to analysing the multibeam images of the wreck.

HMS *Marksman*, the saviour of the survivors of HMS *Sparrowhawk* and HMS *Tipperary* and the *Ardent*'s captain (see page 229), also rescued two raftloads of the *Fortune*'s men, including their chief artificer engineer.[22] According to Harper, 67 of the crew had perished and one survivor was listed as wounded.[16]

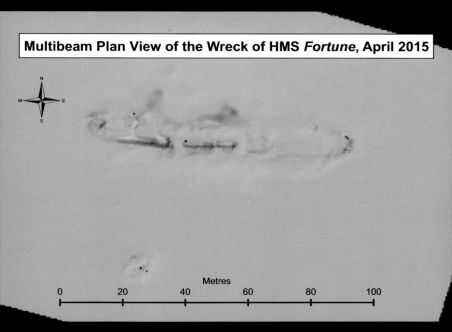

Fig. 14.8 *Plan view of the wreck of HMS* Fortune, *as seen on Vina's multibeam system in April 2015. (Picture: McCartney/JD-Contractor)*

The wreck

The site of the wreck now considered to be HMS *Fortune* was surveyed by multibeam in April 2015 (Fig. 14.8). The wreck was lying in an east–west orientation, with probably the bow to the west. Her overall length and width was commensurate with being a 'K' class destroyer. It looked as if the forward

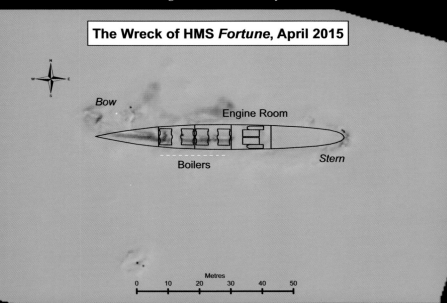

Fig. 14.9 *The hull form and machinery distribution plan for the K class of British destroyer overlaid on the plan view of the multibeam image in Fig. 14.8 reveals that the wreck is HMS* Fortune. *(Picture: McCartney/JD-Contractor)*

20-metre section of the wreck was slightly displaced and broken off from the rest of the wreck.

Once more, the hull form and machinery schematic for the K class destroyers was correctly scaled and then overlaid on the multibeam plan view (Fig. 14.9). The schematic matches well with the multibeam plan of the wreck. Boiler No. 2 to No. 4 line up correctly and what appears to be boiler No. 1 is displaced slightly forward where it seems that the fore section of the wreck has broken away. It would appear that the 2015 survey was not the first time this wreck had been visited (although it was the first time I and JD-Contractor had done so), because the ship's condensers seem to have been removed from the site (Fig. 14.9).

Interestingly, the east–west orientation of the wreck suggests that *Fortune* had in fact followed the Fourth Destroyer Flotilla's column as it turned on to a converging track to the First Battle Squadron in order to launch torpedoes. However, the main question was whether this was actually the wreck of HMS *Fortune* or HMS *Ardent*, which was sunk nearby (see Fig. 14.3). Since both were of a similar design, would it be possible to tell them apart? It turned out that HMS *Ardent* had a surprise in store, as is recounted next.

HMS *Ardent*

Like HMS *Fortune*, HMS *Ardent* (Fig. 14.10) was also a 'special' version of the K class. She was the only one of the class built by William Denny & Brothers of Dumbarton and she too was a 'try-out' for the future L class. So HMS *Ardent* also had some unique characteristics. She was the first ship built for the Royal Navy using the longitudinal frame system, as opposed to the traditional transverse framing system. She remained unique in this respect until 1939, despite the longitudinal framing offering greater strength in these long slim ships, which were subject to sagging and hogging stresses. Longitudinal framing also offered significant weight savings, of which the Admiralty did not take advantage in this 'one-off' ship.[23]

The Denny shipyard also sought to improve on the Admiralty K class design in a number of other ways. Of particular note was its interest in lowering the overall silhouette of the ship. The bridge, funnels and gun mounts were all lowered and, like HMS *Fortune*, the torpedoes were moved aft of the funnels and the central gun was placed between them instead. HMS *Ardent* was also the only ship of the K class to have only two funnels. It has been suggested

that this was so because she was the 'try-out' ship for the two-funnelled variants of the L class.[24]

HMS *Ardent* was sunk as she gamely attempted to torpedo the line of the First Battle Squadron after she had become separated from the rest of the Fourth Destroyer Flotilla. She fired both torpedoes before the searchlights found her and rained destruction on her from very short range. The *Ardent*'s commanding officer, Lieutenant-Commander Arthur Marsden, was one of only two survivors. He was picked up unconscious at 06.00 by HMS *Marksman*. He recounted later in 1916:

> *Smoke was reported right ahead… but as I got nearer realised it was not our flotilla, but a big ship steaming on exactly the opposite course to us. I attacked at once and from very close range our torpedoes were fired, but before I could judge the effect the enemy switched on searchlights and found us at once… Shell after shell hit us and our speed diminished and then stopped; then the dynamo stopped and all the lights went out… I could feel the ship was sinking… A terrible scene of destruction and desolation was revealed to me as I walked aft… Then all of a sudden we were again lit up by searchlights, and the enemy poured in four or five more salvoes at point blank range, then switched off her lights once more. This would be about ten minutes after we were first hit… The* Ardent *gave a big lurch… and the ship heeled right over and threw me to the ship's side… The* Ardent's *stern kept up and then she slowly sank from view.[25]*

Marsden's account reveals that the *Ardent* sank bows first and rolled as she sank. This clue could possibly help in identifying the wreck, although HMS *Fortune* had sunk in the same manner.

Fig. 14.10 *HMS* Ardent *had a length of 269 ft and a displacement of 981 tons, with three 4-inch guns (one forward, one between the funnels and one aft) and two 21-inch torpedo tubes aft of the funnels, with a searchlight between them. Note that there are only two funnels. (Picture: Richard Osborne Collection)*

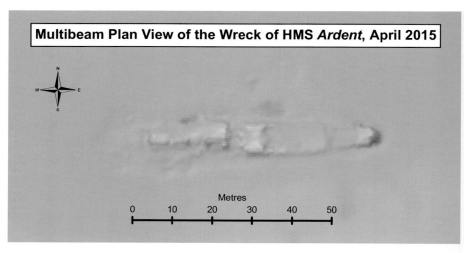

The wreck

The site of the wreck of HMS *Ardent* was surveyed with multibeam in April 2015 (Fig. 14.11). Like HMS *Fortune*, the wreck lies east to west. The bows appeared to point west, which would place the wreck roughly on the reciprocal course described by Marsden. The stern portion seemed to be in better condition, while the bows were flattened or buried.

In the previous year JD-Contractor had surveyed the wreck site with ROV and we consulted the tape for evidence. Of particular interest to me was finding evidence of the ship's unique framing, although the condition of the destroyers so far examined suggested that this would be difficult.

Fig. 14.12 *The hull form and machinery distribution plan for the K class of British destroyers overlaid on the plan view of the multibeam image in Fig. 14.11 reveals that the wreck is HMS* Ardent. *The non-standard number of three boilers, instead of four, proved important in identifying this site. (Picture: McCartney/JD-Contractor)*

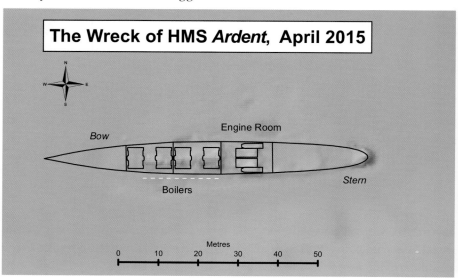

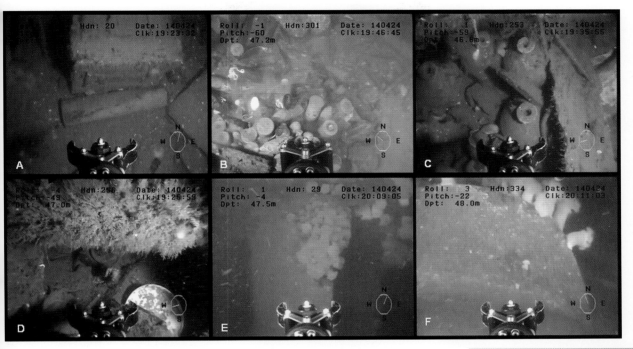

Hdn: 20   Date: 140424   Clk:19:23:32

Roll: -1   Hdn:301   Date: 140424   Pitch:-60   Clk:19:46:45   Opt: 47.2m

Roll: 1   Hdn:253   Date: 140424   Pitch:-59   Clk:19:35:55   Opt: 46.8m

A

B

C

Roll: -4   Hdn:256   Date: 140424   Pitch:-49   Clk:19:25:59   Opt: 47.0m

Roll: 1   Hdn: 29   Date: 140424   Pitch: -4   Clk:20:09:05   Opt: 47.5m

Roll: 3   Hdn:334   Date: 140424   Pitch:-22   Clk:20:11:03   Opt: 48.0m

D

E

F

Fig. 14.13 Features seen around the stern of the HMS Ardent wreck, confirming that this is, with HMS Shark, the most intact and important of the British destroyer wrecks at Jutland.. (Pictures: McCartney/JD-Contractor)

The survey took place in the early evening of 24 April 2014 in dark and muddy conditions with underwater visibility of only around one metre. Nevertheless, the wreck was examined for nearly two hours and much was seen. The wreck had sunk into the mud, with the forward section more buried than the stern. The boilers were partially buried, with only the steam drums clear of the mud. The engine room also looked partially buried. But, most interestingly, the stern portion of the wreck was in relatively good condition compared with other wrecks of this type. Sadly the visibility made it difficult to ascertain the extent to which the framing could be examined and will have to wait for another occasion.

The extent to which the stern portion was intact was shown by a number of features (Fig. 14.13). The stern was characterised by many smaller items, in some cases still stowed as they would have been when the ship was operational.

Fig. 14.12A shows one of a number of expended 4-inch shells in the stern, illustrating that the *Ardent* had put up a fight before she sank. B shows the remains of a crate of pom-pom ammunition. The pom-pom gun must have been a post-design addition because none of the published works consulted reveals that the *Ardent* was so armed. Of everyday items, C shows stoneware bottles of the type used by the Royal Navy at this period and D shows an intact china plate in a hole under the deck. Of particular note during the ROV survey was the 'A' bracket of the port-side propeller (E) and the blade of the port propeller sticking out of the seabed (F). This was the only propeller seen on any of the destroyers or torpedo boats until July 2015 when JD-Contractor recorded HMS *Shark* on ROV.

The multibeam scan seemed to show that the wreck had only three boilers. The K class were, as seen on the wrecks of HMS *Shark*, HMS *Fortune* and in the Admiralty plans for the class, built with four boilers.[26] When the hull form and machinery schematic was scaled to size and overlaid on the multibeam image (Fig. 14.12) the boilers did not correctly line up. This opened the possibility that the wreck might be HMS *Turbulent*, also sunk nearby (see Fig. 14.3) and known to have been fitted with three boilers. However, the dimensions of the site did not fit well for the *Turbulent* and her wreck was thought to have been satisfactorily identified elsewhere during the 2015 survey (as explained later in this chapter) so another explanation was needed.

The experimental nature of the K class 'specials' proved to be the answer. Further consultation of the records showed that, in addition to her other peculiarities, HMS *Ardent* had been fitted with only three boilers. This was confirmed by the details held in the 'Denny List' and by Andrew Choong at the National Maritime Museum who assured us that the *Ardent*'s specific plans (now too fragile to copy) show three boilers, two of which fed into the ovoid forward funnel and the aftermost boiler into the smaller circular one. This might explain the supposed marginal weight saving seen in this class, which had been previously attributed to her unique framing.[23] With the three boilers now satisfactorily explained, the wreck's identity could be confirmed as HMS *Ardent*.

The wreck's engine room is in good condition and the condensers and other features seem to be still in place. The excellent condition of the wreck, compared with the other smaller warship wrecks, and her unique characteristics make this wreck a special case, worthy of further research and perhaps even monitoring. Certainly there is much more that could be learned from careful examinations of the hull in decent underwater conditions.

HMS *Turbulent*

HMS *Turbulent* (Fig. 14.14) was also of a unique design among the destroyer wrecks sunk during the Battle of Jutland. Like the *Tipperary* which was taken over while being built for Chile, *Turbulent* was one of four destroyers being

Fig. 14.14 HMS Turbulent
had a length of 309 ft and a
displacement of 1,098 tons, with
five 4-inch guns (two on the
forecastle wings, one between
the funnels, one on the upper
deck aft and one on a platform
aft) and four 21-inch torpedo
tubes in double mounts aft of
the funnels. (Picture: Richard
Osborne Collection)

built for Turkey by Hawthorn Leslie in Newcastle upon Tyne and was taken over by the Admiralty in November 1914. She was launched in 1915 and completed in early 1916 in time to take part in the Battle of Jutland, having been temporarily transferred from the Harwich Force to the Thirteenth Destroyer Flotilla.

HMS *Turbulent* was sunk when she followed a turn made by the leader of her line, HMS *Lydiard*, bringing her right under the bows of the First Battle Squadron. Although Harper stated that 13 of the crew ended up as prisoners of war, no survivor's account appears to exist.[16] However, there were witnesses to the destruction of the ship and it is to them we must look for clues as to how she sank.

The crew at the stern of HMS *Petard*, the nearest British ship, reported seeing that the *Turbulent* had been run over by the leading German ship SMS *Westfalen*.[27] Contradicting this, HMS *Nicator* reported that the *Turbulent* blew up under heavy fire from the German line. Sinister echoes of the 'ripple of flame' seen when the *Defence* blew up were reported as a flicker that apparently ran along the ship's length before she too was 'blown right out of the water'.[28] The German official historian, Otto Groos, stated that the *Turbulent* was destroyed by gunfire after apparently turning to avoid being rammed and ending up on a parallel course on the port side of the First Battle Squadron. It was reported that the first salvo swept away the after gun and within a few seconds the *Turbulent*'s boilers were seen to explode.[10] The only way to try to understand what really happened was to locate her wreck.

The wreck

The wreck now considered to be HMS *Turbulent* was scanned by multibeam in April 2015 (Fig. 14.15). The wreckage was extremely broken up and flattened

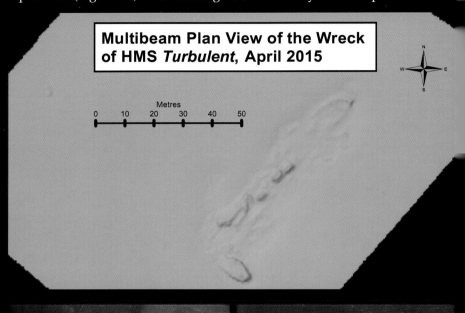

Fig. 14.15 *Plan view of the HMS Turbulent wreck, as seen on Vina's multibeam system in April 2015. (Picture: McCartney/JD-Contractor)*

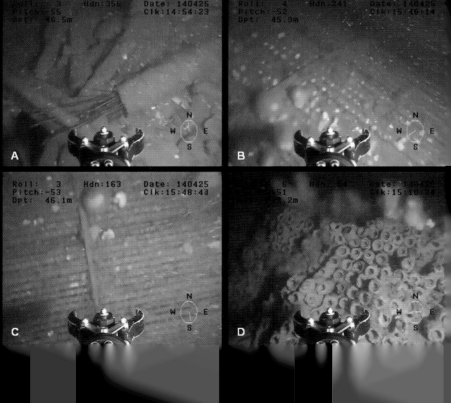

Fig. 14.16 *Features seen on the HMS Turbulent wreck, confirming her nationality and perhaps confirming the boiler explosion described by Groos. (Pictures: McCartney/JD-Contractor)*

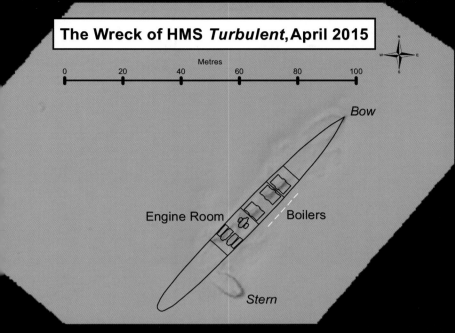

The Wreck of HMS *Turbulent*, April 2015

Metres
0   20   40   60   80   100

Bow

Engine Room   Boilers

Stern

Fig. 14.17 *The hull form and machinery distribution plan for HMS* Turbulent *overlaid on the plan view of the multibeam image in Fig. 14.15 reveals that the wreck is HMS* Turbulent. *(Picture: McCartney/JD Contractor)*

nto the seabed. The high points seemed to resemble the boilers as seen in other heavily degraded cases, such as the wreck of HMS *Tipperary*. The real challenge was to see if it was possible to identify this wreck satisfactorily.

D-Contractor had looked at this site with an ROV on the afternoon of 24 April 2014 and we consulted the tape for evidence. The conditions were as poor as on the *Ardent,* with underwater visibility not much more than one metre. Nevertheless, enough could be seen to confirm the wreck to be British and to assist in explaining what may have happened to her. Some images from the ROV survey are shown in Fig. 14.16. The survey began at the south-westerly point of the wreck, which turned out to be the stern. The highest point was the bent rudder pin. Around it lay a number of 4-inch shell cases.

The shell case (Fig. 14.16A) had the British type of 'spaghetti' sticks of cordite projecting from the open end. As the ROV passed over the area of the engine room the unmistakable shape of a condenser was seen (B and C), with its tightly bundled copper tubing and overall shape similar to the British design. Finally as the ROV worked its way forward, it found a boiler (D) in a similar condition to those seen on the wrecks of SMS *V27* and *V29* (which the *Turbulent* had helped to sink, see Chapter 3), with the steam drum zone and only the piping leading upwards from the water troughs visible

This may be evidence supporting the description by Groos that there was a boiler explosion on the ship before she sank.

The ROV survey confirmed the wreck was British and suggested that the wreck was pointing to the north-east. The hull form and machinery distribution schematic for HMS *Turbulent* was laid over the multibeam image: The match was a good one (Fig. 14.17). It seems most likely that HMS *Turbulent* turned sharply to starboard and was attempting to escape, turning end-on to the enemy when she was sunk. This is similar in some ways to the fate of HMS *Black Prince*. The extremely damaged nature of the stern suggests that most of the enemy fire was concentrated in that area and that, in all probability, once disabled the ship rapidly sank stern first, with the stern snapping off on impact with the seabed.

Once in the glare of the searchlights, the *Turbulent* had little chance of escape and her sad remains represent the tomb of 90 of her crew. Wrecks of this type should naturally be given a certain degree of respect and not treated as an economic resource. It is perhaps a moot point to speculate just how long the condenser shown above will remain on the wreck once this book has been published. Looking at the way so many of the other Jutland wrecks have been treated, the prognosis is not encouraging. We will return to this issue in Chapter 15.

Destroyer wrecks of the Night Action: in summary

This chapter looked at four British destroyers sunk during the Night Action. Each case presented its own challenges, but through a combination of rigorous archival research and archaeological survey they have now been satisfactorily accounted for. Of particular interest was the somewhat non-standard build of both HMS *Fortune* and HMS *Ardent*. In the *Ardent*'s case, this actually helped to identify her wreck, distinguishing her from HMS *Fortune* by being a 'special' with only three boilers. The *Ardent* proved to be the most important of the British destroyer wrecks because of her state of preservation and rarity.

The most degraded of the wrecks were the two largest: HMS *Tipperary* and HMS *Turbulent*. There was never any doubt about the *Tipperary*'s identity once all the evidence was brought together. Her six boilers made her unique among the wrecks. The *Turbulent*'s remains are worthy of further inspections to learn more about her before she is degraded any further. The wrecks of HMS *Sparrowhawk* and SMS *V4* await discovery in the future.

Notes

1   National Archives (various dates). Groos O. *The Battle of Jutland: Official German Account*. Translated Bagot WT. ADM 186/626. London: Admiralty; 1926. p.177.

2   *Ibid.*, p.180.

3   Campbell NJM. *Jutland: an Analysis of the Fighting*. London: Conway; 1986. p.394.

4   Fawcett HW, Hooper GWW. *The Fighting at Jutland*. Glasgow: Maclure, Macdonald & Co.; 1921. pp.348–53.

5   *Ibid.*, p.362.

6   *Ibid.*, pp.353–57.

7   National Archives (various dates). Groos O. *The Battle of Jutland: Official German Account*. Translated Bagot WT. ADM 186/626. London: Admiralty; 1926. p.183.

8   Harper JET. *Reproduction of the Record of the Battle of Jutland*. London: HMSO; 1927. p.88.

9   Gordon A. *The Rules of the Game*. London: John Murray; 1996. pp.483–84.

10 National Archives (various dates). Groos O. *The Battle of Jutland: Official German Account*. Translated Bagot WT. ADM 186/626. London: Admiralty; 1926. p.191.

11 *Ibid.*, p.203.

12 *Jutland: Reports of Flag and Commanding Officers*. ADM 137/302. National Archives (various dates), London. pp.540–42.

13 *Ibid.*, p.238.

14 Battle of Jutland, press and survivors' reports, press cuttings, extracts from letters etc.Vol. I. ADM 137/4808. National Archives (various dates), London. pp.44–45.

15 Fawcett HW, Hooper GWW. *The Fighting at Jutland*. Glasgow: Maclure, Macdonald & Co.; 1921. p.355.

16 Harper JET. *Reproduction of the Record of the Battle of Jutland*. London: HMSO; 1927. p.117.

17 March EJ. *British Destroyers: a History of Development 1892–1953*. London: Seeley Service & Co.; 1966. p.124.

18 *Ibid.*, p.130.

19 Church Papers Misc 1010. TW Clifford correspondence, Imperial War Museum (various dates), London.

20 Dorling T. *Endless Story*. London: Hodder and Stoughton; 1936. p.207.

21 Fawcett HW, Hooper GWW. *The Fighting at Jutland*. Glasgow: Maclure, Macdonald & Co.; 1921. p.363.

22 *Ibid.*, p.368.

23 *The Denny List Part III: Ship Numbers 769–1273*. National Maritime Museum (various dates), London. p.648.

24 Manning TD. *The British Destroyer*. London: Godfrey Cave Associates; 1979.

25 Fawcett HW, Hooper GWW. *The Fighting at Jutland*. Glasgow: Maclure, Macdonald & Co.; 1921. pp.363–67.

26 Constructor's plans of New torpedo boat Destroyers 1911–12. Ship's plans collection, National Maritime Museum (various dates), Controller's Department, Admiralty (undated), London.

27 *Jutland: Reports of Flag and Commanding Officers*. ADM 137/302. National Archives (various dates), London. p.324.

28 Fawcett HW, Hooper GWW. *The Fighting at Jutland*. Glasgow: Maclure, Macdonald & Co.; 1921. pp.379–80.

With Gert Normann Andersen, Nick Jellicoe, two television crews and the JD-Contractor team on MV Vina at the conclusion of the ground-breaking April 2015 multibeam survey. This was the culmination of 16 years of diving, survey and research and finally enabled this book to be completed. (Picture: JD-Contractor)

PART FOUR

JUTLAND ONE HUNDRED YEARS ON

15 CONCLUSIONS: THE ARCHAEOLOGY OF A NAVAL BATTLEFIELD

With the Jutland battlefield now surveyed and recorded and all wrecks except HMS Sparrowhawk *and SMS V4 accounted for, it is time to take stock of what it all amounts to. This falls into three broad subject areas: the contribution of the wrecks to studies of the history of the Battle of Jutland; the study of First World War shipwrecks and their current condition; and the debates surrounding salvage, protection, legislation and enforcement of underwater cultural heritage.*

Informing the historical record of the battle through archaeology

In the Introduction I suggested there were at least two main areas of study where the shipwrecks of Jutland could contribute to a greater understanding of the battle. Firstly, comparative analysis of the wrecks could be measured against the circumstances of their losses (including the reports of eyewitnesses) and could potentially reveal new detail over what was known before the wrecks were discovered, when the battle resided only in books and on maps. Secondly, the positions of the wrecks could potentially add to our understanding of the battle and be a benchmark against which to examine the accuracy of the *Harper Record* and other sources.

What the shipwrecks are telling us

The 22 shipwrecks examined and identified in this book have significantly contributed to the history of the Battle of Jutland. In several cases, the wrecks themselves have, once surveyed, revealed much about how they were destroyed – which was not known from eyewitnesses. By now readers will be aware of what the wrecks are contributing to the historical record of the battle so not all the results bear repeating here. However, some examples are particularly worthy of note. Highlights of the Battlecruiser Action include:

- The knowledge that HMS *Indefatigable*'s fore part exploded as she rolled over and sank;

- The discovery, in the case of HMS *Queen Mary*, that subsequent to the ship breaking in half, the stern stayed afloat, moving forward under the power of the still rotating propellers to sink beyond the wreckage of the bows. This is consistent with Cave's description of a 'rising bow wave' and shows that descriptions of the stern exploding were not correct;

- The identification of HMS *Nestor*, which seems to show that Bingham in his final Victoria Cross-winning foray most probably attacked the First Scouting Group and not the van of the German fleet. SMS *V27* and SMS *V29* both show archaeological remains consistent with possible boiler explosions.

Readers of my two academic papers will be aware of the amount of new data acquired relating to HMS *Defence*[1] and HMS *Invincible*.[2] The clear benefit of multibeam over any other readily available technology is evident from the more accurate site maps presented in this book as a result of the 2015 survey. Highlights of new knowledge from the wrecks sunk in the Fleet Action include:

- Understanding how HMS *Defence* was destroyed. The concentration of magazines in the forward and aft areas of the ship matches the points at which the bow and stern sections of the wreck have broken away. Both ends of the ship must have exploded. This possibly started forward and was propagated through the ship via the ammunition passages producing the flicker seen by Captain Poland on the *Warspite*. The ship then sank in no less than 12 seconds;

- The chance discovery of HMS *Invincible*'s 'P' and 'Q' turrets away from the main wreck area, which allowed for a scenario of her last moments to emerge. The two side turrets were bodily ejected out of the ship and she too subsequently sank in no less than 12 seconds;

- SMS *Wiesbaden*'s actual position, noteworthy for its distance from Harper's position (see page 128).

The wrecks of the Night Action are generally of a slightly different historical complexion. This is primarily because the German ships were scuttled, with the exception of SMS *Pommern*, and the circumstances were documented at the time. Nevertheless, there are some significant cases that have contributed to the history of the battle:

- The wreck of HMS *Black Prince* proved the most revealing. The dives before 2015 had only hinted at what this wreck could reveal. The multibeam and ROV survey has shown that the ship managed to turn away from her tormentors before 'X' magazine exploded, condemning the ship and her crew to destruction;

- The multibeam survey of SMS *Pommern* revealed that she completely exploded when hit by a torpedo. One turret at least was ejected out of the ship during this time;

- The scuttled German wrecks' actual positions have contributed to building a more accurate map of the battle.

- The upright wrecks, SMS *Frauenlob,* SMS *Elbing* and *Rostock*'s stern portion, are arguably among the best preserved of the German wrecks. Conversely, SMS *Lützow* has been extensively salvaged and is upside down;

- The four British destroyer wrecks all had stories to tell. It is perhaps the wreck of HMS *Turbulent* that adds the most to the history of the battle. Like HMS *Black Prince*, the *Turbulent* seems to have managed to turn stern-on to the enemy in an attempt to escape before being destroyed. Contrary to some British accounts of the battle, she was not rammed and sunk.

In overall terms, looking at the historical contribution of the wrecks, it is perhaps not surprising that it is from the cases where the ships sank with the least known about them that we have learned the most. Because of the circumstances of the battle, in nearly every case these have turned out to be British; most significantly HMS *Indefatigable, Queen Mary, Defence, Invincible, Black Prince* and *Turbulent.* On the German side, most significantly, the losses of SMS *Pommern* and *Wiesbaden* are better understood.

While it is certain that more can be done to gather further historical and archaeological data about the wrecks, it is important to bear in mind that there is a limit to what the wrecks can realistically tell us, as many have now greatly collapsed. For example, it would be very challenging to find a means of contributing to the knowledge of the British mismanagement of cordite in the fleet beyond the discovery of a single Clarkson case in the gun house of one of HMS *Invincible*'s turrets (see Chapter 5).

This is because the turret structures of the larger wrecks are not in a condition to allow us to see the flash arrangements in their original configurations or, as Lambert has suggested, to see whether the turrets and handling spaces were overstocked with exposed cordite in order to facilitate rapid firing.[3] This is primarily because where such evidence may have been found, it is also likely to have blown up at the time. Nevertheless, in broad terms, the wrecks of the three British battlecruisers manifest damage patterns commensurate with the detonation of magazines with explosions of varying power. This should be of no surprise to anyone, as it was known at the time.

In the cases of the two armoured cruisers, it is not possible to say whether HMS *Defence* was destroyed by a round striking a turret roof, subsequently igniting of exposed cordite in a gun house and the handling passages of the ship, or whether her side armour was penetrated, directly igniting some vulnerable spot internally and then causing the same effect in reverse. In either scenario, propagation of flash through the ship would have probably occurred.

However, the case of HMS *Black Prince* is slightly different. This is because at the short range at which the ship was destroyed, the flat trajectory of rounds fired means that she could only, it seems, have been hit side on. Side armour penetration of either hull or turret appears to be the likely cause for her destruction, igniting cordite somewhere along the chain from magazine to gun. The fact that 'X' turret has neither gun nor roof is evidence that it violently burned out, but it cannot be established whether this was at the beginning or the end of a chain reaction.

This book has highlighted what is realistically possible, but it is far from being the final word on the subject. Just as my earlier papers highlighted the archaeological potential of the Jutland wrecks, this book is merely an interim point, as it is certain that more historical and archaeological data will emerge in the future.

The *Harper Record* re-examined

It is now possible to look at the *Harper Record* with fresh eyes. With the accurate positions of so many Jutland wrecks now known, it is interesting to compare where they fall in relation to where Harper estimated they had been, back in 1919. Currently this analysis is in its earliest stages, but what follows is a summary of the work being undertaken. One of the truly outstanding qualities of the *Harper Record* and its supporting charts is that all of the tracks and wreck positions are presented with proper lat/long

TABLE 1. ACCURACY OF HARPER'S ESTIMATED POSITIONS OF SHIPS SUNK BY DISTANCE FROM THE ACTUAL SHIPWRECK			
WRECK	**ACTIONS**	**DAY/NIGHT**	**HARPER DISTANCE (Nautical Miles)**
HMS *Invincible*	Fleet Action	Day	0.7
HMS *Ardent*	Night Action	Night	1.0
HMS *Queen Mary*	Battlecruiser Action	Day	1.3
SMS *V27*	Battlecruiser Action	Day	1.9
HMS *Tipperary*	Night Action	Night	2.1
HMS *Defence*	Fleet Action	Day	2.1
HMS *Black Prince*	Night Action	Night	2.3
SMS *V29*	Battlecruiser Action	Day	2.5
SMS *Pommern*	Night Action	Night	2.8
HMS *Shark*	Fleet Action	Day	2.9
HMS *Fortune*	Night Action	Night	2.9
HMS *Turbulent*	Night Action	Night	3.0
HMS *Nomad*	Battlecruiser Action	Day	3.1
SMS *Elbing*	Night Action	Night	4.5
SMS *Frauenlob*	Night Action	Night	4.7
SMS *Rostock*	Night Action	Night	4.8
HMS *Indefatigable*	Battlecruiser Action	Day	5.0
SMS *V48*	Fleet Action	Day	5.2
HMS *Nestor*	Battlecruiser Action	Day	6.1
SMS *Lützow*	Night Action	Night	6.7
SMS *Wiesbaden*	Fleet Action	Day	8.1
SMS *S35*	Fleet Action	Day	n/a
HMS *Sparrowhawk* (W)	Night Action	Night	unknown
SMS *V4* (W)	Night Action	Night	unknown

references. Naturally, you would expect to see this in the work compiled by the Admiralty's director of navigation as Captain John Harper was when assigned to compile the *Harper Record*.

I can find no evidence that Harper's positions for where the ships sank was later amended in any way and the list on page 110 of the *Harper Record* is identical to his original manuscript.[4] Importantly, if you accept Harper's version of events, it would be wise to treat the track of the Battlecruiser Fleet on the Harper Charts during the 'Run to the North' and afterwards with suspicion.[5] Fortunately, this has little effect on the analysis of the shipwrecks because the Battlecruiser Fleet did not suffer any losses after HMS *Queen Mary* and hardly features in this book's narrative after that time.

In the maps in each chapter there is a slight difference in the positions of the printed losses on the Harper Charts and the black crosses denoting the position as given in lat/long on page 110 of the *Harper Record*. Aside from minor differences caused by having to georeference the charts into a GIS software package, the primary reason is that the losses marked on the charts have been drawn so that they do not overlap other tracks of ships and so on.

In that regard, the actual compilers of the charts (the Operations Division of the Naval Staff) and the publishers (The Hydrographic Office) seemed to have some degree of artistic licence. The differences between the actual known wrecks and Harper's estimates of where they sank have been based on the lat/long positions in the text (that is, the black crosses), not the artistic representations on the charts themselves. The true positional differences in each case are shown in Table 1.

The table lists the wrecks in order of accuracy. Naturally, HMS *Invincible* is at the top, because she was located in 1919 and her position fixed as accurately as possible for the time, which turns out to be 0.7 nautical miles from the actual wreck. What is quite remarkable is how many of the wrecks have been found within 3 nautical miles or so of the Harper positions. The average positional difference across the entire battle is 3.5 nautical miles. The average of 3.5 nautical miles remains consistent during the day and night segments of the battle.

The more inaccurate cases mostly have logical explanations. For instance, there was no possibility of accurately plotting the position of SMS *Wiesbaden*, because she drifted throughout the night from where she was last recorded in British sources. Similarly the positions of the scuttling of the German ships at night could only be estimated from the Admiralty data available in 1919, which included intelligence material, and brief reports by Scheer and Hipper. The cases that raise the most interest would appear to be HMS *Nestor* and HMS *Indefatigable*.

In the case of HMS *Nestor*, it seems inevitable that some degree of error would creep into Harper's work when estimating the movements of ships that sank, leaving no physical record of the battle and few British witnesses. This challenge was compounded by the shortage of navigational data available from the destroyers, whose movements were probably plotted by Harper on the *Harper Record*'s charts from their known relative positions to the tracks of the squadrons of larger warships. Inevitably then, there was no navigational plot for the destroyer action that took place around the time of the sinking of HMS *Queen Mary*.

From the position Harper gives for HMS *Nestor*'s loss it seems that the source on which Harper relied (probably because little else was available) was the report of the *Nestor*'s action written by Commander Bingham when he was interned in Holland.[6] Dated 14 May 1918, it is the most detailed account of the destroyer fight during the Battlecruiser Action I have found, but understandably it is not without error.

The track chart appended to Bingham's report must have been the source of the position of the *Nestor*'s loss as it plots it in a similar spot, to the east

Fig 15.1 *Cmdr. Bingham's drawing of the destroyer action. Position (F) shows where he estimated* Nestor *sank. The wreck actually lies just to the west of the path of the British battlecruisers, as shown in Chapter 3 (Crown Copyright).*

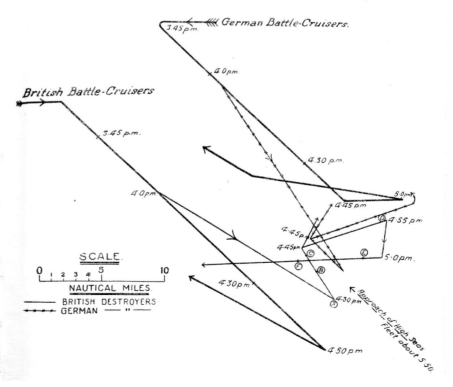

of the wreck of HMS *Queen Mary*.[7] The track chart was duplicated in *Jutland Dispatches*[8] (as shown in Fig. 15.1) and in Bingham's autobiography.[9] As discussed in Chapter 3, the *Nestor*'s actual movements had been called into question by Campbell, among others.[10] The discovery and identification of the wreck seems to confirm Campbell's analysis. The conclusion seems to be that the reliability of the source material led Harper off course in this instance. The case of HMS *Indefatigable* also reveals some interesting elements about the compilation of the *Harper Record*.

Indefatigable's mysterious position

Of note in the *Harper Record* is Harper's assertion that the positions of the wrecks of HMS *Invincible*, *Queen Mary*, *Indefatigable* and *Defence* were considered by him to be accurate.[11] As previously noted, HMS *Invincible* was found in 1919. Because Harper's position for HMS *Queen Mary* is accurate to 1.3 nautical miles it seems possible that her position may have been fixed on

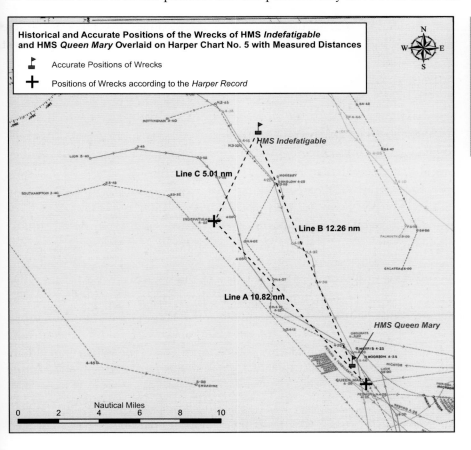

Historical and Accurate Positions of the Wrecks of HMS *Indefatigable* and HMS *Queen Mary* Overlaid on Harper Chart No. 5 with Measured Distances

⚑   Accurate Positions of Wrecks

✚   Positions of Wrecks according to the *Harper Record*

HMS Indefatigable

Line C 5.01 nm

Line B 12.26 nm

Line A 10.82 nm

HMS Queen Mary

Nautical Miles
0   2   4   6   8   10

Fig. 15.2 *The historic and actual positions of the wrecks of HMS* Indefatigable *and* Queen Mary, *with the measured distances by which they differ, as seen on Harper Chart No.5.*

1 June by ships returning to base by the large oil patch she was known to be giving off. In the case of HMS *Defence*, which sank while surrounded by a large number of ships, Harper had much data to work with and an accuracy of 2.1 nautical miles is well above the average. It is the position of HMS *Indefatigable* that stands out as odd. In this instance, something really is not right.

Fig. 15.2 re-examines the map shown in the Chapter 1 (Fig. 1.3). The distances in nautical miles between the actual and historic positions of the *Indefatigable* and the *Queen Mary* are shown in lines A and B. Line C shows that the wreck of the *Indefatigable* is actually 5.01 miles 18 degrees from Harper's position. This is peculiar compared with the relatively minor difference of 1.28 miles between the actual and Harper positions of the *Queen Mary*.

A key question that emerges is related to timing. According to Harper, the *Indefatigable* sank at around 16.02 and the *Queen Mary* at 16.26, 24 minutes apart. This is difficult to reconcile with the actual known positions of the wrecks. Fig. 15.3 shows the distance between the two wrecks to be 12.26 nautical miles. To cover a distance of 12.26 nautical miles in 24 minutes (i.e. for the Battlecruiser Fleet battle line to have been in both places) requires a speed of 30.65 knots. This also assumes no changes in course that would elongate the track, of which the Battlecruiser Fleet made several.

The maximum speed of the slowest ship in the British line was the *New Zealand*'s 26 knots and no straggling occurred.[12] So, allowing for 26 knots, no changes in course, the negligible tidal stream and seven cables' (1,500 yards) distance between the two ships, there still appears to be a timing difference of at least five minutes. It is worth noting that the distance between Harper's two positions for the wrecks (line A on Fig. 1.3) is 10.82 nautical miles. By the same measurement, the timing difference is negligible at one minute.

One possible answer to this mystery lies in the times recorded for the ships being destroyed and the time it takes for them to actually sink and become wrecks. Much happened behind smoke. Was the *Indefatigable* slowing down early on? Did the *Queen Mary* sink later than supposed? That the *Indefatigable* was already falling behind the Battlecruiser Fleet line when she finally blew up is known and clearly she was totally incapacitated when the Carne photograph was taken (see page 36). More interestingly, SMS *Von der Tann* recorded that she may have hit the *Indefatigable* as early as her third salvo.[13] Was she slowly losing way from this point? John Roberts has suggested that the 'X' magazine explosion may have destroyed the control shafts and steering gear.[14] We cannot know for sure, but the distance between the two wrecks continues to pose questions about the opening minutes of the battle and how the first two battlecruisers met their ends.

How does Harper's Chart compare with HMS *Lion*'s original one? Oddly, there is more than one version of the *Lion*'s track chart at Jutland. In *Jutland Dispatches* there are four. A copy, readied for printing, of the first track resides in the National Archives[15] and is reproduced in *Jutland Dispatches*.[16] This track is drawn from magnetic compass readings. Although the *Lion* was surely fitted with gyro compasses by the time of Jutland, perhaps damage mitigated their use.[17] After the battle her track must have been converted to true north where it appears alongside HMS *Iron Duke*'s track in *Jutland Dispatches* and was signed by Jellicoe, dated 18 June 1916.[18]

Curiously there is another seemingly identical chart, signed by Jellicoe the following day, that features an amended track of HMS *Lion*.[19] The amendments are also shown in yet another chart showing the *Lion*'s track and also printed in *Jutland Dispatches*, which Harper believed was a somewhat clumsy attempt (presumably by Beatty) to hide the full circle made by the Battlecruiser Fleet at 19.00 on 31 May.[20] The inference being that Beatty was attempting to hide the fact that he was not in contact with the enemy at this time, because a 32-point turn would not be carried out under fire.[21] This 'doctored' track is also signed by Beatty, but the facsimile in *Jutland Dispatches* is undated.[22] Crucially, however, for the purposes of this analysis, there is no great positional difference in the *Lion*'s track during the 'Run to the South' in any of these versions. The alleged 'cover-up' appears to begin during the 'Run to the North' and the intervention of the Fifth Battle Squadron into the fight, an episode of the battle not covered in this book because no ships were sunk during this period.

In order to compare it with Harper, Fig. 15.3 shows the same geographic region as Fig. 15.2, but with the *Lion*'s track from *Jutland Dispatches* in place of Harper Chart No.5. The first thing that stands out is the 13.13 mile distance between the locations of the supposed losses of HMS *Indefatigable* and HMS *Queen Mary* (line A). This is longer than the true distance between the wrecks (Line B, 12.26 nautical miles) and longer than the Harper Chart, which shows his estimated distance as 10.82 nautical miles (Fig. 15.2, Line A).

As discussed above, the true distance between the two wrecks is difficult enough to reconcile with the maximum speed of the Battlecruiser Fleet. It

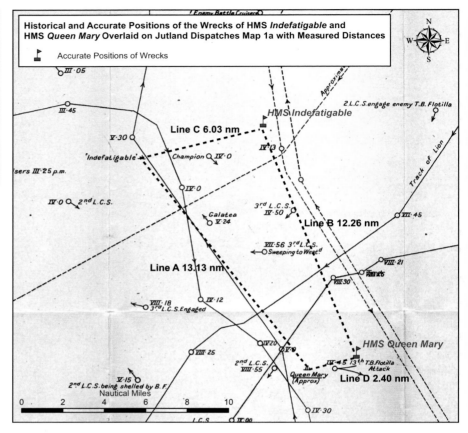

Fig. 15.3 *The historic and actual positions of the wrecks of HMS* Indefatigable *and HMS* Queen Mary, *with the measured distances by which they differ as seen on the* Lion's *track of the battle, as depicted in* Jutland Dispatches.

would appear that Harper noticed that the 13.13 mile difference on the *Lion's* track chart was also improbably long. He must have either moved the wreck location of HMS *Indefatigable* to the shortened 10.82 nautical miles distance from the *Queen Mary* on Fig. 15.2 and adjusted the *Lion's* track accordingly, or adjusted the track and then moved the wreck. If this was how Harper worked out the *Indefatigable's* position, it is difficult to see how he could have been so confident in its accuracy.

Just how inaccurate some of the track charts were that Harper had to work with and why this happened has been ably described by Andrew Gordon and in this light it seems remarkable just how broadly consistent Harper was able to make the *Harper Record*.[23] It certainly seems that each track chart available was checked for improbable timings and corrected. This process would clearly have removed a number of understandable errors made in navigational logs compiled on open bridges while under fire and created more accurate lines of movements, from which presumably some consensus must have emerged.

This was then augmented by checking gunnery ranges, which slowly built up an interlocking matrix of tracks.

Of course, what could not have been done is to accurately place the revised tracks on a chart, because, aside from the located wreck of HMS *Invincible* (and possibly HMS *Queen Mary*), all other positional data was derived by 'dead reckoning' during and after a passage across the North Sea and during a naval battle. As seen in the case of HMS *Nestor*, the less evidence to work with, the higher the chance of error. So it must have been at the outset of the Battlecruiser Action where there was only limited data available from the Battlecruiser Fleet's accompanying cruisers and destroyers. This is perhaps the reason why the *Lion*'s track was plotted by Harper too far west and south of the now known position of the HMS *Indefatigable* wreck. There was no other data to check it against.

There is no implied criticism of Harper here. If anything, the case of HMS *Indefatigable* is the exception that proves the rule that, in the circumstances of the time, the *Harper Record* is a remarkably reliable chronology of the Battle of Jutland. Without a greater number of fixed data points to work with, it is difficult to see how a better job could have been done with the tracks and logs available in 1919.

Identifying Jutland's shipwrecks

The process of identifying the Jutland wrecks was initially a simple one, because it was the larger ones that appeared first. When the torpedo boats and destroyers began to be located, things got a little trickier. The larger wrecks are quite widely dispersed and are of types that easily lend themselves to being identified. The only challenge was finding them and, as this book shows, that part of the story is now over.

The original locators of HMS *Invincible* aboard HMS *Oakley* in 1919 clearly had no difficulty in identifying her wreck, although it is currently not known whether divers were used to check the wreck site or in fact how they concluded she was the *Invincible*, which she certainly was. Similarly there was no question whether the identities of SMS *Lützow, Pommern, Elbing, Rostock, Frauenlob, Wiesbaden* or HMS *Defence, Indefatigable, Queen Mary* or *Black Prince* were wrong because they could not, in fact, be anything else. You only had to inspect these sites and see some relatively unique feature, such as a gun turret, to be certain which wreck it was.

The 13 smaller warship wrecks at Jutland offered a much more challenging proposition. This is primarily because they tend to be concentrated into confined areas of the battlefield where it is possible that the actual locations of the wrecks are close as to make it impossible to distinguish one from the other, as, for example, in the cases of the destroyers lost in the Night Action. Furthermore, the remains of these wrecks are now very broken down and not easily distinguished from one another by the untrained eye.

As this book has shown, the 2015 multibeam survey offered a means by which the destroyers and torpedo boat wrecks could be identified down to the class level. This was achieved by developing a typology of each ship type based on her size and the number and distribution of heavy machinery that was likely to show up clearly on the multibeam scans of the wrecks. Ironically, the multibeam scan was also able to show when certain pieces of machinery had been salvaged. The absence of the condensers on several of the wrecks bears witness to this.

This approach worked satisfactorily on the remains of 11 of the 13 wrecks because the machinery on the seabed could be matched to the hull form and machinery distribution schematics of the relevant class of vessel. Only HMS *Sparrowhawk* (which broke into three pieces some hours before sinking) and SMS *V4* (which was probably much salvaged, being close to shore) were not satisfactorily picked out using this methodology. So while this approach can work, there are reasons to be cautious.

Multibeam has its limitations because in practical use it is only as good as the resolution of its images. *Vina*'s state-of-the-art equipment had no problem picking out any feature on the destroyers down to around one square metre. This was perfectly good for our purposes, but it would not work nearly as well when attempting to identify smaller mass-produced vessels, such as submarines, where in my long experience the key identifying items can be as small as the shape of a flooding hole cut into the outer casing of the hull.[24]

Most of the smaller wrecks were also examined by diving or ROV, giving an additional level of verification and therefore strengthening the confidence that the identifications made are, in fact, correct. But even then, this is not the final word. In the case of closely situated wrecks such as SMS *V27* and SMS *V29*, there still lingers the possibility that their identities might have to be substituted for each other in the future. Similarly, this is the case with SMS *S35* and SMS *V48*.

This is because while all the evidence from the wrecks, supported by archival research, points to the current identities, I do not consider them to be 100 per cent certain. In these cases, an outcome similar to the case of HMS *Nomad* and HMS *Nestor*, where the name on the bell from one site effectively identified both would be necessary for ultimate confirmation. This, of course, requires human interaction with the wreck sites.

So, as a rule of thumb, multibeam can lead to identification at the class level. If that is all that is needed for a positive identification, such as was the case with HMS *Tipperary* which uniquely had six boilers, then the job is done. However, if further work is required beyond class level, a visual means of inspection is essential.

The wrecks' ongoing condition

Over the past 17 years, as each shipwreck has been surveyed, her current condition has been recorded. Unsurprisingly, the state of collapse in some sites has increased. This is natural, because all shipwrecks must ultimately succumb to the sea. The battlefield at Jutland is relatively shallow, with the deepest wrecks being in around 60 metres of water. The North Sea can be a very hostile place, even to the extent that a heavy swell can be felt on the seabed when diving.

These sorts of conditions do not lend themselves to the healthy preservation of steel shipwrecks. Still, the armoured ships have fared better than their smaller counterparts, which, as this book has shown, are no longer recognisable as ships but only as assemblages of machinery, which in the years to come will inevitably be swallowed up by the seabed or be carted off by scavengers to be melted down. There will be no destroyer or torpedo boat wrecks at Jutland to examine when the bicentenary of the First World War comes around.

Of the larger shipwrecks, the best data available extends as far back as 1991 when the 75th Anniversary expedition briefly reported on the condition of HMS *Queen Mary* and HMS *Invincible*.[25] As described in Chapter 4, the evidence shows clearly that the *Invincible* is now in an extremely advanced state of collapse over what was seen in 1991. It is impossible to predict when she will fall to the seabed, but inevitably this will happen and the site too will slowly bury.

In the case of the *Queen Mary* the rapid collapse of the hull from her reported high point of 45 metres in 1991 to the highest point recorded by multibeam in 2015 of 51 metres bears testament that this site is also degrading. In 25 years the wreck has collapsed by around 6 metres. It should also be noted in this case that the wreck was recently attacked by a salvage company using a grab to recover at least one condenser and numerous other items. As described in Chapter 2, this has extensively altered the stern portion of the wreck and will certainly have done nothing to slow down the rate at which this wreck site too is succumbing to the marine environment.

The point to be made here is simply that there will never be a *Mary Rose* moment for the Jutland wrecks. We will never see a Dreadnought battleship lost in battle recovered, conserved and reconstructed. The cost and logistical issues make it impossible. So the truth is that once the wrecks are collapsed and buried in the seabed they will be gone for all time and we will never learn anything else from them. That day is a lot closer than many presume. In archaeological terms, it is time to 'use it or lose it'.

The truth about salvage

To simply see the remains of the shipwrecks as a means by which the history of the Battle of Jutland can be revised and refined, or to see them as subjects of archaeological study is only half the story. The discovery of the wrecks now means they exist outside of the library and on the seabed of the real world. To many, they are now physical extant memorials to the battle and the graves of many of its brave participants. To others, they are a way of making money by melting down metals from the wrecks.

Even 100 years after the event there is an emotive element attached to the wrecks that cannot easily be ignored. Undoubtedly some readers will be shocked to see the distasteful extent to which the wrecks have been subject to salvage for profit and that in practical terms nothing has been done to prevent this.

Table 2 shows the extent of the salvage seen on the Jutland wrecks up to and including 2015. It should be pointed out that I was not looking for evidence of salvage when examining the wrecks but in fact looking for what was present, not what had been removed. Nevertheless, it is sometimes obvious when items have been taken away. In these cases, the table shows what has been observed to have gone, but this list is far from definitive and in some cases probably much more has also disappeared.

TABLE 2. EXTENT OF SALVAGE OF THE BATTLE OF JUTLAND'S SHIPWRECKS	
HMS *Black Prince*	**Extensive**
HMS *Queen Mary*	Extensive
SMS *Lützow*	Extensive
SMS *Pommern*	Extensive
HMS *Fortune*	Condensers
HMS *Nestor*	Condensers
HMS *Nomad*	Condensers
HMS *Tipperary*	Condensers
SMS *V27*	Condensers
SMS *V29*	Condensers
SMS *Wiesbaden*	Propellers
HMS *Indefatigable*	Propellers
SMS *Rostock*	Suspected
HMS *Invincible*	Suspected
HMS *Shark*	Unknown
HMS *Sparrowhawk* (W)	Unknown
SMS *S35*	Unknown
SMS *V4* (W)	Unknown
SMS *V48*	Unknown
HMS *Ardent*	No evidence seen
HMS *Defence*	No evidence seen
HMS *Turbulent*	No evidence seen
SMS *Elbing*	No evidence seen
SMS *Frauenlob*	No evidence seen

The 'suspected' cases are listed as such because, for example, although I have never looked for HMS *Invincible*'s propellers to check whether they are there, conversely I have not seen them either and therefore suspect they may have gone. Aside from Gert Normann's rescue of her guns for the Sea War Museum Jutland, the *Rostock* looks suspiciously 'nibbled' in places.

I believe it is important to distinguish between the recovery of artefacts for museums, public education and research and profiteering from the wrecks by selling artefacts or melting down metal. Salvage for profit at Jutland is not

Fig. 15.4 *The Hydrographic Office record of SMS* Lützow, *showing the salvage operations that took place in 1960. (Contains public-sector information, licensed under the Open Government Licence v3.0, from United Kingdom Hydrographic Office)*

```
Latitude = 56 16'.700 N   Longitude = 005 39'.017 E [EUR] Square Number = 250
State = LIVE

Wreck Number          32344                        Classification    = Unclassified
Symbol                NDW                          Largest Scale Chart = 1404
Charting Comments

Old Number            025000214
Category              Non-dangerous wreck

WGS84 Position        Latitude = 56 16'.660 N   Longitude = 005 38'.937 E
WGS84 Origin          Block Shift
Horizontal Datum      EUR  EUROPEAN (1950) (ED50)

Position Method
Position Quality      Precisely known
Position Accuracy
Area at Largest Scale No

Depth
Drying Height
Height
General Depth         48 metres
Vertical Datum        Lowest astronomical tide
Depth Method
Depth Quality         Depth unknown
Depth Accuracy
Conspic Visual        NO                          Conspic Radar      NO
Historic              NO                          Existence Doubtful NO
Non Sub Contact       NO

Last Amended          29/07/1991
Position Last Amended 29/07/1991
Position Last         Latitude = 56 17'.000 N  Longitude = 005 28'.000 E

Name                  LUTZOW
Type                  BATTLECRUISER
Flag                  GERMAN
Dimensions            Length = 210.0  metres    Beam = 29.0  metres    Draught = 8.2 metres
Tonnage               26600 Displacement
Cargo
Date Sunk             31/05/1916

Sonar Dimensions      Length =                  Width =                Shadow Height =
Orientation

Magnetic Anomaly
Debris Field
Scour                 Depth =                   Length =               Orientation =

Markers
General Comments

Circumstances of Loss
   TORPEDOED BY HMS ACASTA DURING THE BATTLE OF JUTLAND AFTER PREVIOUSLY BEING BADLY DAMAGED
   BY GUNFIRE FROM HM SHIPS LION AND PRINCESS ROYAL.  SHE BECAME UNMANAGEABLE, WAS ABANDONED
   BY CREW AND EVENTUALLY SANK.  (DOD).

Surveying Details
H3468/20 SUNK IN 561700N, 052800E, APPROX.
H3927/60 1.9.60 SALVAGE OPS REPORTED IN PROGRESS IN 561700N, 054100E.  (HAMBURG NM 2582/60)
   NCA YET.
H3927/60 13.9.60 SALVAGE OPS COMPLETED.  (HAMBURG NM 3510/60).  NCA
   31.7.72 WK SHOWN IN 561710N, 052750E ON DANISH FISHERIES 5604 [REC'D 1965]).
   12.1.84 SHOWN AS NDW IN 561700N, 052800E ON DANISH 93 [INT 1044] [OCT'83 EDN].
HH100/351/04 29.7.91 DIVED ON IN 1990 IN 561642N, 053901E BY DANISH DIVERS.  POSITIVELY
   IDENTIFIED - NAME PLATE RECOVERED.  REGULARLY FISHED.  POSN CONSIDERED LIKELY TO BE VERY
   ACCURATE.  (BATTLE OF JUTLAND - 75TH ANNIVERSARY EXPED. REPORT 3.7.91).
```

new. Archivally there is evidence pointing to the fact that SMS *Lützow* was salvaged in the 1960s and the 'Notices to Mariners' posted during salvage operations are recorded as such in the Hydrographic Office record of this wreck (Fig. 15.4). It has also been claimed that the *Queen Mary*'s propellers had been removed long before I began diving on the wrecks in 2000.[26]

What is startling though is the pace at which the scavenging of valuable metals from these wrecks has been increasing in recent years. Cheaper and readily available technologies, such as GPS and underwater imaging equipment, have made it easier to access the wrecks for both legitimate and nefarious purposes.

You only have to look on the internet to see video and photos of the wrecks taken perfectly innocently by the few hardy recreational divers who occasionally visit some sites, to see how easy it is for salvagers to spot valuable items to go and pick up. I am grateful to Kevin Pickering for sharing his video from 2002 of HMS *Nomad*. In Fig. 15.5 a condenser can be seen on Kevin's dive in that year. Both the 2014 ROV survey and the multibeam survey of 2015 on this wreck failed to locate this object and it is now thought that it has most likely been taken away.

The greatest surprise of the 2015 multibeam survey was the number of the small wrecks that were located. The second greatest surprise was to see how many of them had already lost their condensers. These wrecks have been coming to light only in the last decade or so and they already bear the scars of salvage for profit. They represent a second wave of salvage at Jutland which is unlikely to stop without some form of monitoring and enforcement. The question is: enforcement of what and by whom?

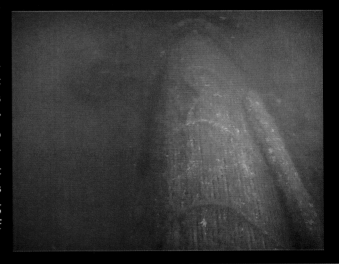

Fig. 15.5 *The top of one of HMS Nomad's condensers, as seen in 2002 by Kevin Pickering. This item was not located in 2014 or 2015 and has probably been taken from the wreck site and melted down for profit. (Picture: Kevin Pickering)*

The paradoxes of protection

The wrecks of the Battle of Jutland are now also participants in a newer battle; the battle over the future of the world's underwater cultural heritage, what should be done with it and how should it be managed and protected.

The Jutland wrecks, like all warship wrecks, are in international law 'Sovereign Immune', which means they are legally protected from salvage or other interference without the consent of either Britain or Germany. In Britain, despite there being evidence of salvage on the wrecks since the 75th Anniversary Expedition in 1991, there seemed little appetite at the MOD to do much about it. The UK government, after all, had a long history of making profit out of its own 'war graves' by selling salvage rights or even the wrecks themselves. The MOD sanctioned salvage of major 'war graves' such as HMS *Edinburgh*, *Natal* and *Vanguard*. Incredibly, HMS *Aboukir*, *Cressy* and *Hogue* were sold for scrap in 1956. These cases are all well documented and need not be repeated here.

However, because of pressure being placed on the MOD from a number of sources, the Jutland wrecks were finally designated under the Protection of Military Remains Act 1986 in November 2006, some two decades after the Act came into force. The Act itself is poorly named because it has practically no power to actually *protect* the Jutland wrecks since they lie in international waters. Only British-flagged vessels and British citizens fall under its auspices.

Salvagers from any other country do not come under the Act. In theory, the wrecks are also 'Sovereign Immune' in international law, but in practice foreign salvagers may seemingly still do as they please, with little practical chance of getting a knock on the door from the MOD Police wanting back its bits of these historic ships. Non-British salvagers may still have an obligation to report their recovered items to local 'Receivers of Wreck', depending on the salvage laws in force where the items are landed. In practice, this means little.

In 2014 the extent to which the MOD took its responsibilities seriously under the 1986 Act was severely shaken by the HMS *Victory* 1744 case. In this instance, the MOD deemed it appropriate to 'gift' a 'Sovereign Immune' shipwreck, HMS *Victory* 1744, by any measure an important part of British naval history, to a charitable 'foundation', with no significant financial resources and which has contractual salvage connections to a company with a long history of salvaging wrecks for profit.[27]

In March 2015, under pressure from a privately brought Judicial Review, the MOD withdrew the charity's permissions to recover artefacts from the wreck, but the 'gifting', seemingly, could not be undone. Kevan Jones MP commented: 'This has been a scandalous episode which has tarnished Britain's name internationally. We not only need to know how it happened, we need to put in place a process that ensures these sites are properly protected in future.'[28] We wait on events.

In the meantime, the Jutland wrecks endure with only the veneer of any genuine protection in place, administered by a body in which it is currently difficult to have much confidence. Ideally, the custodians of so much cultural heritage should perhaps be demonstrating something more of a proactive and imaginative approach towards its monitoring, recording and management.

Another possible route that could afford protection to the Jutland wrecks is the UNESCO Convention on the Protection of Underwater Cultural Heritage 2001, which in simple terms seeks to preserve and not exploit shipwrecks. It

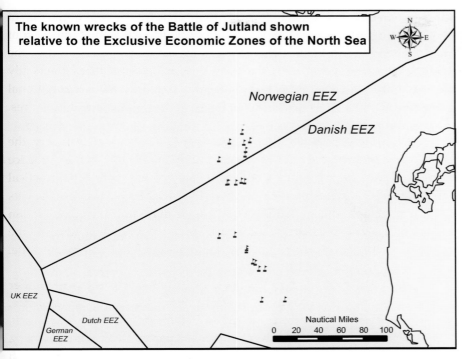

The known wrecks of the Battle of Jutland shown relative to the Exclusive Economic Zones of the North Sea

Norwegian EEZ

Danish EEZ

UK EEZ

Dutch EEZ

German EEZ

Nautical Miles

0   20   40   60   80   100

Fig. 15.6 The known wrecks of Jutland showing in which Exclusive Economic Zones they reside.

requires that each country wishing to bring the Convention into force in its own Exclusive Economic Zone must have it ratified by its national government. Britain has consistently declined to ratify the UNESCO Convention reputedly on the grounds of resourcing, that to do so would potentially undermine its bargaining rights under a number of other international treaties and agreements and that it would undermine its 'sovereign rights' over its sunken warships, which, as we have seen, they have done practically nothing to protect in the past.

As Fig. 15.6 shows, the wrecks of Jutland fall into the Exclusive Economic Zones of both Denmark and Norway. The wrecks of the Fleet Action and HMS *Indefatigable* are in the Norway zone. Neither Denmark nor Norway has so far ratified the Convention and it is currently unknown if there are plans afoot to do so. However, as this book goes to press I am advised that Denmark is proposing to give Jutland wrecks some form of protected status; again, we wait on events.

The legislative options, such as they are, represent only one aspect of this debate. For whatever laws are ratified and whatever speeches are made, some degree of monitoring, management and enforcement is essential to ensure adherence to the rules. A willingness to do this has been absent in the past, as is evident throughout this book. Currently the prognosis for the future seems no more encouraging than it was 17 years ago when I first began to record the wrecks and report on what was there then. A lot less is there now. Partly because of this, the reader will have noticed that none of the actual positions of the wrecks is listed in this study. In the current circumstances it would be unwise to do so. While the political inertia remains, the form of culture theft seen on the Jutland wrecks and elsewhere will sadly continue.

Final reflections

In their time the Dreadnought warships were not only the measure of a nation's prestige but the single most complicated structure built by human hand. Yet for many years there was in certain archaeology and naval history circles the notion that 20th-century shipwrecks are not real archaeology, because we know everything about them anyway. This has always struck me as nonsensical and it is very encouraging to see that it is a perspective now mostly out of fashion.

I am reminded of a talk recently given by the naval historian Rear-Admiral James Goldrick in which he refreshingly noted that while we could recommission Nelson's flagship HMS *Victory* in a few weeks, it would be practically impossible to recommission a Dreadnought (if one existed) because we simply do not now possess the requisite skills and knowledge to do so.

As I hope this study has shown, surveys of the Jutland wrecks offer the opportunity to fill in some of this knowledge gap, and contribute to a more accurate historical text about the battle in general, and perhaps even reappraise the work of our forebears, but as time passes, this opportunity will continue to fade. The Battle of Jutland has now passed from human memory and, by the time of the bicentenary, much of its physical remains will also be beyond our sight. Jutland will have returned to the virtual world of the archive and much that we could have learned will have been lost for all time.

Dr Innes J McCartney

Penzance, March 2016
imccartney@bournemouth.ac.uk

Notes

1   McCartney I. The armoured cruiser HMS *Defence*: a case study in assessing the Royal Navy shipwrecks of the Battle of Jutland 1916 as an archaeological resource. *International Journal of Nautical Archaeology* 2012; 41(1): 56–66.

2   McCartney I. Jutland 1916: The archaeology of a modern naval battle: the wreck of HMS *Invincible*, the world's first battlecruiser. *Skyllis* 2012; 2: pp.168–76.

3   Lambert NA. 'Our bloody ships' or 'our bloody system'? Jutland and the loss of the battle cruisers, 1916. *Journal of Military History* 1998; 62:29–56.

4   Jellicoe Papers MS49019 Harper manuscript. British Library (various dates), London. p.109.

5   Temple Patterson A, editor. *The Jellicoe Papers*: Volume II *1916–1935.* London: Navy Records Society; 1968. pp.477–82.

6   Jutland: additional papers, 1916. ADM 137/1643. National Archives, London. pp.237–57.

7   Battle of Jutland, 31 May 1916: plans, diagrams, track charts and photographs. ADM 137/303. National Archives (various dates), London. p.49.

8   Admiralty. *Battle of Jutland: 30th May to 1st June 1916: Official Dispatches with Appendices.* London: HMSO; 1920. p.345.

9   Bingham B. *Falklands, Jutland and the Bight.* London: John Murray: 1919. p.140.

10 Campbell NJM. *Jutland: an Analysis of the Fighting.* London: Conway; 1986. pp.55–56.

11 Harper JET. *Reproduction of the Record of the Battle of Jutland.* London: HMSO; 1927. p.110.

12 Gordon A. *The Rules of the Game.* London: John Murray; 1996. p.116.

13 Staff G. *German Battlecruisers of World War One.* Barnsley: Seaforth; 2014. p.46.

14 Roberts J. *Battlecruisers.* Annapolis: Naval Institute Press; 1997. p.116.

15 Battle of Jutland, 31 May 1916: plans, diagrams, track charts and photographs. ADM 137/303. National Archives (various dates), London. p.31.

16 Admiralty. *Battle of Jutland: 30th May to 1st June 1916: Official Dispatches with Appendices.* London: HMSO; 1920. plate 10.

17 Gordon A. *The Rules of the Game.* London: John Murray; 1996. p.604.

18 Admiralty. *Battle of Jutland: 30th May to 1st June 1916: Official Dispatches with Appendices.* London: HMSO; 1920. chart 1a.

19 *Ibid.,* chart 4a.

20 Roskill S. *Admiral of the Fleet Earl Beatty.* New York: Atheneum; 1981. p.327.

21 Temple Patterson A, editor. *The Jellicoe Papers*: Volume II *1916–1935.* London: Navy Records Society; 1968. p.478.

22 Admiralty. *Battle of Jutland: 30th May to 1st June 1916: Official Dispatches with Appendices.* London: HMSO; 1920. chart 8a.

23 Gordon A. *The Rules of the Game.* London: John Murray; 1996. appendix II.

24 McCartney I. *The maritime archaeology of a modern conflict.* New York: Routledge; 2014.

25 Moor G. *Battle of Jutland 1916. 75th Anniversary 1991: the Expedition Report.* 1991. Unpublished copy in author's collection.

26 Gordon A. *The Rules of the Game.* London: John Murray; 1996. p.601.

27 Odyssey Marine Exploration Executes Agreement with Maritime Heritage Foundation for Admiral Balchin's HMS *Victory* Shipwreck [online]. February 2012. Available at: http://www.shipwreck.net/pr240.php [Accessed 7 December 2015]

28 ThePipeLine. HMS *Victory* Decision 1744 Rolling News. [online] March 2015. Available at: http://thepipeline.info/blog/2015/03/05/hms-victory-decision-1744-rolling-news/ [Accessed 7 December 2015]

BIBLIOGRAPHY

Admiralty. *Stokers' Manual*. London: HMSO; 1912.

Admiralty. *Torpedo Drill Book*. London: HMSO; 1915.

Admiralty. *Battle of Jutland: 30th May to 1st June 1916: Official Dispatches with Appendices*. London: HMSO; 1920.

Admiralty. *Narrative of the Battle of Jutland*. London: HMSO; 1924.

Amos Papers, Liddle Collection, Leeds University (various dates), Leeds.

Anon. *Fallen List SMS Lützow*. Undated. Unpublished copy in the author's collection, provided by Gary Staff.

Anon. *Photographic Records of the BCF August 1914 – December 1916*. Undated.

Anon. *Medical Report of SMS Lützow*. Undated. Translation by Gary Staff, in the author's collection.

Arbuthnot R K. *Commander's Order Book for a Mediterranean Battleship*. Portsmouth: Griffin & Co.; 1900.

Battle of Jutland, 31 May 1916: plans, diagrams, track charts and photographs. ADM 137/303, National Archives (various dates), London.

Battle of Jutland: press and survivors' reports, press cuttings, extracts from letters etc. Vol I–II. ADM 137/4808, ADM 137/4809, National Archives (various dates), London.

Battle of Jutland: extracts from reports, logs and signal logs from the Fleet. ADM 137/4825, National Archives (various dates), London.

Bingham B. *Falklands, Jutland and the Bight*. London: John Murray: 1919.

Brooks J. *Dreadnought Gunnery and the Battle of Jutland*. London: Routledge; 2005.

Brown DK. *Warrior to Dreadnought*. London: Chatham; 1997.

Brown DK. *The Grand Fleet*. London: Chatham; 1999.

Brown DK. HMS *Invincible* – the explosion at Jutland and its relevance to HMS *Hood. Warship International* 2003; 40(4):339–49.

Brownrigg D. *Indiscretions of the Naval Censor*. London: Cassell; 1920.

Burr L. *British Battlecruisers 1914–18*. Oxford: Osprey; 2006.

Burroughs Papers, Liddle Collection, Leeds University (various dates), Leeds.

Burt RA. *British Battleships of World War One*. Barnsley: Seaforth; 2012.

Campbell NJM. *Jutland: an Analysis of the Fighting*. London: Conway; 1986.

Cave Papers, Liddle Collection, Leeds University (various dates), Leeds.

Church Papers Misc 1010. H Bonatz correspondence, Imperial War Museum (various dates), London.

Church Papers Misc 1010. RH Bowden correspondence, Imperial War Museum (various dates), London.

Church Papers Misc 1010. TW Clifford correspondence, Imperial War Museum (various dates), London.

Church Papers Misc 1010. H Fischer correspondence, Imperial War Museum (various dates), London.

Church Papers Misc 1010. BW Gasson correspondence, Imperial War Museum (various dates), London.

Church Papers Misc 1010. E Sheard correspondence, Imperial War Museum (various dates), London.

Church Papers Misc 1010. WJ Wilkins correspondence, Imperial War Museum (various dates), London.

Clash of the Dreadnoughts television programme. Ideal World Productions, 2004, distributed by Channel 4.

Constructor's plans of HMS *Black Prince*. Ship plans collection, National Maritime Museum (various dates), London.

Constructor's plans of HMS *Indefatigable*. Ship's plans collection, National Maritime Museum (various dates), London.

Constructor's plans of HMS *Invincible*. Ship's plans collection, National Maritime Museum (various dates), London.

Constructor's plans of HMS *Marne*. Ship's plans collection, National Maritime Museum (various dates), London.

Constructor's plans of HMS *Minotaur*. Ship's plans collection, National Maritime Museum (various dates), London.

Constructor's plans of New torpedo boat Destroyers 1911–12. Ship's plans collection, National Maritime Museum (various dates), London.

Constructor's plans of HMS *Queen Mary*. Ship's plans collection, National Maritime Museum (various dates), London.

Constructor's plans of HMS *Tipperary*. Ship's plans collection, National Maritime Museum (various dates), London.

Constructor's plans of HMS *Trident*. Ship's plans collection, National Maritime Museum (various dates), London.

Constructor's plans of SMS *V25–30*. Ship's plans collection, National Maritime Museum (various dates), London.

Corbett JS. *History of the Great War based on Official Documents: Naval Operations, Vol. I–III, with maps*. London: Longmans, Green and Co.; 1920–25.

Croome Papers Doc. 5141, Imperial War Museum (various dates), London.

Daily Weather Reports 17–31 May 1916. Meteorological Office, Exeter.

Daily Weather Reports 1–16 June 1916. Meteorological Office, Exeter.

Delgado JP. Recovering the past of USS *Arizona*: symbolism, myth and reality. *Historical Archaeology* 1992; 26(4):69–80.

Delgado, JP. *Lost Warships: an Archaeological Tour of War at Sea*. London: Conway; 2001.

The Denny List Part III: Ship Numbers 769–1273, National Maritime Museum (various dates), London.

Dohm A. *Skagerrak: die größte Seeschlacht der Geschichte*. Gütersloh: Bertelsmann; 1936.

Dorling T. *Endless Story*. London: Hodder and Stoughton; 1936.

Fawcett HW, Hooper GWW. *The Fighting at Jutland*. Glasgow: Maclure, Macdonald & Co.; 1921.

Friedman N. *Naval Weapons of World War One*. Barnsley: Seaforth; 2011.

Friedman N. *British Cruisers of the Victorian Era*. Barnsley: Seaforth; 2012.

Frost HH. *The Battle of Jutland*. Annapolis: Naval Institute Press; 1936.

Gardiner L. *The Royal Oak Courts Martial*. Edinburgh: Blackwood; 1965.

German surface craft: specifications, movements, details of damage and losses sustained at Jutland. ADM 137/3881, National Archives (various dates), London.

Goodenough W. *A Rough Record*. London: Hutchinson & Co; 1943.

Gordon A. *The Rules of the Game*. London: John Murray; 1996.

Gould RA. Beyond exploration: underwater archaeology after the year 2000. *Historical Archaeology* 2000; 34(4):24–28.

Gröner E. *German Warships 1815–1945. Vol. I*. London: Conway; 1990.

Groos O. *Der Krieg zur See 1914–1918. Nordsee Band 5* and *Nordsee Band 5: Kartenband*. Berlin: Mittler & Sohn; 1925.

Groos, O. *The Battle of Jutland: Official German Account*. Admiralty translation. 1926. ADM 186/626. National Archives, London.

Grove E. The Autobiography of Chief Gunner Alexander Grant: HMS *Lion* at the Battle of Jutland, 1916. In: Rose S, editor. *The Naval Miscellany*. Vol. VII. Aldershot: Ashgate; 2008.

Haldane Papers, Liddle Collection, Leeds University (various dates), Leeds.

Harder V. *Report concerning the Battle on 31 May 1916*. Translation by Gary Staff, in the author's collection.

Harder V. Letter to E von Mantey. 1930. Translation by Gary Staff, in the author's collection.

von Hase G. *Kiel and Jutland*. London: Skeffington & Son; 1921.

Harper JET. Reproduction of the Record of the Battle of Jutland. London: HMSO; 1927.

Harper JET. *The Truth About Jutland*. London: John Murray; 1927.

Hit diagrams: SMS *Lützow*. Bundesarchiv-Militärarchiv (various dates), Freiburg.

Hydrographics Department of the Admiralty. Record of Wreck No. 31507 SMS *Pommern*. Taunton: Hydrographics Office; 2000.

Hydrographics Department of the Admiralty. Record of Wreck No. 32334. SMS *Elbing*. Taunton: Hydrographics Office; 2000.

Hydrographics Department of the Admiralty. Record of Wreck No. 32344 SMS *Lützow*. Taunton: Hydrographics Office; 2000.

Hydrographics Department of the Admiralty. Record of Wreck No. 32345 SMS *Frauenlob*. Taunton: Hydrographics Office; 2000.

Hydrographics Department of the Admiralty. Record of Wreck No. 32350 HMS *Queen Mary*. Taunton: Hydrographics Office; 2000.

Hydrographics Department of the Admiralty. Record of Wreck No. 32352 HMS *Nestor* [Probably]. Taunton: Hydrographics Office; 2000.

Hydrographics Department of the Admiralty. Record of Wreck No. 32354 HMS *Indefatigable*. Taunton: Hydrographics Office; 2000.

Hydrographics Department of the Admiralty. Record of Wreck No. 32367 HMS *Nomad*. Taunton: Hydrographics Office; 2000..

Hydrographics Department of the Admiralty, 2000. Record of Wreck No. 32378 HMS *Black Prince*. Taunton: Hydrographics Office; 2000.

Hydrographics Department of the Admiralty. Record of Wreck No. 33019 HMS *Invincible*. Taunton: Hydrographics Office; 2000.

Hydrographics Department of the Admiralty. Chart No. 1404, *Esbjerg to Hanstholm: Including Offshore Oil and Gas Fields*. Taunton: Hydrographics Office; 1999.

Jane's Fighting Ships of World War I. London: Studio Editions; 1990.

Jellicoe Papers, British Library (various dates), London.

Jellicoe Papers MS49019 Harper manuscript, British Library (various dates), London.

Jung AK. *Skagerrak: Mit Schlachtkreuzer 'Lützow' an der Spitze*. Leipzig: Reclam; 1942.

[Skagerrak with the Battlekreuzer *Lützow* at the Head.] Translation by Gary Staff in the author's collection.

Jutland: additional papers, 1916. ADM 137/1643, National Archives (various dates), London.

Jutland: later reports, 1916. ADM 137/1664, National Archives (various dates), London.

Jutland: reports of Flag and Commanding Officers. ADM 137/302. National Archives (various dates), London.

Kennedy R. *The Book of Modern Engines. Vol VI*. London: Caxton; 1912.

King-Hall S. *My Naval Life 1906–1929*. London: Faber & Faber; 1952.

Lambert NA. 'Our bloody ships' or 'our bloody system'? Jutland and the loss of the battle cruisers, 1916. *Journal of Military History* 1998; 62:29–56.

Liddle PH. *The Sailor's War 1914–18*. Poole: Blandford Press; 1985.

Loss of HMS *Hood* in action with German battleship *Bismarck*: Boards of Inquiry. ADM 116/4351. National Archives (various dates), London.

Manning TD. *The British Destroyer*. London: Godfrey Cave Associates; 1979.

March EJ. *British Destroyers: a History of Development 1892–1953*. London: Seeley Service & Co.; 1966.

Marder AJ. *From the Dreadnought to Scapa Flow: Volume III*. Oxford: OUP; 1966.

Marshall PA. The *Invincible*'s explosive photo. *Naval History* 2012; 26(1):44–46.

McCartney I. The armoured cruiser HMS *Defence*: a case study in assessing the Royal Navy shipwrecks of the Battle of Jutland 1916 as an archaeological resource. *International Journal of Nautical Archaeology* 2012; 41(1):56–66.

McCartney I. Jutland 1916: The archaeology of a modern naval battle: the wreck of HMS *Invincible*, the world's first battlecruiser. *Skyllis* 2012; 2:168-76.

McCartney I. *The maritime archaeology of a modern conflict: comparing the archaeology of German submarine wrecks to the historical text*. New York: Routledge; 2014.

Mearns DL. *The Search for the Sydney*. Sydney: Harper Collins; 2009.

Moor G. *Battle of Jutland 1916. 75th Anniversary 1991: the Expedition Report*. 1991. Unpublished copy in the author's collection.

Odyssey Marine Exploration Executes Agreement with Maritime Heritage Foundation for Admiral Balchin's HMS *Victory* Shipwreck [online]. February 2012. Available at: http://www.shipwreck.net/pr240.php [Accessed 7 December 2015]

Oram HK. *Ready for Sea*. London: Futura; 1976.

Parkes O. *British Battleships*. London: Seeley Service & Co.; 1970.

Paschen G. SMS *Lützow* in the Skagerrak Battle. *Marine-Rundschau* May 1926. Translation by Gary Staff, in the author's collection.

Philbin TR. *Admiral von Hipper: the Inconvenient Hero*. Amsterdam: BR Grüner; 1982.

Preston A. *Battleships of World War I*. New York: Galahad Books; 1972.

Pollen A. *The Navy in Battle*. London: Chatto & Windus; 1919.

Pumping plan SMS *Lützow*. Ship's plans collection, National Maritime Museum (various dates), London.

Rasor EL. *The Battle of Jutland: a Bibliography*. Greenwood: Westport; 1992.

Roberts J. *Battlecruisers*. Annapolis: Naval Institute Press; 1997.

Roskill S. *Admiral of the Fleet Earl Beatty*. New York: Atheneum; 1981.

Royal Navy. *German Warships of World War I*. London: Greenhill; 1992.

ScapaMAP 2000–2002: Report Compiled for Historic Scotland on the Mapping and Management of the Submerged Archaeological Resource in Scapa Flow, Orkney. Orkney: Scapa Flow Marine Archaeology Project; 2003.

Scheer R. *Germany's High Sea Fleet in the World War*. London: Cassell; 1920.

Staff G. *German Battleships 1914–18*. Vol. I. Oxford: Osprey; 2010.

Staff G. *Battle on the Seven Seas*. Barnsley: Pen & Sword Maritime; 2011.

Staff G. *German Battlecruisers of World War One*. Barnsley: Seaforth; 2014.

Steel N, Hart P. *Jutland 1916*. London: Cassell; 2003.

Surgeon Parkes Collection. SP2469, Imperial War Museum (various dates), London.

Tarrant VE. *Battlecruiser* Invincible. London: Arms and Armour Press; 1986.

Tarrant VE. *Jutland: the German Perspective*. London: Arms and Armour Press; 1995.

Temple Patterson A, editor. *The Jellicoe Papers*: Volume II *1916–1935*. London: Navy Records Society; 1968.

ThePipeLine. HMS *Victory* Decision 1744 Rolling News. [online] March 2015. Available at: http://thepipeline. info/blog/2015/03/05/hms-victory-decision-1744-rolling-news/ [Accessed 7 December 2015]

Thomas RD, Patterson B. *Dreadnoughts in Camera*. Stroud: Sutton; 1998.

Wyllie WL, Owen C, Kirkpatrick WD. *More Sea Fights of the Great War*. London: Cassell; 1919.

Yates K. *Graf Spee's Raiders*. Annapolis: Naval Institute Press; 1994.

Yates JA. *The Jutland controversy: a case study in intra-service politics, with particular reference to the presentation of the Battlecruiser Fleet's training, conduct and command*. PhD thesis. University of Hull; 1998. Available at: http://core.ac.uk/download/pdf/2731830.pdf [Accessed 7 December 2015]

INDEX